D1566469

All·of·the·People
All·the·Time

ALL·OF·THE·PEOPLE
ALL·THE·TIME
Strategic Communication and American Politics

JAROL B. MANHEIM

M. E. Sharpe, Inc.
Armonk, New York
London, England

Available in the United Kingdom and Europe from M. E. Sharpe,
Publishers, 3 Henrietta Street, London WC2E 8LU.

Library of Congress Cataloging-in-Publication Data

Manheim, Jarol B., 1946–
   All of the people, all the time / by Jarol B. Manheim.
      p.   cm.
   Includes index.
   ISBN 0-87332-796-9
   1. Communication in politics. 2. Public relations and politics. I. Title.
JA74.M35   1991
302.2—dc20   90-39657
                                                                              CIP

Printed in the United States of America

MV 10   9   8   7   6   5   4   3   2   1

For Amy

who waited twenty years for the right book to come along

CONTENTS

ACKNOWLEDGMENTS

Writing a book is at best a daunting experience. All those words to invent—all those pages to fill. And, at least ideally, one must actually *say* something, and say it with logic, rigor, reason, and panache. As a result, authorship is necessarily at once a solitary activity and a social one. In Washington, it involves locking oneself away from everything but the noise of the jets flying in and out of National Airport—which is inescapable—yet at the same time talking with as many people as possible in search of insight and verification. Writing involves reading—everything from newspapers and scholarly tomes to multipage contracts with "what-if" clauses that make nuclear Armageddon seem attractive by comparison. There are days when one would rather visit the dentist.

But writing a book can also be extremely rewarding—not so much in financial terms, though I do appreciate your having purchased this book—but in the sense of satisfaction it can afford when the words do seem to work, and in the opportunities it provides to make and renew friendships.

In that context, I am grateful for the comments, suggestions, assistance, and support of many people who shared in the collective enterprise that is *All of the People, All the Time*. Among them: Irv Rockwood, the solidity of whose surname testifies to his role in the project; Lance Bennett, whose early support was of special value; Michael Weber, Helen Albert, Susanna Sharpe, Alexandra Koppen, and others at M. E. Sharpe, who made the book a reality; Mark Siegel, Les Francis, Bill Garrett, Steve McCurry, David Broder, Larry Hanson, Jerry Post, Bob Kenny, Kurt and Gladys Lang, and David Osterlund for the insights they provided, some intended and others not; and Montague Kern for her critique of an early draft. As an indication of my genuine appreciation, I will not publish their unlisted telephone numbers here—only my thanks. Any brilliant gems that might have mistakenly found their way into these pages are undoubtedly their collective responsibility. What's left is mine.

J.B.M.

If you once forfeit the confidence of your fellow citizens, you can never regain their respect and esteem. It is true that you may fool all of the people some of the time; you can even fool some of the people all the time; but you can't fool all of the people all the time.

Abraham Lincoln

ALL·OF·THE·PEOPLE
ALL·THE·TIME

1 ... SOME OF THE PEOPLE

It was vintage Harry Truman. Under a clear Missouri sky, the powerful engine slowly backed onto the siding of the St. Louis railyard and toward the platform of Union Station. Thrust before it was the special campaign car used by the candidate for this whistle-stop tour of the great Midwest, patriotically bedecked, as one might expect, in red, white, and blue, and bearing a banner proclaiming it the campaign special. The crowd waved its signs and surged forward in anticipation, while a choral group harmonized lightly to the strains of the campaign theme: "Doo doo doo doo doo doo doo doo doo. . . . Don't worry. . . . Be happy . . . ." It was a freshly scrubbed Republican crowd filled with freshly scrubbed Republican faces, and they were eager for their first glimpse of the candidate. And suddenly, there he was—smiling, waving, making his way from the railcar platform to the impromptu stage which had been constructed for his visit.

But wait a minute! Harry Truman? Republicans? Don't Worry, Be Happy? What was this . . . a badly colorized film on Turner Network Television?

Actually, the year was 1988, not 1948, and the candidate wasn't Harry Truman at all, but George Herbert Walker Bush. And those *were* College Republicans and Jaycees in the audience, not unionists. And that music really *was* the *Happy Days Are Here Again* of the eighties. Don't worry. Be happy. (For the record, songwriter and performer—and ardent Democrat—Bobby McFerrin wrote to the Bush campaign objecting to its adoption of his tune as its theme.) It wasn't the *reality* of the scene that was Trumanesque, but merely the *image*. Indeed, the only things missing for C-SPAN viewers watching this spectacle from the comfort of livingrooms all across America were the sepia tones of Movietone News.

As a matter of fact, George Bush's whistle-stop tour of the Midwest covered a total distance of 300 yards. It began in the St. Louis railyard a mere three football fields from its conclusion, rolled out on time, and brought the candidate into the station right on schedule.

The St. Louis rally of October 31, 1988, was the quintessential event of the year's presidential campaigning, scripted for brevity, staged with care—complete with a bevy of high school cheerleaders and a pair of Bush grandchildren who looked more than a little bewildered—and structured to convey simple messages. In addition to its upbeat theme and Missouriana flavor, it was designed to serve as the centerpiece of Candidate Bush's response to charges then extant that he was running a campaign heavy on images and light on issues. For there on the stage with him, piled high on a table, in plain view, were dozens of copies of a book issued by the campaign that day purporting to show the many issue statements the candidate had made. "George Bush," proclaimed its cover, highlighted by a sketch of a firm but friendly candidate. "Leadership on the Issues." Three hundred and forty-seven pages of the collected wisdom of the candidate, as expressed in speeches and position papers covering a period of some two years. A package of Bushthink. "A presidency can shape an era—and it can change our lives. A successful presidency can give meaning to an age." Anybody, the wall of books seemed to say, who could say this much *must* be saying something.

◆ ◆ ◆ ◆

Politics is the art of getting what you want at the least personal expense. Political communication is the art of getting it merely by expending words.

This is a book about the uses and abuses of political communication in contemporary society. It is a book about the ways that governments, politicians, corporations, terrorists, special interests, highly paid lobbyists, and others manipulate words, pictures, events, and one another to get what they want; about how and why that manipulation works; and about what it means for those of us who live in an ostensibly free and open democratic society.

The argument of the book can be stated succinctly: Politicians, governments, and others have become increasingly sophisticated in their ability to anticipate how the news media will report their words and deeds, and how the public will respond to those reports. They have developed increasingly effective strategies for managing or circumventing the news, shaping their images, and channeling public perceptions. This has reduced the role of journalists and the so-called free press almost to the point of complicity, and it has deprived the public—never highly motivated toward politics to begin with—of the tools it needs to make informed judgments about world and national affairs. The result is a democracy of the uninformed, one that is ever more vulnerable to the wispiest breezes of political expediency.

Some would have us believe that this state of affairs is the product of a conspiracy. Media critics of the left and the right, alike, make a comfortable living decrying ideological bogeymen of opposing stripes, and, not incidentally, soliciting our more or less tax-exempt dollars to do it. Nor do politicians lack for constructive suggestions from political gadflies. Fairness and balance, it seems, are in the eye of the beholder—the question seems only to be: Which eye?

Here, as elsewhere in life, however, overly simple conspiracy theories explain little, and our tendency to focus on them draws attention away from important things that are happening around us. What is at work here is not an ideological conspiracy, but a confluence of social forces—subtle, but nonetheless potent, enduring, and all-encompassing social forces. They include professional self-interest on the part of politicians, journalists, and others; an odd blend of both hypersensitivity and insensitivity to demographics, or the distribution of such attributes as income and education through our society; and the seemingly contradictory forces of institutional advancement and institutional conservatism—the tendencies of news organizations, government agencies, political parties, and other institutions of American society in the first instance to get everything they can (power, money, or whatever the stakes may be), and in the second to play it safe.

The element that binds these forces together and gives them political leverage is information—not just any information, but information that can be used to advantage. Information that can be manufactured and sold as news or political advertising. Information that can be selectively cast and distributed to persuade or cajole or manipulate the public. Information that can be managed or controlled to manipulate the media. Information, in short, that can be used as a source of power.

Those who are enabled to use information in these ways by their positions or capabilities, and who are rendered willing by their motivations, are, in our contemporary, media-centered society, the ones most favored. Those without the ability, opportunity, or drive to control information *as a political resource* are the disadvantaged.

In its essence, the argument of this book is an argument about skill and opportunity—specifically *political* skill and opportunity—and about those who have and use it . . . and those who do not. At one end of the pipeline, it is an argument about the growing capabilities of an elite group of political operatives who think of themselves as "strategic communication" professionals, people who combine knowledge and experience in the selling of political images with the bottom-line–oriented, short-term and short-sighted mentality of the M.B.A. At the other end of the pipeline, it is an argument about a society that is being deprived, not merely of information about the realities of political life, but of the ability to recognize, use, or even value that information, even if it were available. In between, it is an argument about the ways in which groups of professionals who are presumed to be adversaries often use one another for mutual advantage, irrespective of the impact their actions may have on the public interest.

Now, if I were a prosecuting attorney, my nose for justice might, in fact, begin twitching, for it does seem that some elements of conspiracy are present here: Some of the people gaining advantage over others (the few over the many). The manipulation of a public resource (information). Frequent contacts among the key participants (reporters, politicians, backstage political operatives). Pure limburger.

But there are two key elements missing—a sense of common purpose and a sense of direction. As we shall see, for example, politicians and journalists may often find it in their interests to cooperate with one another, even while appearing to be adversaries, and both groups may find advantage in misinforming, or at best underinforming, the public. But the motives and objectives of the two differ considerably. They are, in effect, following the same road, but to different destinations. And, as we shall argue, neither group, in the aggregate, cares very much about where the road leads since neither looks more than two to three steps ahead at any one moment. And there goes the case.

From the public's point of view, then, it is the driving force of *inadvertence*, an *absence* of purposefulness, rather than conspiracy, action for a hidden purpose, that distinguishes the argument here. And it is that very same inadvertence, and the all but total absence of recognition of, or concern for, the consequences of their actions that typifies so many political communicators—far more than any conspiracy we might reasonably conceive—that places our political system at risk. Our task in this book is to examine the sources and nature of that risk, and the things we can do to alleviate it.

To explore those issues, we need to understand some basic ideas about the use of information in politics, about the process of political communication, and most especially about the techniques of what has come to be called "strategic political communication." Building on the discussion to this point, let us say that political communication refers to the creation, distribution, use and control of information as a political resource, whether that is done by governments, by organizations like pressure groups or the media, or by individuals. What sets *strategic* political communication apart from other types is the way in which those engaged in it use sophisticated knowledge about human behavior to mold information to accomplish very specific, and often very short-term, objectives. Their emphasis is very much on controlling the messages that are sent, the circumstances of their transmission, and the roster of recipients. Their objectives can be to persuade or to influence, to integrate or to isolate, to mobilize or to demobilize, to unify or to divide, to seek out or to avoid, a defined group of people, where doing so is thought to be somehow advantageous. Their methods are entirely utilitarian—if it works or holds promise of doing so, do it. Strategic political communication involves not only the selective distribution of political information, but, under certain circumstances, the prevention of its distribution (e.g., news management) as well. There is a cliché that says talk is cheap. But to strategic political communicators, talk, and the control of talk, is power.

The notion that talk, or, more generally, image, is potent is not an invention of late-twentieth-century America, nor even of our era generally. Indeed, it can be traced at least as far back as the time of Vlad the Impaler—now remembered through the Dracula legend—who reputedly ordered the decapitation of some ten thousand of his most loyal subjects and the literal posting of their heads around the borders of his domain. The message to would-be invaders was clear: If this is the way he treats his friends. . . . Nor was his the only instance of such communication. The Greek historian Herodotus, for example, tells of Harpagus, a Median general of the sixth century B.C. who was selected by Astyages, the Median king, to kill the king's infant grandson Cyrus, whom he saw as a future rival for power. Harpagus delegated the task to a herdsman who chose instead to keep the child alive. Needless to say, this angered the king, who responded by serving to his general as a dinner entree the head of his own son. The message was potent, but not altogether effective—Harpagus later became Cyrus's most trusted commander when the grandson (soon to be known as Cyrus the Great) deposed sweet old grampa Astyages. Then, too, there is the similar story of Richard I of England, who, during the Crusades, plucked out the eyes of hundreds of prisoners and sent them to his rival, the Saracen sultan Saladin, as a communiqué. A picture, it has been said, is worth a thousand words.

Nor can we lay claim to having first introduced a more subtle touch into the exercise of talk as a base of power. It was, after all, Niccolo Machiavelli who (posthumously) advised the Medici princes of Italy in 1532 that

> The prince must . . . avoid those things which will make him hated or despised; and whenever he succeeds in this, he will have done his part and will find no danger in other vices. He will chiefly become hated . . . by being rapacious, and usurping the property and women of his subjects, which he must abstain from doing, and whenever one does not attack the property or honour of the generality of men, they will live contented; and one will only have to combat the ambition of a few, who can be easily held in check in many ways.[1]

Then, later,

> Besides this, he ought, at convenient seasons of the year, to keep the people occupied with festivals and shows; and as every city is divided into guilds or into classes, he ought to pay attention to all these groups, mingle with them from time to time, and give them an example of his humanity and munificence, always upholding, however, the majesty of his dignity, which must never be allowed to fail in anything whatever.[2]

What we *can* claim as our own, however, is the pervasiveness with which manipulative communication is used in our society today *with effect* for political purposes. We are history's greatest perpetrators of the act, and its greatest victims.

It is tempting to say that one need look no further than the headlines or the nearest television set for evidence of this fact: Spin doctors who flood journalists with prepackaged ''spontaneous'' assessments of political events and who, themselves, are hired by news organizations to provide commentary. The Willie Horton show that toured the country for George Bush in Campaign '88, and the narcissistic ''handlers'' spots—those purporting to show Bush's managers plotting strategy in a smoke-filled room—mounted by the Democrats. Will the real Dan Quayle please stand up?

Tempting, yes, but not a little bit naive. For implicit in the temptation is the assumption that, in fact, what you see is what you get. The news may be managed to some degree, but there it is for all to see and judge. If you don't like Peter Jennings, watch Dan Rather. If you don't think Dan is telling all, read the *Times* or the *Post*. Better yet, watch and read them all.

But there is ample (and growing) reason to believe that what we see is *not* what we get, that we are in fact treated to Machiavellian ''festivals and shows'' that distract us, whether purposely or not, from the underlying reality of politics. The techniques by which this is accomplished can range from control over the definition of news to denial of access to it. When, for example, the Tory government of Margaret Thatcher wanted to convince the British people of the need to accept the stationing of Cruise missiles in their country, it hired the American advertising and public relations firm of J. Walter Thompson to boost the image of the Reagan administration in Britain.[3] It then employed the Official Secrets Act to try to prevent this arrangement from becoming public knowledge. And closer to home, recall that roughly a million dollars of the booty from the Iran-Contra arms deal was channeled to a Washington public relations firm operated by a former Reagan campaign aide for the purpose of improving the image of the Contras in the United States, perhaps with the complicity (in violation of U.S. law) of the State Department's Office of Latin American Public Diplomacy. Nicaragua, we were reminded, was but a two-day drive from Harlingen, Texas.

And there is reason for concern. Voter turnout in American presidential elections, already among the lowest of all the Western democracies, has declined steadily since the end of World War II. And, perhaps more telling, the confidence that Americans express in their national institutions, governmental and otherwise, is less than half that reflected in the polls just two decades ago. People are not thinking or acting about politics as much, or in the same ways, as they once did, and the change is invariably toward withdrawal from political life. Americans seemingly have so little interest in government and politics that, in 1990, approximately two-thirds of the potential electorate failed to vote in the congressional elections, one tax dollar of every five owed was being evaded, and nearly forty percent of the population did not even go to the trouble of returning their Census forms.[4] Walter Lippman once observed that people carry around with them "a repertoire of stereotypes," images that guide the understandings they attach to experience.[5] The evidence suggests that the American political repertoire is changing. The question is whether substantial changes in the meaning and practice of American democracy can be far behind. That is the question to be explored here.

Although essentially an exercise in pessimism, the argument to be developed here is not without its optimistic elements. It was, after all, Abraham Lincoln and not P. T. Barnum who gave us our title and the aphorism with which we began, the latter a clear expression of confidence in the ultimate regenerative powers of democracy. And, to be sure, some journalists and some members of the public are coming slowly to recognize the trends we shall delineate in these pages and the risks they entail. But the emphasis of this book will be on the danger posed to democracy by our very great dependence on information from the mass media and by the very great susceptibility of those media to manipulation by the emerging elite of strategic political communicators.

◆ ◆ ◆ ◆

The key to understanding how and why strategic political communication works so effectively is to realize that words and pictures generate images that do shape popular perceptions of political reality. That is why politicians and others are able to use them to create and exercise political power. When Walter Cronkite, anchor of the CBS Evening News for many years (and for much of that time shown in public opinion polls to be the most trusted man in America) would end his newscasts with the words "That's the way it is . . . "—well, it *was*! More than anything Cronkite said, it was the fact that *he* said it that gave his words their potency.

We also need to understand, as the Cronkite example makes clear,

... SOME OF THE PEOPLE   11

that political talk comprises more than mere words. In fact, sometimes the words themselves are irrelevant.

Political talk includes *actions* that are designed more to send a message than to accomplish any "real" objective. Why, for example, during the early days of the Reagan administration, were U.S. marines in Lebanon based in the low-lying coastal plain, probably the single most vulnerable piece of real estate in the area? Certainly it was not for military advantage. To the contrary, it was to make clear the limited intentions of the American intervention. Their vulnerability to attack was not a mistake—it was the whole point of the exercise. And it failed because the administration badly misjudged its audience. The message was understood all too well.

Political talk includes the *packaging* through which words are conveyed. It was no accident that Jimmy Carter (and later Dan Rather) appeared on national television in a sweater. It was part of a concerted effort to portray the president as common man, Carter's effort to help the nation out of its "malaise" in the wake of Watergate. Nor was it an accident that the Reagans adopted a pointedly more formal posture four years later with the same objective in mind.

Political talk includes visual *images*—starving children in Ethiopia, Willie Horton, and aging Ayatollahs—images that convey emotion more than knowledge, and holistic messages rather than isolated bits of information. Read my lips!

And political talk includes *visualizations*—words used not to convey ideas, but to paint mental pictures. In an era of "duck tests" in which we were assured by Richard Darman, President Bush's Director of the Office of Management and Budget, that no new taxes would waddle or quack our way, thank goodness for "revenue enhancements" and "user fees." At least one can still use what the president himself termed a "semi-automated hunting rifle" like the AK–47 assault weapon or the Mack 10 to "harvest" deer. Never doubt the power of a good euphemism.

Then there are the words themselves. Political scientist Murray Edelman, who has made a lifelong study of the use of words in politics, suggests that there are four different kinds of political language.[6] They differ in the extent to which they appeal, alternatively, to emotion or to reason, and in the ways that they blend ambiguity and specificity. What they have in common is that each is employed to establish, maintain, legitimize, and represent various types of power relationships.

One of these types of political language, which Edelman calls "hortatory," is of particular interest to us here. Hortatory language is, as the name implies, a language of exhortation, one that appeals to the emotions and that may often be deliberately vague. It is a language used by individual politicians to establish a claim to leadership of some segment of the public by forging very personalized bonds of support. The best examples of this type of language are provided by such charismatic figures as Dr. Martin Luther King, Jr., or John F. Kennedy. I have been to the mountain, and I have seen the promised land. Ask not what your country can do for you. . . . The objective here is to appeal to the audience at an emotional level, and words are chosen that will resonate with the shared feelings and experiences of the specific audience that is being addressed. The elements of delivery—timbre of the voice, facial expression, staging—are very much a part of the use of hortatory language, but it is the words that set it apart.

Many politicians attempt to use hortatory language, but not all are successful, and not all circumstances lend themselves equally to hortatory appeals. For one thing, it is sometimes easier to lead people against something than for it. Jim Hightower, Agriculture Commissioner of the State of Texas, for example, delivered a classic political attack speech at the 1988 Democratic National Convention, describing George Bush, at the time the presumed Republican candidate, as "a toothache of a man" who was "born on third base and thought he'd hit a triple," and in other, even less flattering terms which had evident appeal to his highly partisan audience. Arkansas Governor Bill Clinton, on the other hand, in what may have been an early allegory for the coming campaign, fumbled around for more than half an hour in nominating the eventual Democratic standard-bearer, Michael Dukakis. In the process, he squandered both his audience and his own reputation. It is one thing to say that hortatory political language *can* be used with effect, and quite another to make it happen.

The other forms of political language, though less directly related to the argument at hand, are nevertheless worthy of mention in the present context because they, too, are designed to establish or represent power relationships, and can, on occasion, become instruments of strategic political communication.

"Legal language," Edelman's second category, is, as the name implies, the language of the courts and of the legislative process. It employs words that convey an appearance of precision, but a reality of ambiguity. Indeed, legal language is deliberately employed to mask ambiguity. The objective is to require that those who do not "speak" the language, when confronted with the need to do so (for example, when they are arrested or served with legal papers), to become dependent upon a minority of educated linguists whom we call attorneys. In this sense, law schools are merely language laboratories where aspirants learn to "interpret" laws and precedent, and courts exist only because of the latent ambiguity of the codes. If the law were plainly stated and invariant, after all, we would need a lot fewer of both, much to the chagrin of the American Trial Lawyers Association. The most blatant acknowledgment of this came, interestingly enough, in a syndicated television commercial that was aired in a number of markets some years back.

Recall that, until fairly recently, it was considered unethical for attorneys to advertise their services, or even their specialties, to the public. Bar associations nationwide took the position that such advertising was demeaning to the legal profession. When that barrier was finally overcome in the 1970s, television advertisements for law firms, especially those dealing at the "retail" level (criminal law, wills, divorce, and individual-level civil litigation), became increasingly commonplace and, as had been predicted, came to look more and more like other commercial advertising. Since most such firms were relatively small operations and unlikely to have much expertise in image-smithing, some media consultants offered syndicated advertising formulas into which a local firm needed merely insert its own name and logo. One such advertisement showed a judge at a high bench peering down over two lawyers. "Mumbo jumbo mumbo jumbo mumbo jumbo," said the judge. "Mumbo jumbo mumbo jumbo mumbo jumbo," said the opposing attorney. Cut to a medium shot of the featured counsel, who offers a reassuring summary of the firm's services and abilities. Cut back to the courtroom, where, to the judge's heartily agreeable concluding "Mumbo," the featured counsel, *our* attorney, replies with a resonant "Jumbo," then turns to the camera with a satisfied smile. "The Law Offices of [fill in the blanks]." Language is power. I have it; you don't. You need me.

The third class of language, which Edelman terms "administrative," is similar in form and purpose to legal language. It is, if anything, even more precise in appearance than its cousin, but can hide just as much ambiguity. Its objective is to legitimize the power held by bureaucrats. Think back to the last time you filed an income tax form with the Internal Revenue Service. Subtract the amount on line 54(b) of form 1040X from the amount on line 16(d) of form 1056Y, but only if the income referred to on line 17(k) of form 8079 exceeds the amount subject to the alternative tax (ever wonder what that tax was alternative to?) as specified in instruction 4.3 (page 47) and the sections of the tax code cited therein. How much more precise can you get? But recall that, in one test of the tax system during 1989, IRS personnel whose job it was to assist taxpayers in completing the forms gave "correct" advice only about 30 percent of the time. The gulf between language and meaning was so vast that even those ostensibly trained as linguists could not bridge it, much to the embarrassment of the agency.

The fact is that nobody elected the employees of the IRS, the Department of Veterans' Affairs, college admissions offices, city zoning offices, or of an almost limitless host of other bureaucracies to positions of authority, yet they surely do exercise that authority. Linguistic obfuscation through the development and enforced use of highly stylized forms and regulations creates a dependency among the public on those knowledgeable few who understand and can guide one through "the system." Even apparent simplicity can mask deliberate ambiguity. Perhaps you recall the insurance advertisement some years ago, during the heyday of so-called "plain language" insurance, which asserted that the company in question would pay claims against you arising from an automobile accident "even if it was not your fault." Well, more to the point, what would they do if it *was* your fault?

Finally, Edelman talks about the language of negotiation. Here the situation is a bit different in that the principal parties to a given exchange are roughly coequal in the amount of power they hold vis-à-vis one another. If they were not, there would be no need to negotiate. The stronger participant would simply impose his or her will on the weaker. Negotiating language appears in such places as labor agreements or treaties among nations, and in the public statements that accompany the completion of such documents. It is a blend of specificity and ambiguity designed to codify or put on the record the relationship that exists. Where there is agreement, the language is very precise: By 1 September 1995, you will remove and dismantle one hundred SS–20 missiles from Czechoslovakia and we will redeploy two hundred F–16 aircraft from advance bases in Great Britain to Omaha,

Nebraska. Where there is continuing disagreement but an apparent need exists among the parties to make it appear as if agreement has been achieved (for example, to satisfy public opinion or other governments in an alliance), the language is ambiguous: Both parties agree to promote peaceful development in sub-Saharan regions of Africa, and both support national self-determination for the peoples of that region. The latter is most common in international relations, where arms negotiations, peace plans, and the like tend to be reported in terms of agreements "in principle," diplomatic code for a failure to agree on details. Everyone sleeps better at night knowing that "progress has been made."

As Edelman suggests, political language is employed in these various ways to establish or reflect power relationships. But political language has other important uses as well. Not least of these is the setting of standards of judgment. Put most simply, what we call something can have a lot to do with how we think about it. Consider, for example, the ongoing debate over abortion, a medical procedure causing the expulsion of a relatively undeveloped fetus from the womb of the mother. In medical or biological terms, there is general agreement on the meaning of the term. But in politics, that is not the case at all. On one side of the issue, we find those who view the issue in terms of the rights of the mother to be free of an unwanted medical condition—pregnancy—and its long-term consequences—childbirth and the responsibilities of child-rearing. On the other side of the issue, we find those who view the fetus from conception as a functioning human entity entitled to rights, and legal representation and protection, of its own. But in the court of public opinion, those are not the terms of debate. Rather, we are presented with two carefully crafted and artfully posed choices: "freedom of choice" and the "right to life." What could be more inherently *American* than the former? Isn't this country, after all, *built* on the very foundation of free choice? Didn't we fight a revolution about that very thing? And what could be more inherently *American* than the latter? Is that right not now as *inalienable* as it was when the Declaration of Independence was drafted? If it weren't so difficult to get past the packaging of the issue, we might actually be able to resolve it. But that is the very point of the language. By tapping feelings or values that are widely shared in our culture, the proponents of each side rally support to their respective causes, or at the very least shore up their political defenses, not on the basis of reasoned argument so much as on that of conditioned responses to powerful words.

Nor is the abortion debate unique in this regard. Is the Palestine Liberation Organization an association of terrorists or of freedom fighters? Is the Israeli army a defense force or an army of occupation? It is very much a matter of perspective. Which is politically the more defensible: social *welfare* or Social *Security*? Both are programs that redistribute wealth from the haves to the have-nots. If anything, Social Security is the more regressive of the two programs, based, as it is, only on earned income. But try to tell that to the advocates from the American Association of Retired People. We don't hear much about "Social Security Cadillacs." Again, it is a matter of perspective. And other words serve equally judgmental purposes. Communist. Immigrant. Carpetbagger. Labels like these do much more than describe. And for that very reason, they have political potential. As Republican Phil Gramm of Texas once put it on the Senate floor, "If government does one thing well, it is that it distorts the language to try to affect the outcome of a debate."[7]

Language can also be used to frighten or reassure the public, depending on the needs of the moment. Do we have the best defenses money can buy, or are we on the short end of a missile gap, a tank gap, or some other vulnerability, real or imagined? The answer, insofar as the Department of Defense has one, is very much a function of where we happen to be in the budget cycle at the time the question is raised. Similarly, we may be experiencing ever-rising rates of crime and ever more efficient crime fighting. The Federal Bureau of Investigation will tell you either or both, again depending on when you ask.

This particular game extends as well to international affairs. During the Carter administration, for example, Saudi Arabia asked for an expression of American support as it found itself confronted across the Persian Gulf with a hostile and unpredictable revolutionary regime in Iran. The response, after some political battling in Washington, was to dispatch four "AWACS" aircraft, high-powered surveillance planes, to the area. The practical effect of this action was to extend from five to perhaps eight the number of minutes of warning Saudi forces would have of any impending Iranian air raid against oil facilities that were, in any event, all but indefensible. But the political effect was to extend what was referred to at the time as the "American security umbrella," in essence merely an overt expression of concern, to the Saudi oil fields. Whether for this or other reasons, the Iranians turned their attention elsewhere. The Iraqis, of course, proved somewhat more difficult to convince a few years later.

Efforts to reassure the public through such symbols do not always work as intended, of course, as the government of the Philippines discovered in September 1990. In response to charges that the national lottery was rigged, Philippine President Corazon Aquino asked the director of the National Bureau of Investigation, Alfredo Lim, to investigate, and the government moved to restore confidence in the integrity of the lottery by holding the drawing of the winning number in full public view on live television. The winner of the first televised lottery, worth about $200,000? The same Alfredo Lim. Coincidence is a marvelous thing.[8]

Finally, political language can be used to unify us as a people, or to divide us into factions. Consider the differences in news coverage between times when the president is in Washington, focusing on domestic policy, and when he is traveling abroad, focusing on foreign policy. In the first instance, the language of politicians, president, and the media alike typically centers on issues that divide one American from another. Who benefits from this legislation, and who is disadvantaged? Which special interests have the ears of the president, the key senators, the House committee chair? But on the road, dealing with foreign leaders and strange customs, the president represents all of us—our hopes, our aspirations, our very freedom and security. We are very pointedly reminded that what we have in common is more important than where we differ. Robert Lichter of the Center for Media and Public Affairs recently reported to a panel of political scientists, for example, his observation that news coverage of President Bush is evenly divided between positives and negatives when he is at home, but is eighty percent positive and twenty percent negative when he travels abroad.[9] And, if the polls are to be believed, at such times we often feel better, at least about the president, perhaps about ourselves.

The important point here is this: Political language does not just drop from the sky. It is created. It is molded. It is fashioned into messages designed to accomplish more or less clearly defined ends. It is distributed wholesale to the media. It is sold at retail. And we buy it. We demand it. And we fool ourselves into thinking it is something that it is not.

We do this for a number of reasons, not least of which is the fact that we have each been told, over and over again, that we have a civic responsibility to follow issues and events. Watch the news. Read the newspaper. Know what is going on in the world around you. Be informed. Sound familiar?

The difficulty is that, on most questions of political significance, those are the *only* ways that we *can* be informed. We are, quite simply, *dependent* on the news media for our knowledge and understanding of political affairs. They are our eyes and ears, our observers and interrogators. How, in fact, could it be otherwise? But in fulfilling that function, the news media have two weaknesses. First, for reasons that we will explore over the entire course of this book, they do not do a very good job of observing. And second, they have a vested interest in obscuring that first fact from us—indeed, in making us believe that quite the opposite is true.

News and other media occupy a position of particular privilege in American society. Not only are their rights expressly guaranteed in the Bill of Rights, they are guaranteed in the very *first* amendment. That tells us two things. To begin with, it tells us that the free press was seen by the Founding Mothers and Fathers as very important, worthy of first mention. But it also tells us that the press was not altogether trusted. It did, after all, require an *amendment* to the Constitution to codify its protected status.

Over the years since, the independence of the free press has achieved mythic standing, sufficient even to extend to pornography and clearly antisocial content. That is a tribute to the tolerance of the American people—or at least to that of their political elites—but it also gives rise to a pointed concern on the part of those in the media over the need, continually, to reinforce the legitimacy—the great perceived social value—of their privileged status. Why should this small and vulnerable group, once dubbed by Spiro Agnew, himself hardly a paragon of vice-presidential virtue, as "nattering nabobs of negativism" and, in any event, hardly representative of the diversity of American mass opinion, continue to be afforded special treatment? Because it is in the national interest and that of the public, whom they serve, to do so. It is vital to the survival of the press as presently constituted that the public be repeatedly and invariantly drilled in this catechism.

The media accomplish this task by assuming very publicly the posture of loyal adversary to the government and the political leadership of the country. While accepting the established political order—American media are decidedly *not* revolutionary—they exude skepticism about specific leaders and policies. They question, they press, they cajole, they snoop, they generate and express public outrage and concern. They are EveryAmerican. In theory, this is not only a valid, but an important role for the media, and it is a principal component of American democracy. In practice, however, it can also look a lot like self-aggrandizement and self-promotion. Because they *are* Every-American, they argue, the media have Rights, they have Privileges, they merit Special Consideration, they deserve Respect. *They* get the front row seats in the theater of politics. *They* walk the corridors of power and rest in its VIP lounges. And *they love it.* Irrespective of their genuine role in limiting the excesses of government, then, the media also have a significant interest in preserving *for its own sake* the myth of their centrality to democratic life—termed by political scientist W. Lance Bennett the "myth of a free press and a free people"—an interest that sometimes, and perhaps more often than we realize, motivates their behavior.[10]

The media also have an interest in money. U.S. news media are, almost without exception, commercial enterprises—many of them operated by major corporations—with the same needs for profitability as companies in other industries. And, at least in the aggregate, they are successful corporations. In 1987, for example, CBS Inc., parent company of the network, had total sales of $4.38 billion and profits of $235 million; Capital Cities/ABC earned $255 million on sales of a mere $4.2 billion; and Gannett, which published 129 newspapers in 36 states and *USA Today*, and which operated 15 radio and 8 television stations, had a profit of $320 million on sales of $3.1 billion.[11] And those are just three of the many successful companies in the media business. All in all, it is not a bad business to be in.

Increasingly, however, the media's interest in money has come to supercede their interest in journalistic values, or at the very least has increased the awareness among their journalist-employees of the audience-maximizing and cost-cutting concerns of management. The encroachment of business values into the television newsroom is nicely chronicled in *Almost Golden,* Gwenda Blair's account of the rise and fall of Jessica Savitch,[12] and has included everything from simple format changes to a restructuring of personnel requirements to emphasize personal attractiveness and performance skills over journalistic ability. Nor have newspapers, who see themselves as bastions of journalistic tradition, proven immune to the enticements of the bottom line. *USA*

Today, for example, in a remarkable acknowledgement of its niche as the pablum of the presses, is marketed through vending machines shaped like television screens, and even the revered *New York Times* changed its format from eight columns to six in the 1970s in order to increase its appeal to readers. Mammon wanders freely in the Fourth Estate, served by a priesthood of news doctors, pollsters, and people meter readers.

The point here is not that the news media serve no socially or politically redeeming function. To the contrary, their role is truly vital. Rather, it is that the motives of the media are inevitably mixed. Overt public service enhances the myth of the free press, which, while genuinely serving the needs of an open political system, also reinforces the special status we accord to the media. But to some extent, it is the "overt" part, not the "public service" part, that is, from the perspective of the media, the most important. To be seen as doing good is more important than any actual good that may be done. To this end, it is in the interests of the business side of the media to allow a good deal of freedom of action on the journalistic side, so long as audience appeal is enhanced or, at the least, not threatened. Recognizedly good journalism adds to the myth. But good journalism is merely the means to an end, and not the ultimate objective that upper management tends to have in mind. The journalists who work for news organizations are seldom willing, or even knowing, partners in this dual enterprise, but their work is surely judged in some quarters by economic and systemic, as well as professional, standards. And there is a growing body of evidence that suggests that, where good journalism comes into conflict with good business, good journalism is expendable.

If we consider, then, the overall relationship among the political leadership of the United States, the leading news organizations, and the American people, we can detect several cross-cutting interests that have direct consequences for the style of political communication that all will adopt. For politicians, the principal objective is to gain and hold power. This is achieved in our system by developing an image of authority, responsiveness, and responsibility, and converting that image into stewardship of a public office. The development and conversion of images is accomplished by the use of political language conveyed to the people through the news/mass media. For the media, the objectives are, collectively, to sustain their unique position of privilege in the social and political order, and to enhance their economic well-being. The former can be accomplished by appearing as careful, knowledgeable, but skeptical observers of political life; the latter by pandering to the basest interests of the audience. Again, political language can be employed to both ends.

As for the people/audience/voters/consumers/public/citizenry, it would be nice to say that they demand of political leaders and the media alike the highest standards of performance, accountability, and information. The evidence, however, suggests otherwise. Though there are those who have such expectations, most people do not. They simply do not have the interest in politics or the time, skills, or background to make such demands, or to make them stick. As Murray Edelman has put it in *The Symbolic Uses of Politics*,

> For most [people] most of the time politics is a series of pictures in the mind, placed there by television news, newspapers, magazines, and discussion. The pictures create a moving panorama taking place in a world the mass public never quite touches. . . .[13]

Politics, in other words, is in many ways equivalent to a long-running soap opera, a series of dramatized events that only remotely resemble real life. It is performed by a large, and largely unrecognized, cast of characters, all of whom have about them an aura of unreality.

What this means, in practical terms, is that the "people" will shape their expectations about politics and news, and the demands that they place on the purveyors of both, less in terms of policies than in terms of drama. Politics is expected to be good theater because, for most people, that is *all* it is. And in a democracy—economic as well as political—the will of the people must prevail. Translation: By working together to generate a continuing drama, spiced from time to time with new players and plot lines, political leaders *and* the media can achieve their separate objectives. And the means to that end? The effective use of both the verbal and nonverbal aspects of political language.

It is in this context that we can best comprehend the subject of this book: the purposeful manipulation of political language for political gain, and the people—the so-called strategic communication professionals—who do it. This group includes political campaign consultants, political public relations practitioners, direct mail specialists, press relations officers and publicists, lobbyists, communication consultants, media specialists, and others whose livelihood is based on their ability to manipulate political images in their own behalf or that of their respective clients. In effect, these folks have made a specialty of divining public opinions, moods, or appetites, and of shaping political messages to suit them. They are political engineers, not of policy, but of the process. And their numbers—and degree of sophistication—are ever increasing.

The task of strategic political communicators is something like that of a dating service trying to arrange a ménage à trois. They must first figure out what it is that each of the three parties—politicians, media, and public—wants out of its relationships. This they do through research—focus groups, surveys, discussions—which, in general, leads them to very much the conclusions that we have already developed. From this analysis, they must identify the points upon which the diverse interests of the parties coincide. Defining the relationship as narrowly as possible, they then develop communication strategies that meet the needs upon which there is agreement. They do this without calling attention to areas of disagreement, and, importantly, without addressing larger social concerns. The view they have of the political process is invariably a very short-term and very near-sighted one. Serve the client by pleasing the public today; worry about the consequences only when they arise. It is a political version of the hedonistic maxim: If it feels good, do it.

It is difficult to know what to make of people whose job it is to give the public what it wants. It is, for instance, quite tempting to see them as parasites clinging to the body politic, drawing personal gain as they siphon away its life's blood and demean its values. To be sure, few enter this particular profession out of a sense of altruism, and fewer still bill their clients on that basis. Indeed, the *New Republic* once headlined a feature on the Graduate School of Political Management, a New York school offering training in strategic political communication, with the sobriquet "School for Sleazeballs." But is it less accurate to portray them instead as the grease that lets the political wheel turn, the clutch that meshes the gears of democracy? Are they not translators of the ever-growing complexity of political life into terms that all citizens can understand? It could be argued, in fact, that if such persons did not exist, we would have to invent them.

The emergence of an entire industry of strategic communicators—a phenomenon of the last decade or so—raises these and a series of related questions. Just what is it that strategic communicators do? Who are their clients? What services do they provide? Are they guided by any sense of professionalism or ethics? How have they changed the ways that politicians and media organizations behave? What impact has their emergence had on the political system? These are the issues to be addressed in the pages that follow.

Notes

1. *The Prince* (New York: Mentor Books, 1952), p. 95.
2. Ibid., p. 113.
3. "U.K. Plans Ads to Support Deployment of Missiles," *Wall Street Journal*, 31 January 1983, p. 33.
4. Paul Taylor, "For Disconnected Americans, Citizenship Fades," *Washington Post*, 6 May 1990, pp. A1, A18.
5. His point is developed in *Public Opinion* (New York: The Free Press, 1965), pp. 3–22.
6. Murray Edelman, *The Symbolic Uses of Politics* (Urbana: University of Illinois Press, 1964), pp. 132–49.
7. 3 August 1989.
8. "Manila Lottery Investigator Wins It," *Washington Post*, 17 September 1990, p. A18.
9. Annual Meeting of the American Political Science Association, Atlanta, Georgia, August 1989.
10. W. Lance Bennett, *News: The Politics of Illusion,* 2d ed. (White Plains, N.Y.: Longman, 1988), pp. 182–87.
11. As reported in *The Value Line Investment Survey* (New York: A. Bernhard, 1987).
12. Gwenda Blair, *Almost Golden* (New York: Avon Books, 1988).
13. Edelman, *Symbolic Uses of Politics*, p. 5.

2 ALL THE NEWS THAT'S FIT TO PRINT

It was four o'clock in the afternoon of June 26, 1987, and I was seated at a table in the lobby of the Chosun Hotel in Seoul. The pepper gas that had permeated the air of the Korean capital for more than two weeks still hung heavy in the lobby, and the expectation of more to come as the hour of the climactic ''Great Peace March,'' promised for six o'clock, approached added to the atmosphere of tension. It was difficult to breathe.

If not at the center of the storm of protest that had swept the South Korean capital since President Chun Doo-Hwan's April 13 suspension of talks on constitutional reform, the Chosun was surely to the windward side. The Chosun was the unofficial headquarters for many of the foreign correspondents dispatched to Korea from Tokyo, New York, Rome, Hong Kong, and Melbourne, correspondents who were described to me by one Seoul-based Western journalist as ''the Saigon boys,'' those who follow the frontline stories from continent to continent; and the hotel was a target of opportunity for those who would reach a worldwide audience.

In the Chosun on that summer afternoon, the Saigon boys (I did not see any women among the press corps) were clearly in their element. They began appearing in the lobby alone or in groups of two or three, and within a few minutes were busy comparing the black-market gas masks and other regalia each had procured for the evening's festivities. There ensued what I can only describe as a fashion show, as one reporter or cameraman after another strutted back and forth from elevators to entranceway, ostensibly to check out the action in the street, but in truth, it seemed, to be seen by his colleagues. Small groups collected to judge the merits of one mask design over another, or to wrap towels around one another's necks to prevent gas-irritated skin.

The uniform of the day, which, allowing for differences of individual taste, was sufficiently standardized to suggest that it was issued from a central storehouse somewhere in the upper reaches of the hotel, was comprised of the mask (these ranged from World War I style black-rubber/charcoal-filter units to boxy canvas entries with large plastic visors reminiscent of the protective gear worn by workers repairing defects in nuclear power plants), a khaki vest or flack jacket with a turtleneck underneath to protect the neck and arms, a towel around the neck between shirt and mask, khaki trousers, heavy boots, and a yellow armband with "Foreign Press" printed on it in Korean.

The armbands were a story in themselves. Early in the demonstrations, as the number of foreign reporters swelled, the Korean Overseas Information Service (KOIS), the agency charged with assisting foreign journalists, had responded to journalists' requests by issuing official armbands. These were intended to facilitate the movement of reporters across police lines and their ready identification by all parties. It turned out, however, that a number of these armbands had also been provided to police informers. These informers were able to pass as foreign journalists because, since virtually none of the foreigners themselves spoke Korean, all required translators, and because several foreign news organizations are regularly represented in Seoul by Korean nationals. When questioned about this later, a KOIS official told me that the agency had actually obtained the armbands from the police in the first place, and it was likely that, unbeknownst to KOIS, they had retained some for their own use. Whatever the explanation, the incident badly damaged the credibility of KOIS and, since almost all government comment was channeled through the agency, sharply reduced the government's opportunities to persuade journalists to its point of view. By June 26, the correspondents had issued their own armbands.

At about five o'clock, the crowd in the lobby began to thin as each correspondent or camera crew drifted off to its own predetermined vantage point or rendezvous. A half hour later, the action started in earnest in the streets. Motorists began honking their horns in sympathy with the demonstrators, and student protesters began to appear in the downtown area. Lacking protective gear myself, and not wishing to exercise my tear ducts any more than was absolutely necessary, I retreated to my room, which commanded a view of three centers of activity in the streets, to observe.

To help place subsequent events in context, let me briefly describe a "typical" demonstration in downtown Seoul during this period. For all of their apparent violence, these clashes between students and police were highly stylized and mutually restrained. One might almost characterize them as "polite riots." Typically (and there were exceptions), the action began daily at about three in the afternoon. The riot police, comprised of college-aged conscripts diverted from military service, would arrive in specially equipped buses and occupy a number of intersections in the downtown area. The buses had steel mesh over all the windows to protect the occupants, and included such comforts as television sets on which, for example, the policemen watched Korea defeat Australia in the President's Cup soccer match while awaiting one day's activities. Supplies of juice or other drinks were kept cool in the shade under the buses. Sometime between 4:30 and 5:00, the students would arrive. They would emerge in small groups from the honeycomb of subway stations and underground shopping arcades that lies beneath the downtown area. When sufficient numbers had gathered, they would move toward the police and begin chanting slogans. In response, the police line, looking for all the world like an assembly line at the Darth Vader factory, would move toward the demonstrators, and one or two policemen would lob gas canisters. Both sides would then retreat until the scene repeated itself some minutes later. By about seven o'clock the students would disperse, and an hour or so later the police would leave.

What was really striking about this was that, as the demonstrations took place, stores and shops in the middle of the "riot area" were conducting business as usual; pedestrians, even mothers with small children, were going about their affairs, albeit suffering the discomfort of the lingering pepper gas; and traffic police, armed only with whistles and wearing no protective gear, kept the flow of downtown traffic nearly normal. The political life of the country may have been disrupted by these events, but its daily urban life was not. In effect, the demonstrations took place in a kind of bubble that floated here and there in the streets. Quite clearly, had the citizenry risen up to take on the police, the police could not have contained them. And quite clearly, the citizenry, including the demonstrating students, were not rising up.

What was happening in Seoul in June was an extension of an established device of the Korean political culture, the resort to violent protest by university students as a means of expressing public dissatisfactions. Such a device has proven necessary because, historically, Korean governments have not been open or responsive to less vehement expressions of public sentiment. Letter writing, petition signing, and the like have proven inefficacious and sometimes dangerous. Accordingly, there has developed a long-standing tradition of student activism, and the participants therein are accorded a degree of legitimacy by the public and the government alike. In this context, what was unique about the June 1987 demonstrations was not that they occurred, but that they spilled from the campuses, where they are usually contained, into the downtown area of Seoul, and that they continued for an extended period, even after the universities were closed. These two facts registered on all concerned.

That brings us to the events of June 26, which proved to be pivotal. On that Friday afternoon, some things were different. The arcade shops, which had gone about their business as usual in the preceding days, closed early, and the underground passages were virtually deserted of shoppers. Vader clones filled the strategic intersections in larger numbers than usual, and pedestrian traffic on the street level was reduced.

As the action began, two to three hundred students, many wearing protective masks or handkerchiefs, roamed the area I was observing. They moved in clusters from place to place, first attracting and then avoiding volleys of gas. The pattern was much like that of earlier demonstrations, with groups of ten or twenty (or, on rare occasions, as many as one hundred) gathering to chant rhythmic slogans or to sing. The police would respond by advancing their line and sending out runners to toss some gas. They would chase the students into the arcades, then stop at the entrances and retreat. Only once during the early stages of the demonstration did I see a policeman lob a gas canister into an arcade, and he was reprimanded on the spot by another officer.

About an hour and a half into this ritual, a camera crew came on the scene, its members easily identified by their armbands, yellow helmets, and other gear. While the camera crew got prepared, the small group of students gathered at one arcade entrance called to a second group which had been resting in a nearby plaza. This resulted in a tripling of their numbers, and represented by far the largest gathering of the evening at this particular location. On cue from a leader, the group began to chant much more emphatically than any group had previously. The effect was to goad the police into a much greater response than they had previously made, which included chasing the students into the arcade and tossing three gas canisters in after them, and, not incidentally, directing a gas canister at the television crew as well. All of this was captured on videotape, after which the journalists departed and the more passive pattern of confrontation set in once more.

In observing these events, I was reminded of a classic study conducted in 1951 by two sociologists at the University of Chicago, Kurt and Gladys Lang, that compared the perceptions of those watching television coverage of a Chicago parade welcoming General Douglas MacArthur on his triumphant, if involuntary, return from service in Korea, with the perceptions of eyewitnesses on the scene. The Langs placed observers along the parade route at each location where a television camera was stationed, and assigned others to watch broadcasts of the event.[1] In a comparison of reports by the two groups, they found that those who watched the parade on television saw a dramatic, intense welcome for a returning hero, while those who watched on the street had a far more reserved experience (if they could see anything at all).

The Langs offered two explanations for these differences. First, by using close-ups and cutting from shot to shot, television concentrated the potential drama of the proceeding, indeed, even added to it by speeding the *apparent* pace of events. Second, according to the on-scene observers, people watching the parade on the street actually behaved differently when they knew they were on camera than at other times. Television, after all, was a new phenomenon in 1951. Most people did not own a set, and many had not seen one. The prospect of actually having one's image captured for television was, for much of the population, every bit as thrilling as it clearly is today for those youths who regularly cluster behind correspondents doing live reports, and their behavior—jumping around, clapping, smiling, and panning for the camera—was similar. They knew little about the medium—Did your body vibrate slightly when the camera was pointed at you?—but they understood that when the red light was on, so were they. As a result, the crowds that the television audience saw were systematically unrepresentative of most persons along the parade route. The net effect was that the televised image of the parade was very misleading.[2]

That is essentially the phenomenon I observed in Seoul. I can say this with some confidence because of a unique feature of television in the Korean capital, the availability (after a time delay of some twelve to thirty-six hours) of much U.S. domestic news programming over AFKN, the Armed Forces in Korea Network. Operating as a third domestic television network (the others are owned or controlled by the Korean government), AFKN presents such news fare as CNN's "Headline News," NBC's "Today," ABC's "Nightline," and CBS's "60 Minutes," along with locally produced military news, a full complement of soap operas and prime time entertainment, and more baseball games than even Bob Eucker could care to watch, good seats or not.

In this case, AFKN brought pictures of the Korean riots back to Korea on the next day's news. The images conveyed are best described as a distillation of the most confrontational aspects of the most confrontational events of the period. This impression was confirmed for me and broadened when I overheard two conversations. In one, a correspondent for a prestigious American daily was entreating his Korean translator to search the Korean-language newspapers of the day, not for the general thrust of their content, but for the most vitriolic phrasing he could find, so that the correspondent could incorporate this in his own dispatch. In the second, a member of a U.S. camera crew just returned from an unsuccessful hunt complained in some seriousness, "We couldn't find any good action out there today. . . . They're trying to put us out of business."

Business was, in fact, quite brisk. Seoul was usually covered on a regular basis by only ten Western news agencies, with a total of nineteen journalists, only five of whom at that time were not Korean nationals. In June of 1987, their ranks were swelled to 350 as the Saigon boys descended. Virtually all official news of Korea was channeled through a single agency, KOIS, which also processed all news film and controlled the available satellite uplink for video. Virtually all unofficial news came from one of two sources, principal opposition leaders Kim Dae Jung and Kim Young Sam, and most of that from the former, who had three advantages as a source: he spoke English very well, having studied at Harvard; he understood American media, having lived in the United States; and he was always by the telephone, having been placed under house arrest by the government. Together with their observations of events in the streets and the translations they could obtain of the Korean press, itself not noted at the time for its independence from the government, these sources constituted almost the entire body of raw material from which the news of Korea was fashioned.

◆ ◆ ◆ ◆

There are two lessons that we can learn from the coverage of these events in Seoul and from many similar instances of news coverage. The first has to do with the nature of news itself, and the second with its impact on the audience. Let us take each of these in turn.

Though for competitive purposes they might have us believe otherwise, most American news organizations have a great deal in common with one another. They hire journalists from the same general pool of prospects, persons of similar social background and training. They organize to gather and process news in similar ways, and rely, by and large, on the very same sources for their raw materials. They compete with one another for the same or comparable audiences. And, perhaps most important of all, they define news itself in essentially the same terms. They are, quite simply, all in the same business. While each of these characteristics might seem self-evident, collectively they have some important consequences that tend to escape our notice. To explore these, let us begin with what seems to be a simple question: What is news?

There are several ways we could go about answering this. A literalist view, for example, might hold that news is comprised of whatever information gets published or broadcast in the news media. If an arms control treaty negotiation is reported to the public, it is news. If it goes unreported, it is, by definition, not news. We might think of this as the "800-pound gorilla approach" to defining news (so-named, for those who have mercifully reached their present stage of life without having heard the old children's joke, for the query, "Where does an 800 pound gorilla sit?" and the response, "Anywhere he wants to"). If it is *in* the news, it is—by the sheer weight of its presence there—*news*. Though compelling in its simplicity, the shortcoming of this definition is evident—it suggests no criteria for distinguishing news from nonnews other than a single fact—that it was reported.

A second approach might hold that news, or more correctly, "newsworthiness," is an inherent characteristic of certain information—that, for example, in which the public has some interest. In this view, the arms treaty negotiation mentioned above would, in fact, be news, *even if it went unreported.* This is more of an "ivory tower approach" in that it attaches no importance whatever to whether "news" ever appears in the media or reaches the public. Instead, it sees newsworthiness in idealized terms—as an *inherent* characteristic of certain events—a notion that is intellectually elegant, perhaps, but of limited practical value.

So far we have the makings of a good fairy tale—an 800-pound gorilla and an ivory tower—but no clear guidance with respect to the problem at hand, coming up with a useful way to think about news. Now, if this *were* a fairy tale, somewhere between the gorilla and the tower, there would doubtless lie a moat—deep, slimy, stagnant, and, if the tale-teller were truly talented, dragon-infested. But since the objective here is overcoming fantasies rather than promoting them, let us fill the void between gorilla and tower not with a moat, but with a synthesis. Let us find there something of a compromise view, one that sees newsworthiness partly as an inherent characteristic of certain events, and partly as a product of media decision making, but above all as the result of a social process, the product of three contributing factors: events, the needs of news organizations, and the professional values and actions of journalists.

Though we tend not to think of it in these terms, news is a manufactured commodity almost in the same sense as are automobiles and toasters. The world is filled with raw materials—events, official pronouncements, great social trends, and the like—any one or more of which can be converted into news on any given day. These supplies of raw materials are distributed geographically much in the way that iron ore or bauxite are, with especially rich deposits to be found in such media capitals as New York or Los Angeles, or such political capitals as London, Moscow, or Washington. Some raw news—the assassination of President Kennedy, for example, or the state funeral that followed—is pure and unadulterated, sprinkled on the surface in plain view. The hunter-gatherers must do little more than pick it up and pass it along. Other news stuff—such as the presence and outline of an assassination conspiracy—is mixed with impurities and hidden from view. It requires both digging and refining. The manufacturing companies—from Capital Cities/ABC to the Des Moines *Register*—send out crews (or contract with press syndicates) to track down the best material of both types and ship it to the central factory, the newsroom. There it is processed—given a particular form that the news organization is prepared to market to its particular audience. Just as steel can be shaped into a Mercedes or a Yugo, raw information can be shaped into the *New York Times* or the *National Enquirer*.

And just as an automobile plant cannot operate without steel, a newsroom cannot operate without a constant flow of external happenings about which to report. But not all events are equally (or even somewhat) newsworthy, and some criteria must be applied to determine which ones will merit time or space on a given day, and the manner in which each will be presented. Students of the newsmaking process have identified several criteria of this type. Among these are location, dependency on sources, timing, timeliness, predictability, dramatic content, and audience appeal. Let us say a word about each one in turn.

Because they are easier and less expensive to cover, stories that occur in a convenient location are more likely than others to be included in the news and to receive the most complete coverage. The major newspapers, news magazines, and television networks maintain bureaus in selected cities around the country and the world—cities like New York, Washington, Chicago, Los Angeles, London, and Moscow, which we described earlier as being news-rich. Most of the news they present originates in these cities, partly because it is in such places that news ore lies closest to the surface, but also because a significant portion of the total national news audience resides there (London and Moscow aside) and is chauvinistic enough to appreciate frequent reassurance that their hometowns merit journalistic notice. In this regard, it is interesting to note a front-page story by David Broder in the February 18, 1990, issue of the *Washington Post* that noted a decline in the number of minutes devoted to Washington stories on network newscasts. The headline: "Nation's Capital in Eclipse as Pride and Power Slip Away." It has been said that "all politics is local." Clearly, the same is true of much news.

Our diet of news-capital concentrate is supplemented by reports of events that occur in places that can be easily reached from these same cities, or that are taken from one or another wire service. But the more remote the location of the story or the more dependent a news organization is on a wire service account, the less likely a given report is to be prominently featured or accompanied by the visual addenda that attract audience attention and connote importance. Remoteness and difficulty of access kept even a long-running, full-scale war—that between Iran and Iraq—out of the news for almost a decade.[3]

At the very end of this pipeline are local newspapers and radio or television news programs, which draw very heavily on wire services or syndication as a source of raw material. In effect, when dealing with national or international affairs, these local news organizations trade in secondhand goods, news that has been gathered and shaped by others for their own purposes.

In addition to a story's location, the availability of sources of information—whether to stimulate coverage in the first place or merely to fill it in—is crucial. One important difference between a news maker and a reporter is that the former does things, the latter reports them. In the absence of a news maker ready and able to provide information to a reporter, there is, quite literally, no story. And it follows from this fact that whatever story a reporter writes will be in no small measure determined—and that is the correct word—by the source(s) he or she is able to employ.

This is a point of particular vulnerability for the media, and one of opportunity for those who would influence them. Daniel Schorr may have put the point most succinctly in a 1983 report on the massacre of American marines in Beirut when he observed that "We can only tell you what people in authority tell us."[4] Indeed, in a study of the sources to which news reported in the *New York Times* and the *Washington Post* could be traced, for example, political scientist Leon Sigal found that fully 75 percent of all news comes from official sources (the government).[5] And not only must sources be official, they must be proactive news makers. Describing the process of covering Congress, for example, Howard Kurtz of the *Washington Post* has commented that "staff members flack their reports to reporters, saying 'Look at page X, there's a good story there.' *That's what reporters need.*"[6] [emphasis added]. The dimensions of the vulnerability created by relying so heavily on government sources may finally have become clear when Larry Speakes, former spokesman for the Reagan White House, confessed that he had simply made up quotations during Reagan's 1985 summit meeting with Soviet leader Mikhail Gorbachev and attributed them to the president. Reagan, it seems, was not saying much, and Speakes was concerned that Gorbachev was gaining the public relations initiative. So he became—in the very fullest sense—the presidential spokesman. His efforts were widely circulated on the networks and in print. "Luckily," Speakes noted afterward, "the Russians [who had never heard Reagan speak these words] did not dispute the quotes.''[7]

We can see from the reporting in Seoul recounted above that the slant of the news was affected as much by the availability and skills of opposition leader Kim Dae Jung and by what reporters perceived as the unreliability of the government news agency as it was by events themselves. More generally, because all reporters on a given story or beat are likely to have access to the very same sources, their work product, the news in its various guises and packages, reflects a distinct tendency toward sameness. Timothy Crouse, in his book *The Boys on the Bus*,[8] revealed the pressures on reporters to conform to one another's view of events—to practice what has come to be called "pack" journalism—and more recent studies have documented a remarkable similarity in coverage across the three major network news programs, not only in topic selection, but in the styles by which particular stories are portrayed.[9] In effect, then, it does not matter whether one watches Dan *and* Peter *and* Tom *and* reads the *Times and* the *Post and U.S. News*, for in reality, all of them have the very same news, even if it is not, in some larger sense, all the news there is. It is all the news they have, and therefore it *is* all the news.

Perhaps the interdependence of these ostensibly independent news voices was best captured on the evening in February of 1980 when the story of "Abscam" first broke. Abscam, you may recall, was an FBI sting operation in which several members of Congress were snared in apparent efforts to sponsor private bills providing for the immigration to the United States of individuals from the Arab world, in return for which they were to receive rather sizable personal bonuses. Needless to say, this was a politically charged story and, coming on the heels of criticisms of the press during Watergate, was destined in its earliest stages to be handled very delicately. I recall watching the "CBS Evening News" that night. Near the top of the newscast, CBS broke the story that the FBI had reportedly caught a number of members of Congress through an undercover operation of uncertain purpose. Little detail was provided. Hungry for this latest tidbit on the temptations of power, I switched channels to the "NBC Nightly News." NBC had obviously had the story, but had not yet broken it—presumably because of an inability to verify the details. As soon as CBS broadcast its first mention, however, NBC—seemingly emboldened by the apparent congruence of material—weighed in with its own version, which specified the actual number of legislators who had been involved. I then switched back to CBS, which broke in with a bulletin stating the number of legislators *and* naming some names. Be there first, said the journalistic imperative. Be there on solid ground, said the editorial constraint. Be there in good company, said the lawyers. The news is the news is the news.

The timing of events, and their timeliness—not the same thing—are important considerations as well. All news organizations have deadlines, and events that occur in advance of those deadlines will, other things being equal, be judged as more newsworthy than those which would literally require stopping the presses. Interrupting a press run may make for high drama in a movie or television program, but as a business practice it can be a real career ender for the editor who orders it. We are not talking here about stories of obvious importance and immense urgency. Such stories are (thank goodness) extremely rare. Rather, we are talking about the nearly 100 percent of all news that is routine in nature—political campaigns, government reports, speeches, traffic congestion, crime rates, and the like. In such instances, news that misses deadlines is not news.

The existence of deadlines affects timeliness as well as timing. Audiences expect the news to have about it a sense of immediacy, and journalists try to convey the day-to-day flow of events with that expectation in mind. Stories are written so that they focus on what has transpired in the world between the last deadline and the next; where a choice must be made to meet time or space constraints, new is better than old, even in a time frame of no more than twenty-four hours. One effect this has on the news is to emphasize action over context, and events over analysis. Journalists, as a professional group, have an extraordinarily short attention span, and the news that they produce is little more than a collection of isolated snapshots taken on high-speed film.

Yet another criterion that determines the newsworthiness of events is their predictability. While it may, at first, seem counterintuitive given the myth of the free press, events that are routinized and predictable are more newsworthy than those that are unexpected. That is not to say that journalists do not cover, and cover prominently, airplane crashes, coups d'état, natural disasters, and the like. Quite to the contrary, such events are the stuff of banner headlines and "Nightline" features. But if you stop to "think about all the news you have read, heard, and seen over the last week, month, or year, chances are that far and away the largest part of it has not centered on such events. The Commerce Department's Index of Leading Indicators rose sharply last month. The Dow Jones Industrial Average fell 23.10 points today. The General Accounting Office issued its much-awaited report on military procurement practices. The mayor attended a charity gala. The latest round of talks aimed at countering the "Greenhouse Effect" began in Helsinki, Finland. The president traveled to Camp David for the weekend. Congress opened hearings on the budget for the next fiscal year. *None* of these events comes as a surprise. These stories, and, in fact, the overwhelming majority of news stories, are based on events that are scheduled well in advance or even on a regular basis. Indeed, most news organizations maintain calendars—often called "day books"— listing these events days, and often months, before they occur. These lists are compiled from press releases, announcements, established bureaucratic patterns of behavior, combing of previous news accounts, and a variety of other sources. They are management tools—planning documents that editors use to allocate their reporters, researchers, camera crews, photographers, sketch artists, and other resources and to develop initial ideas as to what will appear in the news each day.

To understand the importance of predictability in news stories, put yourself in the place of a news editor. It is eight o'clock in the morning. By eleven o'clock tonight, you must fill the equivalent of twenty newspaper-sized pages with information, none of which you presently have in hand. To assist in this, you have a staff of twenty reporters, three photographers, and a machine that receives wire reports from the Associated Press. What do you do? You could wait for the telephone to ring, and hope for some event that is sufficiently catastrophic to fill the newspaper. Aside from its consequences for the quality of life in a society where such events were daily occurrences, however, there is another drawback to this strategy: What if the phone doesn't ring? The advertising department has already sold all the space around your twenty-page "news hole," and you simply *must* fill the hole. Worse yet, what if the phone rings, but not until 9:30 in the evening. Not only too little, but too late. Is it time to break out the Pepto-Bismol? Not if you have your day book listing of events! Send a reporter over to the police station to cover the day's arrests, and another to the courthouse to follow the action there. Save some space for the Commerce Department report and the president's vacation. And on, and on. More often than not, the day book can fill the entire news hole irrespective of any unexpected events. In fact, precisely because these stories are predictable, they typically have *first claim* on the editorial resources that are available. In comparison, unexpected events are actually held to a higher standard: they must demonstrate that they are worth the cost and aggravation of *redirecting* the available news-gathering resources away from routine stories. "If the Daybook doesn't list it," said ABC's Bill Downs of this decision-making process, "it doesn't get covered."[10] Moreover, because every editor has essentially the same day book—or in the case of those provided by the wire services, *exactly* the same one—all the media in the same market are likely to cover the very same stories, day in and day out.

Added to location, timing, timeliness, and predictability, the inherent drama of events helps to determine their newsworthiness. Indeed, it is one of the most important decision-making criteria editors use. Stories that involve well-known personalities, physical action, controversy, or conflict—especially that which can be portrayed as occurring between the forces of good and evil (America versus Iraq, preservationists versus developers, environmentalists versus industry)—will be far more likely to receive coverage than will those lacking in such built-in drama. Think how dull the news would be without an Ayatollah, a Noriega, or an Ollie North. One result of this dramatic emphasis in the news is to reduce many complex events to simple morality plays. Another is to overemphasize the degree of conflict associated with events.

Occasionally, the media—especially television—get carried away with dramatizing the news and cross the line between fact and fiction. This was surely the case in 1989 in the ABC News coverage of one of the more bizarre espionage cases in recent memory, that involving Felix Bloch. Bloch, you may recall, was a ranking American diplomat who was very publicly rumored to have passed information to the Soviet Union, but never legally accused of having done so. For weeks he was hounded by journalists who followed him everywhere. (He took them on shopping excursions and twenty-mile runs, each of which was dutifully reported on the evening news.) Early in the development of the story, ABC conducted a dramatization of Bloch passing secrets to a KGB agent, which it taped in the style of an FBI surveillance recording, complete with cross hairs on the lens and a digital clock. The tape was aired on "World News Tonight," giving every appearance of being the real thing. Though the word "simulation" was superimposed over part of the tape, it was absent from the key ten seconds—an eternity on network news—when the handoff took place, thus giving the audience the clear impression that Bloch had been caught in *flagrante delicto*. The reaction of CNN's Washington bureau chief, Bill Headline—is that a name that fits the job, or what?—was typical. "Most of us," he said, "think simulations are dangerous. . . . [Using them] would tend to blur in the viewers' minds the difference between real and simulated coverage." But CBS Broadcast Group president Howard Stringer, speaking from the business side of the house, had a different view. "Why," he wondered, "can't television explore new forms of non-fiction?"[11]

Finally, an important criterion in judging the newsworthiness of an event is its prospective audience appeal. The subjects of news stories and the style of news presentation are selected in part because they are of interest to a large number of people. As we have already noted, the idea of serving the public interest is central to the myth of the free press, and it has always been claimed as a paramount objective of news organizations. Even those paragons of journalistic virtue, William Randolph Hearst and Joseph Pulitzer, prayed regularly at the Shrine of the Public Interest, though they defined their religion in rather self-serving terms. Hearst and Pulitzer together created the mass-audience press in the United States, principally through the sort of exclamatory journalism characteristic today of the British tabloids and their Rupert Murdock–owned look-alikes in the United States and elsewhere, and principally for the purpose of commercial gain. That Pulitzer is remembered today with some reverence—through the prize for distinguished journalism that bears his name—may have more to do with the quality of his press agent than with his journalistic spirit, which was as controversial in its time as it was innovative. Together with Alfred Nobel, who invented dynamite (the closest thing to nuclear weapons at the time it was devised) and who is remembered today through the Peace Prize awarded in his name, Pulitzer seems to have hit upon a successful technique of posthumous image enhancement.

Once the mass-audience press matured, however, and until the 1960s, the public interest in news was generally defined in terms of what the people *needed* to know—for instance, in seeking to fulfill their duties as citizens—and the professional values of journalists were paramount in determining the content and format of what was presented. That changed, however, with the advent of Frank N. Magid Associates, McHugh and Hoffman, and the other so-called "news doctors"—communication consultants who showed media organizations, particularly but not exclusively television broadcasters, that by introducing show business values into news production, they could greatly increase their audiences for news and, it followed, the money they received for presenting it.[12] These consultants, who came to the fore some twenty years ago, used a variety of methods to study audience reactions to the news, isolated those aspects of news presentation that people seemed to like most (and least), and proposed—first to broadcasters and later to the print media—that news ought to be styled to fit a profile of characteristics desired by its audience. In effect, what they advised media managers to do was to change the political language of the news.

If you think about it, most news is inherently threatening. It centers on crime, accidents, natural disasters, scandals—in short, the full range of problems confronting government or society. These are not events that make the average citizen feel good. To the contrary, they are troubling, upsetting. And the more we watch, the more troubling and upsetting they become. It is not surprising, for instance, that research finds heavy news consumers to have a disproportionately great fear of crime relative to the actual crime rates in their communities. Crime may strike one citizen in ten or twenty, but it fills every newscast and front page. The natural language of news is a language of cynicism, of discouragement, of problems that defy solution. Its effect on the audience is perhaps best captured in the ironic lyric of a popular song of the 1970s entitled "A Little Good News":

> Nobody was assassinated in the whole third world today,
> And in the streets of Ireland all the children had to do was play,
> And everybody loves everybody in the good old USA.
> We sure could use a little good news today.[13]

In this gloomy pit of pessimism, the news doctors found a source of light. Their great insight was the realization that, although one could not change the raw material from which it was made, one could change the process by which that material was fabricated into news and distributed to the public. More particularly, one could render the content of the news less burdensome by packaging it more attractively. That meant two things.

First, it meant that the news had to derive its appeal not from the nature of events, but from the nature of the audience itself. People were naturally more interested in domestic affairs than in foreign affairs, so the news should emphasize domestic events and personalities. People were more interested in other people than in thoughtful analysis, so news stories should be weighted heavily toward the human-interest aspects of events. News should tell us a great deal more about the families of American hostages held in the Middle East, the good doctors divined, than about the fine points of the political upheaval in Lebanon. *That* is what inquiring minds wanted to know. And, though many Americans, instilled as they are since childhood with a sense of civic responsibility, might need to *feel* informed, when you got right down to it, they preferred to be entertained more than they preferred to *be* informed. News, therefore, should be more entertaining—with slides, photographs, white space and open print formats, video graphics, Doppler weather radars, physically attractive media personalities, and the like—in ways that enhanced its *appearance* of keeping people informed even if some such devices actually had the opposite effect.

Second, the news, especially that on television, had to make people feel better about themselves rather than worse, had to reassure rather than threaten them. The big innovation here was the so-called "Eyewitness News" format—"Eye*witless* News" to its critics—in which the several members of a news "team" shared the camera with one another, and engaged in friendly banter about the news itself, the production of their news program, or some long-running "inside" joke to which the audience was privy. The objective here was to convey to the audience by the context in which it was presented the fact that, even though the news itself might not be so good, we have not lost our ability to enjoy life. We still like each other. We still like you. Tune in again tomorrow. Journalism as group therapy.

In effect, what the news doctors prescribed was for news organizations to consider the extent to which any particular story or story treatment appealed to the emotional needs and entertainment preferences of the audience. They reasoned that news packaged with these criteria in mind would, over time, attract a larger audience and make more money, thereby justifying the cost of their own advice. And they were right.[14] Beginning with television stations owned by Westinghouse Broadcasting and ABC, and expanding rapidly outward, this form of group-grope news came to dominate many local television markets; it was the subject of a brief experiment at the network level at ABC, which adapted a four-way split screen approach first developed by its sports department to produce a program widely and derisively known as "ABC Wide World of News"; and it eventually extended even to the print media, as reflected not only in the *USA Today* vending machines we noted in chapter 1, but in the reformatting of all the leading news magazines and the addition and redesign of specialized newspaper sections intended to appeal to particular segments of the audience. Style. Today. People. World News.

This concern over the audience appeal of events brings us directly to the second general factor in determining what is news: the needs of news organizations. It is a factor that we addressed to some extent in chapter 1, but that nevertheless deserves some added emphasis here. News organizations have two sets of needs. If they were people and we were psychologists, we might term these "love" needs and "subsistence" needs. Since they are not, and we are not, let us use two alternative labels: *power* and *money*.

The power needs of news organizations are, as we argued earlier, less focused on influencing events as an end in itself than on preserving for the press a social position of status and authority. The objective is to maintain the society's *active, affirmative* acquiescence in granting privileged standing to the news media, a continual reiteration of collective acceptance of the myth of the free press. In this, the media are somewhat like the dictator who dominates his country absolutely, but wishes for the love and respect of his subjects lest he feel somehow unfulfilled. "People of Parador," says the brutal and megalomaniacal military ruler of that tiny fictional nation in the movie *Moon Over Parador*, "I love you!"

The money needs of these organizations center on the key to economic survival, bringing in more revenue than is expended, and, more and more in recent years, on assuring favorable comparisons of profitability. As increasing numbers of media organizations have been swallowed up by holding companies or conglomerates, their business environment has taken on new dimensions and the standards of comparison have been raised. Individual newspapers or stations must compete against their corporate siblings, and their parent companies must compete against both one another and the full range of industrial corporations.[15] In an era of merger mania and the leveraged buy-out, to falter in the near term may be to disappear in the long.

As the power needs of the press have been challenged in recent years—openly and systematically by the Nixon administration, with more reserve and subtlety by others since—and as the dangers of financial missteps have grown, pressure from the business side of news organizations on the editorial side has increased, and the ability of editors to withstand that pressure has been diminished. Appearance comes to count for more than content, performance for more than journalistic competence, because these are the values that appeal to the audience, and the audience must be served. The conflict here arises from two very different views of the role of the news media.

From the management perspective, news media are, first and foremost, advertising vehicles. In this, they are no different from other media (*House and Garden,* say, or MTV), nor is the news different from other content in a given medium ("The Cosby Show" or the comics). Advertisers (or "underwriters," the more dignified term applied to the same function in public broadcasting) want to reach an audience—either a mass audience or a demographically select one, depending on the anticipated market for the product in question—and will pay the media based on the size and desirability of the audience they are able to deliver through certain programs or publications. In this view, if news and public affairs content can be presented in ways that enhance the audience that is delivered to advertisers, then this should be done. Without question. Without reason to question. "Geraldo!" draws an audience. What can we learn from him?

From the editorial perspective, news doctors and business managers represent the first wave of an impending darkness, a horror of such indeterminant dimension that it would make even Stephen King proud. People on the editorial side not only accept the myth of the free press, they consider themselves to be its living embodiment. Dimly, they perceive that advertising does fill some time or space in their medium. Remotely, they suspect that a relationship exists between the commercial success of their organization and its ability to pay their salaries. But these things are not important. News media, in their view, have two sets of employees, one of which has an overriding sacred trust. It is the sacred responsibility of the editorial side to assure that "good" journalism be done—whatever that may be. It is the subsidiary responsibility of the business side to maintain—but never ever in any way to impinge upon—an environment where the editorial side is free of all worry except that of meeting the sacred trust. Geraldo and his ilk are

Vandals, looting and pillaging the sacred trust. We are the last civilized folk on Earth.

This editorial perspective is a direct outgrowth of the third general factor that helps to define the news—the professional values of journalists and their own understanding of just what it is they are supposed to be about. As we have already seen, reporting and editing are high-pressure, deadline-driven activities where tremendous emphasis is placed on the short term. Reporters rush from place to place, source to source, story to story, and, in many cases, subject to subject, with scarcely the time to pause, let alone to ponder. They are, for the most part, both educated and intelligent—two distinct traits which are often confused with one another—but most do not have training in law, economics, policy science, languages, or other fields that would provide them with a depth of understanding of the actors and events they cover. They are forced by time, training, and circumstance alike to adopt a very superficial style in the stories they write, a style that often reflects their own understanding of events. ABC's Jeff Greenfield captures this pressure and some of its consequences when he says, "If I'm doing a piece [on the various and distinctive democracy movements in Eastern Europe] for the network news, and it's supposed to run 1 minute and 45 seconds, and I say, 'Can I please have 20 more seconds to explain the pro-democracy movement?' . . . that might put my piece over. That's why people are so desperate for those shorthand terms."[16]

In order to cope with the stresses and other shortcomings of their work environment, journalists have developed a rather extensive set of professional norms, and devote inordinate amounts of time to discussing them with one another. Among other things, journalists see themselves as

• neutral observers, whose job is to transmit to the public information summarizing the policies and actions of the government and of political leaders;

• interpreters of government and politics, whose special expertise or knowledge and extraordinary access carry with them a responsibility to help the public better to understand the flow of issues and events;

• participants in policy making, whose fluidity of movement among the branches and levels of government makes them especially well-suited to serve as intermediaries, carrying messages back and forth between policy makers; and

• guardians of the public interest, unelected representatives of the public whose special responsibility is to protect its members against the errors and excesses of government.[17]

A good example of how these different roles interact with one another is provided by Hedrick Smith in *The Power Game: How Washington Works,* which summarizes the observations of government and politics by the veteran *New York Times* correspondent.[18] While his observations are interesting, it is the book itself that best illustrates the point. In it Smith reports on his personal conversations with junior and senior members of both houses of Congress, senior executive branch officials in several successive administrations, government whistleblowers, bureaucrats at various levels in all areas of the federal establishment, political consultants, defense contractors, and many others. No government official—not even, or, perhaps more correctly, *especially* not the president of the United States—is likely to have so extensive a network, and none can move so freely from contact to contact. Observer, interpreter, participant, guardian—each of these professional obligations is reflected not only in specific incidents but in the book and in the series of television documentaries it spawned, as well.

It is when these high purposes come into conflict with the other roles of the journalist—production worker in the assembly line that manufactures news, and cog in the bureaucratic wheel that is a media organization—that tensions rise on the factory floor. The mix is potentially an incendiary one: Legions of M.B.A.s and lawyers, whose training is in journal entries rather than journalism, liability rather than credibility, and whose loyalty is to a corporate headquarters that may be a short elevator ride away from the newsroom geographically, but light-years away from it philosophically. Journalists pursuing the sacred trust and, not incidentally, the ego satisfaction of seeing their work in print or on the air. Editors schooled in the sacred trust, but nose-to-nose with budget constraints and cautious lawyers. Explosions are few, but the pressures can be intense. The need to coexist—to cooperate, to *accommodate*—can become an imperative. So we sell the newspaper from a television set. So we hire an empty-headed pretty face to read the news. So we add 20 percent more white space to the format. It's still the news, isn't it? The 800-pound gorilla says "yes," and, in at least the narrowest sense, the 800-pound gorilla is right.

Two points here are worth noting. First, the decision-making factors and pressures that we have just described do not operate precisely the same way in every news organization, but they consistently tend in that direction. That means that these elements tell us something useful about the media, but it also means that they tell us something useful about the news. The news on Channel 7 will not be identical to that on Channel 9, in the *Herald* to that in the *Tribune*, but they will look very much alike. Both cover the same events, using journalists with equivalent training and similar perspectives, relying on the same sources of information, trying to appeal to the same audience. Each is an independent voice of journalistic integrity, but on most tunes they sing in harmony. Indeed, they may feel pressured to do so. During the early stages of the Persian Gulf crisis of 1990, for example, NBC News Executive Producer Steve Friedman was asked, in effect, whether he would opt to provide live, unedited coverage of a military conflict between Americans and Iraqis, complete with blood and gore, if there happened to be a camera on the scene. "I probably would," he said. His reason? "Because I'd be looking at three other monitors which also had it on."[19] The apparent choice of voices available to the public is just that—an *apparent* choice. Reading and viewing widely may make people *feel* more informed, but there is little reason to think they will really *be* so.

The second important point is that, for all their sameness and for all their limitations, the media are the only source that most of us have for our knowledge and understanding of events that are happening in the world. We are dependent upon them. This is a big and complex country in a big and complex world. Most people simply do not have direct, daily, personal contact with news events and news makers. And the more remote the events—national rather than local, foreign rather than domestic—the less the likelihood of personal contact, or even relevant personal experience. How many conversations have you ever really had that began, "Well, when I was talking with the secretary of state last week . . . ," or "Hi, George. Sorry to interrupt your meeting with Mr. Gorbachev, but . . . " Not, I dare say, blessed many. To be sure, we do experience certain events first hand—good or bad economic times, voting, and the like—but we tend to be at the end of the line on these, not at the front. We live with the consequences of decisions and policies—who the candidates are, what the tax rate will be—rather than making them.

But those decisions can be very important to us. They affect our personal wealth, health, and general well-being. Taxes take our money, prisons our time, wars our lives. We *need* to know what is going on. We need an inter*media*ry, some person or agency to intercede in our behalf, to keep an eye on what those scoundrels in Washington or the state capital or city hall are up to. We need the news media. And we *need* to believe in them. If it is "them versus us," we need to know, in our heart of hearts, that the media are us. We need to accept the myth of a free press and a free people every bit as much as the media need us to do so. We are dependent. We are addicted. In a sense, we are *all* news junkies.

Some years ago, Jerzy Kosinski captured the essence of our media dependency in his novel *Being There*.[20] The protagonist of the novel, one Chauncey Gardiner, or Chance, had lived all his life in an isolated environment. His only contact with the outside world came through television, and his understanding of every action with which he did not have direct personal experience—everything from politics to sex—came from, but was limited by, what he had seen on television. At first, this made him appear to the reader as having more limitations than others in the society (he did not have cable!). But as the story developed and Chance emerged as a prominent public figure, it became clear that, for all of their apparently greater sophistication and base of experience, the other characters in the novel were equally limited, equally dependent on media stereotypes for their interpretations of reality. Kosinski's point was that those of us who think we are immune to media dependency are merely fooling ourselves.

Are we all characters in a real-life *Being There*? Have we, in fact, been there? We've been on the moon with Neil Armstrong. We've been in Tehran with the American hostages. We've trudged through the snows of New Hampshire with countless presidential hopefuls, visited the Great Wall of China with Richard Nixon, and slipped inside the walls of the Kremlin with Ronald Reagan. We've been in Seoul with students marching for the democratization of South Korea. Or have we?

What we believe we know about such times and places and people—and we do, most assuredly, *believe* it—we have learned in most instances from one source, and one source alone: the news media. We watch, we read, we listen—therefore we know, we understand. But *what* do we know? We know whatever it is we have been able to extract from the content and context of the news. We know things that are timely, predictable, simplified, dramatized, and packaged to appeal to what communication consultants think we already know and believe, and want to believe. We know things that are superficial by design, that titillate and entertain. We know things that make good film at eleven. We know things that come with white space and graphics. We know things that make us comfortable. We know things that the media tell us. We know next to nothing.

As citizens in a democracy, we will use what we know to exercise our rights and to fulfill our duties. We will apply the information we gather from the news media to formulate and act on our preferences through the democratic institutions of government, to frame the standards of judgment that we will apply to select political candidates in elections and to judge their performance once in office. Our political system will be enriched—well, at least affected, which is all that one can reasonably hope for in a democracy—by our participation. And if there is a discrepancy between reports and reality? If events themselves are staged—reality is altered—to influence those reports? If the media cooperate with the news makers in framing those reports so that they will meet more completely the criteria of newsworthiness? Is the myth of the free press endangered? To the contrary—albeit ironically—it is enhanced. For the more the media *seem* to be pursuing their great trust, the more they are *believed* to be doing so. The more they are believed to be doing so, the more popular support there is for the myth of the free press. Appearance is reality. Appearance is the key. Enter stage right: The Strategic Political Communication Professional.

Notes

1. Though this study is still widely cited as one of the earliest applications of formal experimentation in the social sciences, the Langs themselves suggest its design was serendipitous. As graduate students at the University of Chicago in 1951, both were enrolled in a course in mass behavior. As Kurt Lang tells it, when they heard that General MacArthur was to be feted, someone suggested, "Let's go out and study mass behavior." His wife Gladys, however, and a second student in the class were pregnant at the time and were reluctant to stand in the expected curbside crowds for long periods, so they arranged to borrow a television set from the Chicago-based Zenith Corporation, and the two women watched at home. The rest, as they say, is history.

2. Lang and Lang, *Politics and Television* (Chicago: Quadrangle Books, 1968), pp. 36–77.

3. The reasons are set forth in Hodding Carter III, "War Reporting: Path of Least Resistance," *Wall Street Journal,* 18 November 1982, p. 31.

4. Cable News Network, October 23, 1983.

5. Leon Sigal, *Reporters and Officials: The Organization and Politics of Newsmaking* (Lexington, Mass.: D.C. Heath, 1973), p. 124.

6. Scott Shuger, "File Before Reading: When the Inspector General Speaks, Nobody Listens," *Washington Monthly*, January 1990.

7. Ann Devroy, "Things Reagan Never Said," *Washington Post*, 12 April 1988, p. 1.

8. Timothy Crouse, *The Boys on the Bus* (New York: Ballantine Books, 1972).

9. See, for example, Edward Jay Epstein, *News from Nowhere* (New York: Vintage Books, 1973); and "Straying from the Network Pack," *Channels*, July/August 1988, p. 80.

10. Quoted in William Barry Furlong, "The Misleading of America," *TV Guide*, 18 June 1977, p. 6.

11. Eleanor Randolph, "ABC and the Spy Story Simulation," *Washington Post*, 25 July 1989, pp. C1, C4.

12. "The News Doctors," *Newsweek*, 25 November 1974, p. 87.

13. Charlie Black, Rory Bourke, and Tommy Rocca, *A Little Good News*, (Chappell & Company and Bibo Music Publishers, 1983).

14. "Happy Talk," *Newsweek*, 28 February 1972, pp. 46, 51.

15. For one of many examples of the pressures this generates see Tom Shales, "NBC News' Un-Chung Dilemma," *Washington Post*, 28 March 1989, pp. D1, D2.

16. Quoted in John Horn, "Dueling Buzzwords," *Chicago Tribune*, 15 January 1990.

17. Delmer Dunn, *Public Officials and the Press* (Reading, Mass.: Addison-Wesley, 1969), pp. 7–22.

18. Hedrick Smith, *The Power Game: How Washington Works* (New York: Random House, 1988).

19. Interview on CNN "Prime News," 3 September 1990.

20. Jerzy Kosinski, *Being There* (New York: Bantam Books, 1972).

3 BLUE SMOKE AND MIRRORS

American political lore is filled with tales of decisions made by small clusters of cigar-chomping politicos ensconced in smoke-filled hotel rooms. Perhaps the most famous of these sessions was the one held on the thirteenth floor of the Blackstone Hotel in Chicago in 1920 that purportedly selected Warren G. Harding as the Republican party's presidential nominee. Though such a meeting did take place, the nomination was not, in fact, finally decided there. Indeed, Harding's campaign manager, Harry Daugherty, was not even aware of the meeting.[1] Still, it *was* the party bosses rather than the rank-and-file membership who settled on Harding, and the party convention that ratified their decision gave, at best, an illusion of democracy.

Times have changed since 1920. The parties—Republican and Democratic alike—have been weakened over the intervening years, and, what with primaries and caucuses and proportional representation, such political bosses as remain do not generally have the power to control the presidential nomination, or even the use of their respective party labels. Illusion is still very much a part of democratic politics, of course, but today it comes less from blue smoke than from mirrors. That difference has nothing to do with the recent strength of the antismoking lobby, and everything to do with the practice of strategic political communication.

The Democratic National Convention of 1988 was held in Atlanta, Georgia, in July of that year, while the Republicans convened the following month in New Orleans, Louisiana. But in the final analysis, the outcome of the 1988 presidential election was probably settled on the Thursday evening before the Memorial Day weekend in two small rooms in Paramus, New Jersey. The first room held sixteen people at a sitting—fifteen voters and a discussion leader. The second held five of George Bush's most senior campaign aides: campaign manager Lee Atwater, media adviser Roger Ailes, pollster and strategist Robert Teeter, chief-of-staff Craig Fuller, and friend and adviser Nicholas F. Brady. The rooms were connected by a sound system and a one-way mirror; the voters could see themselves in the glass. The arrangement is known as a "focus group." The objective in Paramus was to "focus" on Michael Dukakis.

Strategic communication was very much a part of the Bush campaign even before it *was* a campaign. Two years earlier, in the spring of 1986, for example, the then–vice president's advisers, notably Teeter, had become concerned about Bush's "high negatives"—relatively widespread negative feelings or impressions about him held by the public—and cast about for a strategy to reduce them. Of particular concern were linkages being drawn in the press between Bush and various oil interests. The strategy Teeter and his aides settled on—for reasons we will discuss in a later chapter—was to get the vice president out of the news for an extended period—to make him into the invisible man. The idea was that, if the public lost sight of Mr. Bush altogether for a period of several months, by the time he re-emerged into view his image would be a clean slate, devoid of excess political baggage, and one that could be molded to fit the needs of the 1988 campaign.[2] Given the fact that his client was serving at the time as vice president of the United States, Teeter's was not merely a sophisticated gambit, but a daring one.

With all of the jokes we hear about the vice presidency—John Quincy Adams once described it as "the most insignificant office that ever the invention of man contrived or his imagination conceived" and Harry Truman, in somewhat earthier terms, as "a cow's fifth teat"— making the vice president disappear might seem like a relatively easy thing to do. But in the event, given the pervasiveness and intrusiveness of the contemporary press and Bush's obvious interest in higher office, it presented quite a challenge. Bush and the team put together by Teeter's firm, Market Opinion Research, were mostly up to that challenge. Over a period of almost two years, the vice president rendered himself all but inaccessible. He reduced his calendar and avoided appearances where he might be expected to interact with the media. In effect, he hid from the press. It was a variant of the so-called "Rose

Garden Strategy"—by which a president campaigns for re-election from the relative sanctuary of the White House rose garden—but without benefit of the flowers. And sure enough, despite occasional commentaries about his low visibility, Bush all but dropped from sight in the media, and his worrisome linkages to oil interests disappeared.

Now, the danger in a strategy like this one is that, when a politician decides it is time to emerge from the cloisters, his or her "new" image will be heavily influenced by the first one or two subsequent activities that get reported. Bush's reappearance was necessitated, of course, by the impending presidential primary season, and in the fall of 1987 he cast caution to the wind and went public. Unfortunately, his first public activity was to deliver a speech in the Soviet Union in which he praised the craftsmanship of the mechanics who maintained the Soviets' fleet of tanks and urged that, when they ran out of work, Moscow should send them to Detroit. The clear implication was that American autoworkers could learn a great deal about worker attitudes and quality control from those in the Soviet Union.[3] Needless to say, this did not play well in Peoria, not to mention Detroit, and Mr. Bush paid a price for it in the early primaries and state conventions. He ducked from sight for two more weeks to let the ensuing mini-crisis pass, then reappeared for good.

Did the strategy of invisibility work? It did entail some costs. In particular, it probably contributed to the "wimp" image that dogged Mr. Bush through much of the 1988 campaign, and to the impression that endured into the early years of his presidency that he was indecisive; and it lead cartoonist Garry Trudeau ever afterward to picture Bush in his widely read *Doonesbury* comic strip as an invisible character. But, by the same token, the strategy was so successful in recasting the candidate and breaking his perceived links to the oil industry that even during the extended period of public concern over governmental response to the grounding in Alaska of the tanker *Exxon Valdez* in the spring of 1989 and three other massive spills that followed it in short order—an unplanned acid test of the Bush strategy—few press accounts suggested undue presidential sympathy for the industry, or even noted his connection to it. And while political scientists and others might argue that Bush's presidency itself was weakened by a campaign heavy on distortions and half-truths and light on substantive policy— the books piled high in Union Station notwithstanding—one simple fact remains: George Bush became president of the United States.

Even by May of 1988, with polls showing Bush's positives and negatives roughly in balance, his advisers were confident that they were working with a "new" George Bush. They did, however, face some problems, not least of which was the unexpectedly early emergence from the Democratic pack of Massachusetts Governor Michael Dukakis, and, more troubling still, his five to one ratio of positive to negative voter impressions. Their sense of unease was fed by a recently released Gallup Poll that showed Bush trailing Dukakis by sixteen percentage points. The situation was in flux, but things were not necessarily breaking their way. It was, once again, time for decisive action.

So it was that the Bush team brought to Paramus two groups of voters—fifteen in each—all of them so-called "Reagan Democrats," conservative crossover voters who were thought to be essential for a Republican victory, but who were leaning at the time to Dukakis. They brought, as well, a treasure trove of material they had been collecting about the presumed Democratic nominee. The Massachusetts program for furloughing prisoners. The governor's veto of legislation requiring teachers to lead the recitation in schools of the Pledge of Allegiance. The pollution of Boston Harbor. These issues were presented in an impartial manner by a professional discussion leader, and were mulled and bandied about by each group. By the end of the evening, half of the participants had deserted the Democratic front-runner.

Of such conversions, strategies are made, and the lights that went on in the room behind the mirror were not just electric. Lee Atwater later told the *Washington Post* of that evening, "I realized right there that we had the wherewithal to win . . . and that the sky was the limit on Dukakis' negatives." Over the weekend, the coterie of advisers huddled with the candidate at his home in Kennebunkport, Maine, and a week later, at a Republican meeting in Texas, the vice president came out smoking. From that point forward, attack speeches and attack ads were the order of the day. The Democrats tried to counter—through consultant Stanley Greenberg they arranged some focus groups of their own in California and Texas—but the Dukakis campaign was in a state of some disarray at the time, with leadership changing hands from Susan Estrich to John Sasso, and lines of authority uncertain, and the candidate himself was unwilling to respond.[4] His was a dilemma that is becoming common in contemporary political life—get down and mix it up, even at the risk of demeaning the campaign, or lose. Whether he understood its consequences or not, Dukakis made his choice.[5]

♦ ♦ ♦ ♦

Focus groups like those used by both the Bush and Dukakis campaigns are among the most widely used tools of strategic communication. One of the most important things a political operative needs to know is which themes resonate with the public to the advantage or disadvantage of his or her client. Public opinion polls can be used at times to elicit this information, but they have several disadvantages, not least of which are their cost and cumbersomeness. In order to reflect public opinion accurately, a poll must include interviews with at least several hundred people, and often more than a thousand. That can cost tens of thousands of dollars, and can take several days to accomplish. Even then, because polling requires a very highly structured procedure that forces people's answers into a few summary categories that usually have to be thought of before the poll is taken, it cannot be used effectively to meet some needs for information that arise during a political campaign. Polling does have its place, but strategic communication is a field where quickness and agility are sometimes worth more than accuracy, and where soft and fuzzy can be better than firm and precise. Focus groups—really no more than little groups of (carefully selected) neighbors sitting around with a discussion leader and talking or reacting—offer a quick, soft, and fuzzy measure of the public mood. Focus groups are now a commonplace of consumer research on various products or advertisements, and their role in politics is sure to increase after their successful use in the 1988 campaign. Unfortunately, their 1988 product, the negativism of the campaign, is likely to become more commonplace as well.

Negative campaigns are nothing new in American politics. The campaign of 1884, waged between Grover Cleveland and James G. Blaine, was sufficiently tawdry, for example, to move one observer to describe it as a contest between "the copulative habits of one and the prevaricative habits of the other,"[6] and the California gubernatorial campaign of 1934 led socialist reformer and Democratic candidate Upton Sinclair, target of the nation's first "strategic" media campaign, to complain that "I don't know what there is left for them to bring up unless it is the nationalizing of women." Sinclair had already been portrayed in a cartoon in William Randolph Hearst's *Los Angeles Ex-*

aminer as "The Fourth Horseman [of the Apocalypse]" along with Hitler, Stalin, and Mussolini. Two days after his remark, the *Los Angeles Times* printed a Sinclair comment on cooperative child care under the headline "Nationalizing Children."[7]

A more recent example of the genre is provided by the campaign of 1964, in which the Democrats succeeded (with some inadvertent help from the opposing standard-bearer) in casting Barry Goldwater as a trigger-happy eccentric whose election would bring the world to the brink of nuclear Armageddon. One television commercial in particular—the now-famous "Daisy" spot—captured the essence of the Johnson campaign. It pictured a little girl in a field pulling petals from a daisy and counting up their numbers. As the camera zoomed in on her eyes, a more ominous launch countdown replaced her sing-song voice, and a hydrogen bomb exploded on the screen. Enter the solemn voice of Lyndon Johnson: "These are the stakes: to make a world in which all of God's children can live, or to go into the darkness. We must either love each other, or we must die." Lyndon Johnson was not a man of subtlety. The effect of this spot on the campaign was the same as if Goldwater had been standing at ground zero.

While it is fashionable to decry the use of negative messages and images in political campaigns, it is probably more constructive to consider why candidates continue to use them. There are many possible answers to this question. Negative messages tend, for example, to be entertaining and humorous, and are generally more memorable than positive messages. They seem to stimulate the creative juices of writers and producers, and to enliven the campaign staff and the candidate's most partisan supporters. L. Patrick Devlin, a student of political advertising, describes negative campaigning as a kind of political voyeurism whose appeal is similar to that of pornography,[8] while Montague Kern has suggested that negative messages appeal to the underlying political cynicism of the American public.[9] Perhaps most important, however, is the way in which negative messages, especially in advertising, fit the approach of the strategic communication professionals who have come to dominate the American political scene.

A principal objective of any political consultant is to control the media and public images of his or her client. That is what Teeter, Atwater, and company did for George Bush, and it is what Democratic consultants attempted to do for Michael Dukakis. To that end, as Dukakis adviser Stanley Greenberg put it, "We'll use whatever the press will let us get away with."[10] Among the tools available to consultants to accomplish this noble purpose are two classes of campaign media known as "paid" and "free."

Paid media include the full range of campaign advertising: bumper stickers, posters, radio spots, television ads, billboards, buttons, emery boards, matchbooks—you name it, somebody has put a candidate's name on it. AuH_2O. Nixon's the One. Spiro Who? Where Was George? The advantage of paid media, from the perspective of the consultant, is the control that can be exercised over such key factors as content, placement, and timing. The campaign itself decides which messages go where, when, and how, and, within some limits, who will see them. But the disadvantage is that, precisely because they are so obviously controlled by partisan interests, paid media have relatively low credibility and relatively little persuasive power. Voters tend to see campaign-originated messages for precisely what they are—propaganda—and to dismiss them from serious thought.

Free media, on the other hand, include such items as interviews, media appearances, candidate profiles, and news coverage received by the campaign. As part of its continuing coverage of Campaign '88, CBS News now presents an interview with . . . Sources close to the Democratic candidate told NBC News today that . . . The advantages to the campaign of free media are twofold. First, free media are free. They are infinitely cost effective. And second, free media are highly credible. Because they are provided to the campaign by news organizations, journalists, talk show hosts, and others who have some inherent degree of credibility with their respective audiences, the messages conveyed through free media have relatively more potential influence on voters than does overt campaign propaganda. For the very same reason, however, free media carry some disadvantages from the perspective of the political consultant—the content, placement, and timing of their messages lie generally beyond the control of the campaign. Someone other than the campaigners makes these decisions.

Therein lies the basic dilemma of the media campaign: credibility versus control. And therein lies as well the genesis of strategic political communication: how to give campaign messages the credibility associated with news coverage and other free media, and at the same time retain a significant degree of control over the message that is presented. The objective, then, is a political version of having one's cake and eating it too.

Between election campaigns (and depending on circumstances), consultants may try to control a client's image by avoiding news coverage, just as Robert Teeter did for George Bush. It is a strategy with deep historic roots. In 1904, for example, William Jennings Bryan said of New York State Judge Alton B. Parker, who had practiced an earlier version of now-you-see-me-now-you-don't politics—dare we call this the "Teeter-totter"?—shortly before his nomination as the Democratic candidate for president, "It is the first time in recent years at least that a man has been urged to so high a position on the ground that his opinions are unknown."[11]

In the early days of the country, this strategy even carried over to the campaign itself. Andrew Jackson was advised in 1828, for example, that "candidates for the Presidency ought not to say a word on the subject of the election. Washington, Jefferson, and Madison were as silent as the grave when they were before the American people for this office." And Abraham Lincoln was so disinclined to campaign openly that he refused all entreaties to speak during the 1860 race. "Look over my [previous] speeches carefully," he said, "and conclude that I meant everything that I said and did not mean anything I did not say—and you will have my meaning then and now."[12] (One cannot help but compare this with the rhetoric of Richard Nixon a century later, who said in response to a critic, "I know you believe you understand what you think I said, but I am not sure you realize that what you heard is not what I meant.")

During campaign periods today, however, strategic control of the media almost always means grabbing more and better attention. And that is where the real power of negative advertising comes in. Precisely because of its negative character, this advertising meets all of the basic criteria of newsworthiness we set forth in chapter 2. It is inherently dramatic. It is controversial. It is highly visual. It is readily accessible to reporters. It is timely. It is structurally simple. It involves prominent personalities. It is presumed to be familiar and of interest to the news audience. It is, in short, news, and, like a virus infecting a host, it passes through the membrane that separates paid from free media. It is the fact that these "attack" and "defense" advertisements not only present, but actually *embody*, conflict among prominent persons pursuing significant objectives that gives to them a magnetic attraction which journalists are powerless to resist. This attraction produces two potential payoffs for the campaign.

First, the "multiplier effect" of the campaign's advertising will be increased. Think of the multiplier effect as the number of free-media mentions that an advertisement receives each time it is placed, the extent to which advertising is news. In any political campaign, the very first advertisements are likely to have modestly high multipliers simply because they represent the entry of a new candidate into the field, an event that is newsworthy in its own right. But after that, the novelty of the campaign wears off, and the news value of advertisements proclaiming that "Jane Doe Wants to Go to Washington" declines. Even the most interested of voters get bored with the message. Negative advertising can overcome this decline in the multiplier effect by reclaiming media attention. Indeed, the more numerous and more negative they are, the more media attention these advertisements are likely to attract. The effect is to convert news coverage into an extension of the campaign, one that can be anticipated in its strategy. Lyndon Johnson's "Daisy" spot is a perfect case in point. The advertisement ran only one time. Relatively few people actually saw it during its brief lifetime as "paid media." Because it received so much attention from the *news* media, however, it may well have produced the single most indelible and most widely held image generated by the campaign that year.

Second, because the messages of negative ads that make news are an integral part of the story, the messages themselves will be repeated by journalists. This is especially potent on television. How, after all, can a journalist do a story on the use of such devices without showing examples, and they most assuredly do make good film at six and eleven. They are fun. They are titillating. Peek through the curtains and see if anything nasty is going on in politics this evening. Even if, as is sometimes the case, the content of these advertisements is expressly discounted, or even criticized, in the news accounts or commentaries— Harvard University media researcher Kiku Adatto found that in only 8 percent of the *126* network news broadcasts in 1988 that excerpted political commercials did the reporter address the veracity of any claims that were made[13]—it will nevertheless, *merely by virtue of having appeared there*, acquire not just the audience of the news, but some of its credibility as well. It is a case of truth by association. Many in the news audience—again, especially the television news audience— attend closely enough to pick up simple images of events, but not closely enough to gather in much detail. A picture is not just *worth* a thousand words—it is a *substitute* for them. Didn't I see something on the news last night about the slime in Boston Harbor? Peter Jennings said something about that, didn't he? It does not work this way all of the time, but if it did not work this way most of the time—or if, at the very least, the strategic communicators did not believe that to be the case—we would be seeing less negative advertising rather than more.

What this suggests, then, is that some of the most important effects of negative advertising on voters are likely to be indirect rather than direct. Whether voters are exposed to the ads firsthand is relatively insignificant, since such direct exposure to paid media has very limited impact on those who are not already persuaded to the cause. What matters is whether the ads make the news—whether they enhance the visibility and credibility of campaign themes by transferring them from the rough and tumble of the video hustings into the sanctity of the newsroom—and the strategic objective is to assure that they do.

For all of that, however, the negative character of recent political campaigns may be less important than another of their traits, one that is also a product of strategic thinking and the focus-group mentality—the growing practice of appealing to emotion at the expense of reason. Take *pride* in America. It's *morning* in America. On the boats and on the planes, they're *coming* to America. The era of the touchy-feely campaign is upon us.

Increasingly in recent years—and with evident justification—candidates stand accused of running campaigns that are light on the issues and heavy on imagery. Think of it as a kind of Voter Lite: Tastes great! Less filling! George Bush's St. Louis rally, for example, which we described in chapter 1, was designed to serve as a symbolic counterpoint to the charge that Bush was avoiding the issues during the 1988 presidential campaign, and there is widespread agreement among observers that the so-called presidential "debates" have degenerated into issueless posturing sessions. There are two elements of concern here. First, *are* the candidates running on the issues? Second, *how* are the candidates running on the issues when, in fact, they are? We can answer both questions by employing what we have already learned about the use of political language.

There are two very different ways in which a candidate can address the issues. On the one hand, he or she can use language that treats issues at an intellectual level—language that identifies specific problems and offers specific solutions and reasons for them:

Despite *glasnost'* and *perestroika* and the recent changes in Eastern Europe, the Soviet Union maintains a standing army and a nuclear force that present serious threats to our security. I propose that we increase defense spending by 5.7 percent next year to provide for new and replacement equipment to assure that our own forces are up to the challenge. The money is to be taken from the Social Security Trust Fund, which is in surplus at the present time.

Alternatively, a candidate can address issues at an emotional level by using language that creates a locus of worry or of empathy, and communicates a sense of the candidate's concern, without ever presenting specifics:

There is a bear in the woods.

In both instances, the candidate is, in fact, addressing the issues. But this is being done in two very different ways. The first makes the voter think, the second makes the voter feel. The first offers leadership of the mind, the second leadership of the senses. They are two very different things.

We all agree that it is important to make voters think—to engage them intellectually in the exchange of ideas and to use this exchange mechanism to resolve differences of opinion about which policies the government should follow. That is the essence of democracy, right? But what the strategic communicators have discovered over the years is that most people don't want to do this. It takes time away from other things. It is mentally taxing. It does not seem to matter anyway, so why invest the effort? The news doctors are not the only ones to have concluded that the interests and abilities of the American people to engage in informed self-government may have been overestimated. Using the same tools and asking the same questions, political consultants have come to the same conclusion. If a political campaign were a high school civics class, they realized, most of the voters would be dropouts. Results of the history and civics portions of the 1988 National Assessment of Educational Progress, a nationwide test, found among other things that only 19 percent of all high school seniors could describe in any detail the responsibilities of the president, and fewer than four in ten knew that presidential candidates were nominated by national party conventions, this despite the fact that the test was administered during the primary season.[14] They would rather be hanging around the 7-Eleven sucking slurpies and munching on junk food. That leaves the campaign with two possible roles. It can hire on as a truant officer, dragging recalcitrant students back to class, or it can manufacture and sell junk food.

Now, every so often, a truant officer does come along and offer all the appropriate reasons why any thinking person would want to return to school. At the presidential level, for example, Barry Goldwater tried this with a well-developed conservative ideology in 1964, and George McGovern tried it with a well-developed program of liberal policies in 1972. The common fate of these two seemingly diverse efforts is instructive—both were buried under immense landslides. Goldwater and McGovern alike were shunned, not merely by their traditional opponents, but by the mainstream supporters of their own respective parties as well. Both were candidates of divided parties, and both faced well-oiled opposition campaigns—one, as the Watergate scandal later showed, was "greased" as well as oiled—but both had another key characteristic in common. They asked people to think. Goldwater asked people to think about ideas, philosophies, and he assumed that they wanted to do so if only given the opportunity. McGovern asked people to think about problems and solutions, and he made the same assumption. Both bought into the democratic myth. Both offered leadership of the mind. Both lost. Badly.

There are many interpretations one might put on Goldwater's and McGovern's defeats. One could argue, for instance, that both were extremists. Americans don't like policies that entail change in the status quo, let alone change that might be seen as radical. Americans will simply not elect an ideologue with a plan to change the direction of their society. Someone like, say, Ronald Reagan. Yet, when presented with the opportunity in 1980, that is precisely what they did.

Why Ronald Reagan and not Barry Goldwater (or George McGovern)? Maybe it was party unity. But recall that the Republican contest in 1980 was one in which Reagan wrested the nomination from a former president, Gerald Ford, in a contest so close that, during the maneuvering at the convention, Ford was reportedly offered a position as de facto "co-president." Maybe it was the tenor of the times, and especially the deeply felt frustration over the holding of American hostages in Iran. But recall that Goldwater ran during the turmoil following the assassination of President Kennedy and McGovern during the height of antiwar and pro–civil rights violence.

A third explanation, and the one that is subscribed to by many strategic communicators, focuses less on the substance of these concerns than on the style of the campaigns in each of these years. Extremism in the defense of liberty is no vice, said Barry Goldwater. In lieu of maintaining an elaborate welfare bureaucracy, the government should give every man, woman, and child in the United States $1000, said George McGovern. Take pride in America, said Ronald Reagan. It is not what you say, they concluded, but how you say it. Don't make people agree with you—make them like you. Don't make people think—make them feel. It worked in 1980, and again in 1984. Was it Reagan, or was it the strategy? Nineteen eighty-eight was the test.

What negative (and other strategic) advertising and the Doctor Feelgood School of Political Campaigning have in common is the importance they place on sensing and using to advantage all of the nuances of the communications environment. In part, this requires that those running a political campaign (or any other systematic effort at political public relations) get to know the voters—their audience—very well. What are their likes and dislikes? What makes them feel good? Feel threatened? Feel secure? To what themes or images are they most likely to "resonate"? It almost sounds more like a first meeting at a singles bar than an exercise in democratic governance. What's your sign?

Though Ronald and Nancy Reagan reportedly did use astrology to make their decisions—including at least one report that the selection of George Bush as Reagan's running mate in 1980 was determined by a comparison of the astrological compatibilities with Reagan of the various contenders (perhaps, one is tempted to wonder, because the official vice-presidential residence in Washington is located on the grounds of the Naval Observatory?)—professional strategic communicators have devised or adopted a variety of more mundane tools of the trade to try to divine the future, or at least to tap the public mood. We have already mentioned two of these—focus groups and polls. Another technique is the use of a variety of electronic monitors to test advertisements and other messages. In a typical application of this technique, volunteers will be seated in a room equipped with special measuring devices, and pilot advertisements or campaign video clips will be projected on a screen. The measuring devices will record the responses of the volunteer subjects and will align these with the content of the test messages second by second so that reactions can be attributed to specific words or pictures.

The devices themselves can take a variety of forms. Sometimes they are designed to measure minute changes in the pulse rate or the temperature of the skin which are thought to coincide with changes in peoples' emotional state—for example, when they get excited. Devices of this type typically require that wires be attached to the subjects and connected to a central recording device. They look like lie detectors, and they operate on the very same principle. A less intrusive, but much more expensive system focuses a tiny camera on the eyes of each subject and measures changes in the degree to which his or her pupils dilate (open or close) on the theory that pupil dilation equates with the degree of interest in what is occurring. Perhaps the most popular system at the moment, however, presents each subject with a dial which is to be turned to the left or to the right depending upon whether, at any given moment, he or she is feeling more or less comfortable with, or interested in, whatever message is being presented. Typically, volunteers are recruited in shopping malls or other similar locations to participate in these little experiments, though, as with the Bush focus group in Paramus, more and more such efforts are being applied to carefully selected groups.

Clearly, and all of the most outlandish conspiracy theories or works of science fiction to the contrary notwithstanding, no political campaign could seal up one hundred million Americans in focus group rooms and spy on them through one-way glass, let alone hook up every voter to a "feel-good machine." The time, expense, and effort involved are far beyond their means, and the likelihood of universal voluntary submission is nil. But the strategic communicators have learned yet another lesson. They do not need to do this. Rather, all they need to do is to figure out ways to generalize what they learn from their polling and their small groups of volunteer guinea pigs to the larger population of prospective voters. Much like their news doctor counterparts, they do this through an analysis of audience (voter) demographics.

The idea of this demographic analysis is threefold. First, figure out which portions of the potential voting public are already your supporters, are open to persuasion, or are entirely beyond your reach. Second, figure out which messages will be most effective in mobilizing or influencing key groups. Third, figure out how you can most effectively deliver the right message to the right prospective voter, preferably without delivering the "wrong" message to anyone else. This is called targeting, and the mandamus in Paramus is a good example of its use. Recall that the volunteers in those focus group sessions were selected because they were Democrats who had voted for Ronald Reagan and who were known to be leaning toward a return to the fold. Since the Republican party holds the loyalties of a distinct minority of Americans, its candidate invariably needs to attract (or at least to demobilize) a significant number of nominal Democrats in order to win the White House. The Paramus volunteers had demonstrated that they could be won over. The question that confronted Lee Atwater and company was how to do it. Match the message to the audience. Forget Mister Rogers. Take a walk down the street in Willie Horton's neighborhood.

In reality, of course, it is not quite that simple. Behind the meeting in Paramus lay months, even years, of careful polling and other research, probing the positives and negatives of the various candidates, the emergence and disappearance of diverse public sensibilities, the voting habits of segments of the public, and the media habits of likely voters. What are the chances of a crossover of blue-collar voters in Chicago? How soft is Dukakis's support in New England? Among women? The elderly? Does anyone really use "the 'L' word" any more? Still, the basic idea is a straightforward one. What should we say? To whom should we say it? Out of the hundred million votes floating around out there, where will we find the fifty million and one that we need to win, and how will we harvest them?

The use of these and other techniques all traces to one common assumption on the part of the strategic communicators: we need to give the audience whatever it needs to notice, and to feel an affinity for, our client. Find out what half plus one of the people want, then give it to them. What could be more democratic? What these communication strategists espouse, in other words, or at least what they practice, is a form of democracy in which the people are led in whatever direction they are already moving. In effect, the task of the political leader/candidate is to run with the crowd or risk being trampled. Given the central role played by demographic analysis and the targeting of messages, we might think of this not as democracy at all, but as demogracy—a system of governance based not on the *expression* of the popular will, but merely on its *measurement*. Perhaps E. B. White was close to the truth when he defined democracy as "the recurrent suspicion that more than half of the people are right more than half of the time."

But there is more to strategic political communication than mere demographic analysis and pandering to the public whim. For the public is not the only important component of the communications environment, and the mapping of candidate images onto the public psyche is not the only instrument available to the communication strategist. A second target of opportunity, as we have already suggested, is offered by the media.

Our discussion of negative campaigning made clear the reasons why campaigners and others interested in influencing popular images of politics might want to focus attention on the news media. Depending on circumstance, some may find advantage in avoiding news coverage—in withdrawing from public attention. Others may seek more of it. Still others may hope to shape the attention they expect to receive in one direction or another. One of the hallmarks of strategic political communication, in fact, is its emphasis on identifying the publicity needs of the client and adopting media and other strategies to suit them. This is a point we will come back to in a later chapter. For the moment, however, let us focus on the nature of strategies designed to influence—to manipulate—the media.

All such strategies begin precisely where we have, with an understanding of how and why journalists and others working for news organizations make their decisions as to what is news and how it will be presented. Political consultants with an interest in the media have all, in effect, read chapter 2. More than that, they have come to the realization not only that they cannot change the way that journalists and their colleagues work, but that they should not, *need not,* do so. Rather, they have learned that by understanding the criteria of newsworthiness and the daily routines of the news-gathering profession, *and by shaping their own actions to complement those of the persons they would influence*—by *facilitating* the pursuit of the sacred trust rather than by obstructing it—they can actually exercise a good deal of control over what becomes news. It is a devious, but nonetheless a demonstrably effective, approach.

Publicists have long addressed the task of managing the news by assuming, in effect, the role of journalists. If I were a journalist in this situation, they ask themselves, what would I do? But in *strategic* approaches to news management, the question is pushed back one step further, and the order of operations is reversed. What kind of news coverage do I want? Then, how can I cause journalists to act in such a way that they will, *of their own free will*, provide me with that kind of coverage? These questions are asked *before the circumstance exists*, and events are then purposefully *designed* to accommodate the answers. They become what historian and later Librarian of Congress Daniel Boorstin has termed "pseudo-events."[15]

A pseudo-event—or, as the genre is more commonly known, a "media event"—is one that has been staged either primarily for the purpose of attracting news coverage, or in such a way as to "guide" the coverage it receives in some desired direction. I recall many years ago, for example, attending a series of workshops on political campaigning at which George McGovern, who had not yet announced his candidacy for the presidency but was expected to do so soon, was scheduled to present the keynote address. The first four rows of the auditorium were set aside for the media, and they filled with the usual assortment of print flotsam and broadcast jetsam. ABC, CBS, and the major wires and print organizations were all represented. McGovern's talk was set for 10:00 in the morning, but when that hour came, NBC had yet to arrive. So we waited. And waited. And waited.

Finally, at 10:45, an NBC crew arrived on the scene and set up their camera. At that point, McGovern walked to the podium—clad, incidentally, in the requisite dark suit, light blue shirt, and red tie of the television-era politician—and delivered a very revealing ten-minute oration. It was not the substance of what he said that was of interest, however. It was how he said it. From the perspective of my sixth-grade English teacher, there was not a complete paragraph—yea, not a coherent thought expressed—in the entire piece. Rather, it comprised a collection of two-sentence sound bites, each one of which made sense in isolation, but no two of which made sense when coupled with one another. McGovern, it seems, was practicing strategic communication. He did not know which portion of his "speech" would be reported on any given network (or in print, though that seemed less important). But he did know, *based on an understanding of how journalists work,* that he would be granted one sound bite—one twenty-second snippet of oral expression. Whether he made sense overall before a relatively small audience was of no consequence. Whether each sound bite made sense in isolation for an audience of fifty million was of paramount concern. And sure enough, as I flipped from network to network that evening, three different, but very coherent-sounding, two-sentence gems of McGovernesque wisdom filled the ether.

Perhaps the ultimate example of a recurrent pseudo-event in contemporary American politics, though, is provided by the quadrennial spectacle of the presidential "debates." We have already noted the general public expectation that, at some point during a presidential campaign, the candidates ought to address the issues and perhaps, even, one another. Since 1960, though not without interruption, the established forum for this ritual confrontation has been a series of debates. While much has been written about the conduct and impact of these various contests (Should Richard Nixon have rested more and used makeup for his first meeting with John Kennedy? Did Gerald Ford really mean to say, as he did in his debate with Jimmy Carter, that Poland had not been dominated since World War II by the Soviet Union? Did Jimmy Carter really consult his twelve-year-old daughter Amy when formulating the nation's strategic nuclear policy as he claimed in his debate with Ronald Reagan? "There you go again, Mr. President."), relatively little attention has focused on what may be one of their most revealing aspects, the pre-debate negotiations over whether and how the debates will be staged, and the tactical decisions that are incorporated into debate preparation.

In his book *Political Campaign Debates: Images, Strategies, and Tactics,* Myles Martel, who served as debate adviser to Ronald Reagan for his 1980 meetings with Jimmy Carter, has identified the principal behind-the-scenes considerations.[16] Among them are such grandiose issues as whether to engage in debates at all—democratic myths notwithstanding, there are circumstances under which candidates are well-advised to avoid debates at almost any cost—and such mundane questions as whether to sit or stand, whether to take notes, whether to make eye contact, whether to address the opposing candidate by name, and the like. In each instance, the objective is to seek some advantage in the relative positioning or performance of the candidate. Tall candidates will argue for standing, short candidates for sitting. Articulate candidates will prefer informal exchanges of views, less articulate candidates will want to maximize the predictability of the format. And so forth. Typical of this was the effort by the Bush campaign in 1988 to enlist Dan Rather, anchorperson of the CBS "Evening News," as a panelist in one of that year's debates. Rather, you may recall, had engaged Bush (or been engaged by him) earlier in the year in a rather acrimonious interview/colloquy (more on this in a later chapter), and the Bush camp's feeling was that, for this reason—in order to preserve his apparent objectivity and his journalistic role as *loyal* adversary—he might avoid presenting their candidate with especially challenging questions. As it turned out, Rather removed himself from consideration.

Even sponsorship issues are not always what they seem. From 1976 through 1984, the League of Women Voters, by mutual agreement of the political parties and the television networks, assumed sponsorship of the debates, a convenient subterfuge designed primarily to circumvent the equal-time provisions of the Communications Act that would otherwise have required broadcasters to offer to include in the proceedings all minor party presidential candidates. This arrangement broke down in 1988, and a bipartisan commission took over sponsorship. The League of Women Voters claimed that the candidates wanted to control—and, by implication, to weaken—the debate format. The real issue, however, was the number of tickets each party could distribute. Attendance at the debates, it turned out, was a valued perquisite of support for the league and for the Republican and Democratic parties alike. Tickets translated into contributions. The more tickets one or another group had to distribute, the more money—serious money—it could expect in return. In 1988, the league sought to keep most of the available tickets for itself, and apparently lost sponsorship of the debates as a result.

What all of these various machinations have in common (save, perhaps, the last)—and the thing that assures the place of presidential debates in the Pseudo-Event Hall of Fame—is that they are directed very little at influencing the audience in the hall, and very much at influencing the audience tuned in at home. If there were ever a doubt of that fact, it was dispelled on the evening of the first debate of the 1976 campaign, when the single television audio feed failed just as Jimmy Carter began his final rejoinder, and he and Gerald Ford stood silently on a stage in Philadelphia for some twenty-eight minutes waiting for the problem to be resolved. The audience in the theater sat on its hands. The audience at home probably went out for a cold one.

In addition to pseudo-events, would-be managers of the news have a full panoply of other devices available to them. Some of these include the standard tools of the publicist's trade—press releases, press conferences, deadline-sensitive timing of announcements, and the like—but others, the news leak, for example, can be employed in what amounts to an ''underground'' strategy of media manipulation. While many of these techniques are used in political campaigns, however, they are also widely employed in other forms of strategic political communication, and will be dealt with in other contexts later in this book.

For the moment, what is important is that we begin to recognize the importance of poking around beneath the surface of the messages we receive from and about politics. It is the central tenet of strategic political communication that messages should be shaped to conform to the expectations that exist among the intended audience. If we are not careful, the rewards that seem to accrue to those who subscribe to this rather narcissistic approach to political life will reinforce its practice to a point where we may lose sight of the alternatives. The result will be a superficial, self-congratulatory style of politics, one where we think we are doing a lot better than we in fact are. I'm okay, you're okay. What else matters?

Notes

1. Francis Russell, *The President Makers: From Mark Hanna to Joseph P. Kennedy* (Boston: Little, Brown, 1976), pp. 211–22.

2. Personal conversation with Andrew J. Morrison, Senior Vice President, Market Opinion Research, 1986.

3. Gerald M. Boyd, "Bush Lauds Soviet Workers and Is Assailed by U.A.W.," *New York Times*, 3 October 1987.

4. Paul Taylor and David S. Broder, "Evolution of the TV Era's Nastiest Presidential Race," *Washington Post*, 28 October 1988, pp. A1, A10–A11.

5. Dukakis did later conclude that he had underestimated the impact of the Republicans' negative tactics. See Fox Butterworth, "Dukakis Says Race Was Harmed by TV," *New York Times*, 22 April 1990, p. 31.

6. Jules Abels, *The Degeneration of Our Presidential Election* (New York: Macmillan, 1968), p. 78.

7. Greg Mitchell, "How Media Politics Was Born," *American Heritage,* September/October 1988, pp. 34–41.

8. Lecture delivered at The George Washington University, April 1989.

9. Montague Kern, *30-Second Politics* (New York: Praeger, 1989), pp. 25–26.

10. David S. Broder, "Politicians, Advisors Agonize over Negative Campaigning," *Washington Post*, 19 January 1989, pp. A1, A22.

11. Abels, *The Degeneration of Our Presidential Election*, p. 106.

12. Ibid., pp. 112–14.

13. Cited in David Broder, "Critics Lament 1989 as Another Season of Slash-and-Burn Politics," *Washington Post*, 6 January 1989, p. A4.

14. Kenneth J. Cooper, "Test Suggests Students Lack Grasp of Civics," *Washington Post,* 3 April 1990, p. A5.

15. Daniel Boorstin, *The Image* (New York: Harper and Row, 1961), p. 9.

16. Myles Martel, *Political Campaign Debates: Images, Strategies, and Tactics* (New York: Longman, 1983).

4 THE PERMANENT CAMPAIGN

On April 8, 1913, Woodrow Wilson made history. He spoke to Congress. Directly. In person. Not since the days of Washington and Adams had a president done such a thing. If White House political maps of the day treated the Capitol Hill end of Pennsylvania Avenue as *terra incognita,* Wilson was Christopher Columbus. The topic of his address—the first of several such visits he would pay to the legislative branch over the next few years—was tariffs, a major issue of the day. But its real significance was the opportunity it offered to create a media event of such magnitude—the president did what??—that the journalists and newspapers of the day, whom Wilson regarded as hostile to his interests, would *have* to report it, and would have to do so on *his* terms. In effect, he used the Congress of the United States as a prop, a backdrop, to add drama and to draw attention to his message. Wilson was so pleased with his effort that, when, on the drive back home, his wife mentioned that even his publicity-conscious predecessor had not conceived of so potent a device for managing the news, he commented, "Yes, I think I put one over on Teddy."[1]

But it was another Wilson, Ronald Wilson Reagan, who refined the art of using presidential-congressional relations for political advantage to its purest state. From the very outset of his administration, Reagan wielded his appearances on Capitol Hill and his exchanges with the congressional leadership—particularly with the opposition Democrats—as weapons of his political power. For Reagan—especially in the early years of his presidency—talk really was powerful, and the holding of high office truly was a permanent exercise in campaigning. Perhaps the best example of his style of leadership and his ability to mobilize public support for his policies came in the battle over tax reform that marked the first year of the Reagan presidency.

The opening scene of the drama was set against the same backdrop used by Woodrow Wilson nearly seventy years earlier—the chamber of the United States House of Representatives. The date was February 18, 1981. The lead was played by Ronald Reagan, newly inaugurated president of the United States, who, in a thirty-five minute televised speech, told the nation and the legislators there assembled, "The taxing power of government must be used to provide revenues for legitimate government purposes. It must not be used to regulate the economy or bring about social change. We've tried that and surely we must be able to see it doesn't work." Reagan's proposal? Increase the share of the federal budget devoted to military spending by one-third; significantly reduce expenditures for such programs as food stamps, welfare, student loans, school lunches (remember when catsup was defined as a vegetable?) and capital spending for airports, highways, and mass transit; and—this was the key—*reduce taxes by 30 percent.*[2] In effect, the American people were being invited to rethink their basic ideas about the proper role of government in their society—in return for which they would receive a massive tax cut—and the Democrats were being invited to renounce the philosophy that had bound their party together for fully half a century.

Following the speech that evening, the Republicans mustered while the Democrats blustered. Perhaps the most astute comment was that of Republican Orrin Hatch of Utah, at the time chair of the Senate Banking Committee, who not only predicted the outcome of the battle that had just been declared, but foresaw the strategy that would win it for the president. "I can't believe," he observed, "the American people won't bring the amount of pressure that will be needed [to force the Democrats in Congress to accept the president's proposal]."[3] And so, eventually, they did.

Scene two, however, did not go the president's way. In April, while Reagan was recovering from the gunshot wound he sustained during an attempt on his life by John Hinckley—whose apparent motive was to attract the amorous attentions of actress Jodie Foster—the Senate Budget Committee, under Republican control for the first time in many years, actually defeated a budget resolution that would have begun the implementation of the Reagan agenda. Three Republicans joined the Democrats on the committee in opposing the resolution. It was at this point that the "campaign" for tax reform commenced.

While they waited for the president to resume his own efforts in behalf of his program, the White House staff set in motion a systematic and wide-ranging promotional and lobbying effort. They scheduled briefings for some 900 regional editors and broadcasters, set a heavy schedule of speaking engagements for Vice President Bush and members of the cabinet, and prepared to lobby—a word that does not convey the full force of the pressure that was later brought to bear—the three Republican committee members who had strayed from the fold. These efforts were supplemented by the National Conservative Political Action Committee (NCPAC), which was noted at the time for its independent and highly visible spending on negative campaign advertising targeted at liberals—a group defined by NCPAC to include, in effect, anyone whose politics were to the left of the soup spoon. The NCPAC announced that it would spend a million dollars on a media campaign targeted at three congressmen—House Majority Leader Jim Wright, House Budget Committee Chair James R. Jones, and House Ways and Means Committee Chair Dan Rostenkowski—and one Senator, Paul Sarbanes of Maryland, whose principal crime appears to have been that he represented a state close enough to the nation's capital to give the group an excuse to run its advertisements in a media market where other members of Congress might see and be influenced by them.[4]

For his own part, and for a variety of reasons, it was not until June that the president himself reentered the fray. On the tenth of that month his tax bill was formally introduced in Congress, and on the eleventh he opened his personal campaign—and it was very much a campaign—for its adoption with a speech to some 350 supporters in the East Room of the White House, in which he called upon his audience to help him "give this economy back to the American people."[5] On the fifteenth he met with key congressional leaders of both parties to lobby for his proposals, and on the afternoon of the sixteenth he held his first news conference in three and a half months. There, he took off the gloves, claiming a mandate for his tax program, and labeling Democratic opposition to it as "unconscionable." He then extended the conference beyond the usual thirty-minute limit to launch a personal attack on House Speaker Thomas P. "Tip" O'Neill, whom he labeled a demagogue for having suggested that Reagan did not understand working people.

Following the news conference, the president and the speaker engaged in a remarkable minuet of name calling centered on the nature of their respective childhoods and the understanding that each had about the needs of middle-class Americans.[6] Over the next two to three weeks, Reagan's reputation soared, O'Neill's soured, and the Democratic leadership suffered significant defeats on the budget as a coalition of Republicans and conservative, mostly southern, Democrats emerged—along with a massive outpouring of public sentiment—to support the president. Perhaps Dan Rostenkowski best summed up the situation from the Democratic side, drawing, at least indirectly, on that childhood commonplace of one-upmanship: "My dad was in the marines, and he'll get the marines to beat you up." "Well, my dad was in the navy, and . . ." Rostenkowski observed, "My problem is that the president can gear up his army with just one television appearance. That's fighting the Army, Navy, Marines, and Air Force. He's got all that. . . ."[7]

At this point—the July 4 congressional recess—the Democrats determined to launch a counteroffensive. They opened a telephone bank to contact editorial writers at 230 large newspapers, promoted an alternative Democratic tax package to all 242 House Democrats, identified twenty congressional districts in southern states from Texas to Florida for intensive grass-roots activity, and began to bring pressure on Republicans whose support on the tax plan they hoped to woo away from Reagan. In addition, they prepared speaking teams to tour the country, distributed news releases to the home-district media of moderate Republicans who had supported the president's budget criticizing them for having done so, planned a campaign for more access to the media on morning and weekend public affairs programs, and asked the networks for equal time to rebut any speech the president might make on the tax cut.[8] Ironically, this latter request reiterated a point Reagan himself had made three years earlier, when he was on the outside of the White House looking in. In a *TV Guide* essay, he—this was Ronald Reagan, recall, the Dean of Deregulation—called for a "new federal law to require minute-for-minute equal time for rebuttals to presidential speeches, news conferences, and special messages."[9]

In effect, Reagan's success and political strength forced the Democrats to shift their emphasis from a legislative to a communication strategy. At mid-month they hired a public relations consultant, Patricia Bario, to help them promote their own tax bill, which amounted to little more than a variant on the Draconian Reagan cuts, but which they thought would have broader appeal.

The Republicans, of course, had not surrendered center stage for seats in the second balcony. White House chief of staff James Baker took personal control of the tax reform effort, and such groups as the Chamber of Commerce of the United States and the National Association of Manufacturers rose to the president's defense.[10] In addition, four conservative groups—the Fund for a Conservative Majority, the American Conservative Union, Citizens for Reagan, and Young Americans for Freedom—announced plans to spend about $200,000 to mobilize popular support for the Reagan plan. Their efforts included radio and newspaper advertisements placed in the districts of undecided members of Congress, radio scripts urging the public to write Congress in support of the tax plan, and the distribution of buttons and bumper stickers urging its passage.[11] Within a week, the Republican party added its own half-million-dollar radio effort urging listeners in selected cities to telephone their representatives and express their support for the president, and a Washington-area group headed by Representative Stan Parris of Virginia purchased local radio and television time for commercials portraying Speaker of the House O'Neill as a Christmas miscreant who brings an empty box to a disappointed little girl instead of a tax cut. "Ho Ho Ho," says O'Neill. "I've got this nice big package that looks just like a tax cut." But as she slowly opens the beautifully wrapped package and finds it empty, the little girl begins to cry. Even the Republican National Committee and Congressional Campaign Committee demurred on national distribution of that one.[12]

The outpouring of public sentiment reached new crescendos in late July—Congress was literally inundated with letters, telegrams, and telephone calls backing the president—and on the twenty-ninth Ronald Reagan achieved a crushing victory. After seven hours of debate in the House of Representatives, half a hundred Democrats crossed party lines to defeat their own party's alternative bill, and House and Senate alike approved the President's plan. The vote in the Senate was a stunning 89–11 in support of the legislation.[13] It was a day that might arguably be considered the high point of the Reagan presidency, and one that secured his reputation as "The Great Communicator."

◆ ◆ ◆ ◆

"It's a Grand Old Flag," says the song. "Of the Grand Old Party," says George Bush. As presidential candidate in 1988, Bush set about, with great success, appropriating the premier symbol of the United States and painting Democrat Michael Dukakis as lukewarm on patriotism. As president in 1989, he set about painting the entire Democratic party into the same corner.

Mr. Bush's odyssey with the Stars and Stripes began shortly after the Republican convention when he pointed out that, as Governor of Massachusetts, his opponent had vetoed a bill requiring that state's public school teachers to lead their students each day in reciting the Pledge of Allegiance—a charge Mr. Dukakis seemed powerless to counter. The difficulty of Dukakis's position is understandable. It was not based, of course, as Bush suggested, on a lack of patriotic fervor—though Dukakis seemed remarkably incapable of demonstrating fervor on *anything*—but on an advisory opinion from the Massachusetts Attorney General that the act of the legislature was unconstitutional. As we have seen, however, abstract notions like constitutionalism have no chance against a gut issue like national pride. Bush had the low road, but the high ground.

That the then–vice president had wrapped himself rhetorically in the flag was nothing new in American politics. Indeed, doing so is a commonplace of the political stump, the convention hall, and the television production set alike. But few politicians have gone to the same lengths as Bush, who actually visited a flag *factory* in New Jersey, where he associated himself with all of the patriotic events over which the company's flags had flown since 1849. "Back under Jimmy Carter and Walter Mondale," Bush noted in a speech that day, "times were tough. Flags weren't selling that well." But, he went on to note, sales had "taken off" during the Reagan-Bush years.[14] It was an "issue" that drove Dukakis and the Democrats crazy.

It was also an issue that explained later-president Bush's support—in the wake of an unpopular Supreme Court decision in June of 1989—for an amendment to the Constitution that would outlaw desecration of the flag. In a Texas case, the increasingly conservative Court ruled that the burning of the American flag in the context of an act of political protest constitutes protected speech under the First Amendment. It is not nice, said the Court, but neither is it illegal. Bush's initial reaction was a responsible one: it is a deplorable fact that one can burn the flag, he said, but it is the law of the land and my duty is to enforce it.

Once he had slept on his words, however, or perhaps once his advisers had done so, Bush must have realized what he had said—or more to the point, he must have realized that his own initial position on the flag was *precisely* the same as the one that Michael Dukakis had taken on the Pledge of Allegiance: political expediency must take a back seat to the Constitution. That realization, coupled with the demonstrated political opportunities inherent in a pro-flag campaign, must have been on the president's mind when he came forward the very next day with a promise to amend the Constitution—a promised deemed ill-advised by conservative commentators and constitutional scholars alike. One possibility here was that, in proposing such an amendment, Bush was presenting his true position on the issue. If so, he revealed himself as something other than the civil libertarian second class (non–card-carrying) he had long pretended to be. It is at least as likely, however, that he was merely playing to what he thought initially would be the more conservative elements of his constituency—or at least the feeling as opposed to the thinking conservatives—by donning once again his suit of red, white, and blue. If this was the case, what he revealed was the extent to which he was a true disciple of Ronald Reagan. Reagan, you will recall, had assuaged the right-to-life and militant taxpayer elements of his constituency for eight years with promises of constitutional amendments banning abortion and requiring a balanced budget, neither of which ever quite materialized. If this was Bush's game, however—and there is reason to think so, as White House Chief of Staff John Sununu said in the same week that Bush favored *five* constitutional amendments, adding the line-item veto and school prayer to those already mentioned[15]—it may well have been more dangerous than the one his predecessor had played, given the relative potency of the symbols at issue.

Whichever explanation one prefers, President Bush demonstrated a consummate sense of political symbolism in staking out his position. Within three days, while flag-burning was still a hot issue, he presented the language of his proposed amendment to the American people in a speech he delivered just before the July 4 weekend using Arlington, Virginia's Iwo Jima Memorial—the oft-photographed statue of marines pushing up a flag during the bloody World War II battle—as a backdrop. Describing the flag as ''one of our most powerful ideas,'' Bush proclaimed, ''We can't forget the importance of the flag to the ideals of liberty and honor and freedom. To burn the flag, to

dishonor it, is simply wrong." The Department of the Interior had a
rather more prosaic view. In a memorandum to the United States Park
Police regarding their preparations for the July 4 celebration on
Washington's Mall, Richard Robbins, the department's solicitor, advised "While it is now apparently the law that the demonstrators may
roll Old Glory and fire her up like a Marlboro if they want, we don't
have to permit it in the no smoking section. As you know, the park
regulations at 36 C.F.R. 2.13 prohibit the lighting or maintaining of
fires except in designated areas or receptacles. This regulation is still in
effect. It doesn't matter if they want to burn the American flag or the
Washington Post, unauthorized fires are still prohibited in the
parks."[16]

◆ ◆ ◆ ◆

In their dealings with the news media and the public, political leaders
are always looking for the edge. That, of course, is the reason they so
often seek the counsel of strategic communication professionals, and
the reason that communication strategy so often dominates the political
process. It was, in fact, Leslie Janka, a former Reagan deputy press
secretary, who suggested of the Reagan administration that "This was
a PR outfit that became president and took over the country. The
Constitution forced them to do things like make a budget, run foreign
policy and all that. . . . But their first, last and overarching activity was
public relations."[17]

To some extent, the tools of the political campaign can be applied to
the needs of leadership once in office. Lyndon Johnson, for example,
monitored the television networks with a bank of three sets that he had
installed in the Oval Office, and patrolled the corridors of the White
House with the latest public opinion polls bulging from his pockets.
With something of the same end in mind, Ronald Reagan's advisers
held viewing panels for each of his television appearances throughout
much of his administration, using feel-good machines to determine
which words or phrases had desired or undesired effects on viewers.
The "good" phrases were then continually repeated by the president
and others in the administration in subsequent appearances, while the
"bad" phrases were banned from the presidential lexicon.[18] And similarly, George Bush's advisers indicated their intention to monitor the
president's performance through the reactions of focus groups like the

one they used in Paramus.[19] The era of the permanent campaign is upon us.

To be sure, the obvious tools of campaign communication—such as the media event—are regularly incorporated in the politics of governing. A case in point: President Bush's assertion in a nationally televised speech in September 1989 addressing the drug problem that drugs were available in every neighborhood, even across the street from the White House itself. To prove the point, he held up a plastic bag filled with crack cocaine, which, he said, federal drug agents had seized a few days earlier in Lafayette Park. As it turned out, however, the words of the speech were written before the crack was seized, and agents of the Drug Enforcement Administration (DEA) were instructed by the White House to make an arrest in the park before the president's television appearance. Since little drug trafficking normally occurs in Lafayette Park or nearby areas of the city, agents actually had to lure a dealer from elsewhere into the park to accomplish their task. Their problem was complicated by the fact that the dealer they had selected was unfamiliar with the venue. In a conversation that was secretly recorded by the DEA, when asked to make the deal in the park across from the White House, the dealer responded, "Where the [expletive] is the White House?"[20]

But even some of the more subtle aspects of campaign strategy find their way into leadership efforts. In the campaign for the Reagan tax cut, for example, recall the early emphasis that the White House staff placed on journalists from the regional—as opposed to the national— news media, bringing together some 900 of them for a briefing on the budget and tax plans. This was an extension of a tactic that had been tested during the 1980 campaign and was destined to become more and more important in Republican electoral strategy in later years—the localization of media contacts. The decision to use this tactic was based on four assumptions.

• First, it was assumed that the president (or a presidential candidate) must be *seen* as making him- or herself available to the media. To do otherwise would be to risk being portrayed as violating the expectations associated with the myth of free press and free people, and in the process, creating unnecessary political vulnerability.

• Second, it was assumed that national reporters are better skilled, better prepared, more cynical, and, importantly, less favorably disposed toward Republicans, than are their counterparts in local news organizations. Thus, meeting with local journalists rather than their national colleagues would assure a friendlier, less potentially challenging audience. Indeed, the logic—and the tactic—were extended later in the Reagan administration beyond journalists altogether, as publishers—denizens of the business rather than the journalistic side of news organizations, but nevertheless representatives of the press in the eye of an undiscerning public—were targeted for briefings as well.

• Third, it was assumed that, for local journalists—irrespective of skill or viewpoint—being in the presence of the president or other highly prominent federal officials is a once-in-a-lifetime experience. Unlike national reporters, who take such contacts as a matter of course, they would be more likely to be awed by the trappings of the event and to see attendance per se as adding to their personal prestige, and would be disinclined to risk offending the high-and-mighty ones who had granted this audience by asking untoward questions.

• And finally, it was assumed that the American people themselves are quite cynical about the national media—a view that had been nurtured by a generation of attacks on the press by a host of Republican politicians and by such conservative organizations as Accuracy in Media. But, the assumption continued, the people did retain confidence in their local journalists.

Collectively, then, these assumptions led to an emphasis on providing news opportunities for the local or regional press that excluded—sometimes very explicitly—the participation of national reporters. And when the national press charged—as it did with some regularity even through the Bush campaign, where the same tactic was employed—that the president or the candidate was avoiding them, the proffered defense—that, to the contrary, he was *seeking out* journalists, even widening the circle of those with access, and that the national journalists were merely jealous that some of their privileges were being redistributed to reporters of equal merit but lesser stature—found a sympathetic ear with the public.

Perhaps the most egregious example of the strategy of localism came immediately after the Republican National Convention of 1988, and related to the selection of Dan Quayle to round out the party's ticket. Quayle, it seemed clear, had used his family's influence to avoid service in Vietnam, then, once in public life, had become a vocal supporter of the war and an advocate of military action. The press smelled a hypocrite, and went after Quayle in what was aptly described at the time as a "feeding frenzy." After a few days, Quayle agreed to a press conference to respond to the charges. The "conference," however, was staged in the midst of a political rally in his home town of Huntington, Indiana, with an open microphone. With each challenging question from a journalist, the crowd booed. With each Quayle response, it cheered. [21]

The transference of the assumptions and practices of the campaign into the conduct of high public office that is so much a part of the contemporary political scene carries both challenge and temptation. As the Reagan example clearly shows, these devices can be quite impressively marshaled to accomplish the high purposes for which a political leader can claim to have been elected, and, to be sure, the resources and opportunities that high office provides for strategic communication are manifold. At the same time, however, as Bush's use of the flag suggests, the requirements of leadership do not always precisely correspond with those of electioneering—what is at least arguably appropriate in one setting is not necessarily appropriate in another. What both situations share is the political imperative and the incentive to communicate effectively.

As Leon Sigal pointed out some years ago in his book *Reporters and Officials*, politicians want to make news for a variety of reasons. First, they are publicity hounds—they simply like to see their names in print and their images on television. This is especially true of elected officials, of course, who have an evident need to keep themselves before the home folks. But it is true of those who are merely appointed to their positions as well. James Watt—Ronald Reagan's first secretary of the Interior—you may recall had a genuine penchant for stirring up controversies through the media, so much so that he was eventually presented with a "Golden Foot" award, which commemorated his tendency rhetorically to shoot himself in that appendage, and David Stockman—director of the Office of Management and Budget during the same period—earned himself a trip to the "woodshed" for some of his own public utterances. In fact, Stockman's "crime" was to state some months after the fact that the Reagan budget and tax cut—the very subjects of the publicity and lobbying campaign described above—amounted to a political version of the shell game. "The tax program, where we were going on spending, and the defense program," Stockman said in an interview in the *Atlantic*, were "just a bunch of numbers written on a piece of paper. And it didn't quite mesh. . . . But you see, for about a month and a half, we got away with that because of the novelty of all these budget reductions."[22] Just which shell is the little pea under?

The publicity bug can bite nonpoliticians with an interest in shaping policy or public perceptions as well. For example, Norman Ornstein of the American Enterprise Institute, a Washington think tank, is a frequent guest on such programs as the "MacNeil/Lehrer NewsHour," and is widely quoted elsewhere in the media on matters relating to Congress and public opinion. Stephen Hess of the Brookings Institution, another think tank, is equally prominent on matters of media and elections, while Bruce Fein, a Washington attorney, has, in the words of a *Washington Post* reporter, "institutionalized himself as the conservative . . . sound bite in virtually every major report on the Supreme Court."[23] All three owe their visibility in the media to the three "Ps": prominence, proximity, and pithiness. Would-be media sources must hold positions that establish their authority, must make themselves available to reporters at all times, and must know how to speak in brief, quotable phrases. Fein, in fact, went so far as to rehearse metaphors with his thirteen-year-old son, whom he required to submit to him each evening a newly written paragraph containing "one good metaphor and one colorful or zesty adjective."[24] But, according to Hess, a metaphor must be more than well-turned—it must meet the preconceptions of the journalist regarding the shape of his or her story.

As Hess describes the process, "A producer calls to check me out, asking enough questions to know whether I am likely to say what they are after. If I don't respond appropriately, they say they'll get back to me. Which means they won't. . . . It is important to note that they never tell me what to say. Hence they can believe that they are honest journalists. If they choose to interview me on camera, someone shows up and asks a question in as many permutations as it takes to get the answer that is the chip that I'm supposed to represent in the mosaic that is their 'package.' "[25] His view is reinforced by Janet Steele, a communication scholar who spent a year studying the appearances of academic experts on television. As she sums it up, "Television news organizations constantly turn to academics for expertise—but for their own purposes. . . . They want specialists who not only are personable, presentable, and good on camera, but also can speak in 'sound bites' . . . that fit right into the script of a news program."[26]

In addition to gaining publicity, newsmaking is a means that politicians can use to develop support for their programs—a device for mobilizing public opinion. By visiting a school, a prison, a drug rehabilitation center, a shelter for the homeless, a military cemetery, a naval shipyard, or another similarly symbolic site, a president or any other politician can call attention to some item on his or her agenda and bring it before the public. If the politician is prominent, a simple visit will be newsworthy—at least on a light news day—and can be used, at the very least, to dramatize support or concern. Perhaps the best example of this device at work was its use by John F. Kennedy to stimulate support for the nation's space program in the early 1960s. By setting the goal of a manned mission to the moon within a time frame so short that everyone could identify with it, he captured the imaginations of the press and public. (Compare this with the dull thud that accompanied George Bush's 1990 adoption of 2019 as the target date for a manned mission to Mars—a time as seemingly distant as the destination.) Even dour Walter Cronkite was swept up in the excitement of space exploration and pledged, during a report on one of the earliest manned mission launches, that no matter how mundane manned space flight might become in the future, CBS would provide live coverage of every launch. Forever.

Speaking of flight, politicians also use the news to test public reactions to their policies or plans. They do this by floating the famous "trial balloon"—a hot-air device filled with political talk (and sometimes propelled by a leak) that rises slowly above the horizon on a reconnaissance mission. If no one shoots it down, they reason, it is safe to attempt low-level manned flight themselves. Among the classic practitioners of the art of the trial balloon were Jimmy Carter and Alan Cranston. Cranston was a member of the Democratic leadership of the Senate during the years of the Carter presidency. Every so often, the Democratic leaders would meet with the president to discuss his legislative agenda. Immediately afterward, Cranston would appear on the White House driveway to tell reporters the president's deepest and darkest secret plans. These would be duly reported to the nation. The appearance this created was that of a recurrent leak, and one wondered why the president continued to tolerate the disclosure of confidences by the senator from California.

In reality, what Cranston was doing was blowing up Carter's trial balloon. If his leaks and violated confidences played well, it was safe for the president to claim them as his own a few days later. But if the balloon came under hostile fire, it was not even necessary that Carter distance himself from it. It was, after all, just the flaky senator from the Left Coast who had espoused such a ridiculous proposal, not the president of all the people.

Politicians want to make news to provide information to the public and to comply with the democratic expectation that they consider themselves to be somehow accountable to the people. Yes, Virginia, there are altruistic motives at work in the public sector. They are not unmixed, undiluted, but they are there nevertheless. And they lead some public officials—especially in such agencies as the Consumer Product Safety Commission or the Environmental Protection Agency—to let people know what is happening within their government.

Finally, there is the power motive. If a politician is able to make news with regularity—some would say, with impunity—then ipso facto that is evidence of the politician's power. After all, is he or she not newsworthy? In an age of media politics, notoriety can be its own reward, especially when it can be translated into pressure on other policy makers. I am believed to be powerful because I am judged to be worthy of attention. Watch out for me! Or, as Georgia Congressman Newt Gingrich rather succinctly put it, "If you're not in the *Washington Post* every day, you might as well not exist."[27]

What should interest us about all of this in the present context is not so much that politicians should want to make news—that should be self-evident. Rather, we need to realize that—for the very same reasons that they want to *make* news, they also want to *control* it. As Larry Speakes once put it during a disagreement with the networks over their refusal to cover a Reagan speech shortly before the 1982 mid-term election, "*You don't tell us how to stage the news*, and we don't tell you how to cover it"[28] [emphasis added]. Please talk about me *and* please say what I want you to say. Again, we can trace the impulse to Niccolo Machiavelli, who once offered the following advice and example:

> Nothing causes a prince to be so much esteemed as great enterprises and giving proof of prowess. We have in our own day Ferdinand, King of Aragon, the present King of Spain. He may almost be termed a new prince, because from a weak king he has become for fame and glory the first king in Christendom, and if you regard his actions you will find them all very great and some of them extraordinary. At the very begin-

ning of his reign, he assailed Granada, and that enterprise was the foundation of his state. . . . He has continually contrived great things, which have kept his subjects' minds uncertain and astonished, and occupied in watching their results.[29]

One must wonder whether Ronald Reagan did not at one time play Machiavelli's prince in a "B" movie, for it surely seems he read this script. He, like Ferdinand, entered his office at a time of especially low prestige—Jimmy Carter had just been vicariously held hostage by Iranian militants for 444 days. After some early defeats—notably in the valleys of Lebanon—he too assailed Grenada—though his was spelled rather differently and located on the other side of the Atlantic—ostensibly to rescue some American medical students trapped by a hostile island regime. The distraction that the Grenada invasion provided from the debacle in Lebanon and the boost it gave to the president's image of strength and determination were merely ancillary benefits. And Reagan followed with a series of other dramatic moves to occupy the public mind. His prowess as Leader of the Western World was firmly established.

The point of all this is that public officials, no less than political candidates—and probably more—have reason to find means to structure the ways they are portrayed in the news media. Much of their relationship with journalists—and through journalists, with the public—is guided by this fact. Making news, as much as making or implementing policy, is part and parcel of the business of politics.

On the receiving end of all this news making, of course, are reporters, and they have their own reasons for wanting to help politicians get the word out. For one thing, doing so is consonant with at least part of what journalists believe their job to be. In a survey of several thousand journalists during the 1970s, for example, 56 percent of those questioned said that getting information to the public as quickly as possible was an extremely important part of their responsibilities, and a like percentage said it was extremely important to discuss national policy while it is still being developed.[30] But it is also true that cooperating with public officials and other news makers, rather than confronting them at every turn, makes reporters' own jobs much easier. Journalists, as we have already noted, have a significant stake in seeing their work in print or on the air. Journalism is not a profession of egoless automatons, and publication, in and of itself, is a solid source of instant gratification. To the extent that journalists are dependent on their sources—something we have already found to be the case, and a factor of particular importance for those who work a regular "beat" where they must interact with the same news makers day after day—they will be subjected to a strong incentive to play a cooperative game. Go along to get along. Take the easy route. You still get your work published. In fact, it is probably published more often than that of confrontational "investigative" journalists. Play ball. It is a style of work in which complacency does have its rewards, some of them quite consequential.

In fairness, it must be noted that reporters have adopted a norm of skepticism toward their sources—the survey cited found that 76 percent of journalists think it is an extremely important part of their jobs to *investigate* claims and statements made by the government—and to say that journalists are very sensitive to charges of being manipulated would be to risk terminal understatement. The trade journals of their profession are literally filled with case studies of abuses revealed, intonements for the good of the order, and, in the case of one journal—the *Columbia Journalism Review*—"darts" and "laurels" awarded to those who fail to maintain the high standards of journalism and to those who succeed, respectively. All of this is suffused with the religious spirit of the pursuit of the sacred trust.

The point is not that journalists are unethical, unprofessional, or malfeasant. Quite the contrary, they are among the most conscientious of professionals. Rather, the point is that, on a day-to-day basis, it can be very difficult to withstand the blandishments of the would-be media manipulators, or even to recognize these temptations for what they are. And compared to Eve's apple, the temptations that skilled political communicators offer to journalists are a veritable fruit salad. The media events we examined in chapter 3 are mere garnish. Other items on the plate include news conferences, press briefings, news releases, informal contacts and information trading, and faulty plumbing.

News conferences—and especially presidential news conferences—are a good place to begin taking a look at the tools of news making. They offer a prime example of how the process, when in skillful hands, can be at once obviously open and even-handed, and thoroughly planned and controlled.

The presidential news conference as we know it had its origins in the presidency of Teddy Roosevelt—not incidentally, a contemporary of those twins of the tabloids, Hearst and Pulitzer. Roosevelt, as Elmer

Cornwell tells us in his classic review of the development of presidential public relations, *Presidential Leadership of Public Opinion*, was the first American president to possess what we think of today as a good "news sense"—an idea of what he might do that would interest journalists and the public, and why he might want to do it. Among his other efforts in this direction—which included floating trial balloons, much more a state-of-the-art conveyance in his day—he was the first president to meet with reporters on a systematic basis, the first to understand the new reality of the media: that it was more important to make news than to be the subject of favorable editorial commentary. It was news, he saw, not (usually) editorials, that filled the front pages of the new mass circulation press. More than that, he realized that by boosting his personal *image* through stories of his travels, adventures, interests, and experiences—the Rough Rider and the Teddy Bear were, perhaps, the first *yin* and *yang* of American politics—he could build a personal following that could provide political support for his policy proposals at later times.[31] Though his efforts were rudimentary and crude by today's standards, his insight was significant, and it helped him to become one of the earliest strategic communicators in American politics.

Roosevelt's cousin Franklin developed the strategic aspects of the news conference still more. In the context of political communication, Franklin Roosevelt is most often remembered for his so-called "fireside chats" on the radio, but two of his innovations in the conduct of news conferences may have had at least as significant an impact. By Roosevelt's day, such conferences had become regular features of the presidency, but they were conducted under rules very different from the regimented drill we see today. They were small-scale affairs, typically held in the president's office, at which the president could not be quoted directly, at which mention could not be made that information had been obtained at the White House, and for which all questions had to be submitted in writing in advance. Roosevelt did away with many of the formalities—except for the requirement that he could not be quoted directly—and replaced them with a more subtle and sophisticated set of rules. The most interesting of these had to do with establishing two new categories of news—"background" and "off the record." Reporters were free to publish information that they received on a background basis, but they could not link it to the president or the White House. Information given to reporters off the record could not be published in any form. Journalists who violated these expectations quickly found themselves excluded from the Roosevelt circle.

The first of these devices, background, was, in effect, a reassertion of the old rules in a new package, and the second, off the record, was even more restrictive. It is a wonder that reporters were willing to tolerate this at all. But that is where the strategic genius of Franklin Roosevelt came to the fore. For Roosevelt realized that, as the prime news source for reporters covering the federal government—a government whose role and importance in the daily life of the country was growing rapidly—he had the power to make or break journalistic reputations. Those who were in the know were on the go. Those who were left out were left behind. Roosevelt used background and off-the-record information to fix the race.

For a journalist, being in the know has two components—knowing what is going to happen before it does, and knowing what is not going to happen before it doesn't. We can think of these two elements as, first, being right, and second, not being wrong. Roosevelt used backgrounders to let reporters know what his administration was likely to do in the coming days or weeks. Since they were free to use this information—but not to tell where it came from—journalists tended to present background information to the public as if it were a product of their own reportorial initiative. They became political seers. And since, not incidentally, the resultant predictions tended to be confirmed by events with considerable regularity, reporters and columnists who were privy to the backgrounders developed personal reputations for great political astuteness. They were right. They were credible. They were influential. Similarly, Roosevelt gave reporters information off the record to steer them away from what he regarded as unwanted speculation about what his administration *might* do, which he viewed as political distraction. The consequent absence in their writings of speculations that would likely prove unfounded—they literally could not write about these—not only served the president's political purposes, but further enhanced the reputations of these journalists. They were not wrong. They were credible. They were influential. And they were hooked. White House correspondents became addicted to a supply of "inside dope," but their supplier—the president of the United States—was no dope. He was a virtuoso, albeit one caught, for the present, in a mixed metaphor. By merging background and off-the-record information into a steady flow of more regular forms of news, he played the White House press corps like a violin.[32]

As the news conferences got bigger and the issues confronting an emergent world power less tractable, presidents developed more and more buffers between themselves and the journalists covering them, and more devices for controlling the flow of news. The more the president talked, for example, in a news conference of fixed duration—thirty minutes is now the norm—the less time there was for reporters to ask questions. Give a lengthy opening statement. Give long-winded answers. Control the agenda. News organizations tend to report the answers to questions asked by their own reporters. Be sure to call on reporters from the major organizations and on those known to be friendly. Control the agenda. Beyond that, plant questions. Learn to be evasive. Set the mood of the moment. Control. Control. Control.

Among the most revealing of these techniques was the practice, begun under Harry Truman of, in effect, cramming for the exam. Truman was never comfortable in his dealings with the press, and before each news conference he arranged to be briefed as to the questions he was most likely to encounter. Over the years since, these presidential briefings have become an elaborate ritual. By the time of Gerald Ford's administration, for example, the White House Press Office maintained three large spiral briefing books of material gathered from all the fingers and toes of the federal executive—the best guesses of each agency's press officers as to what might be asked, and the best advice of each agency's leadership as to what ought to be answered. The president, with the assistance of his staff, would then study and rehearse for portions of two or three days in advance of each conference to eliminate surprises and to hit upon the proper political language to apply in each instance. Specifics here, ambiguities there. Duck and weave. Back and fill. Watch your head. Ronald Reagan followed a similar approach, rehearsing up to sixty anticipated questions and answers with his staff.[33] In effect, the president may have become less the leader of the free world than its principal press spokesperson.

Though the news conference is still very much with us—indeed, it is arguably the most visible of presidential activities—its importance as an instrument of *strategic* political communication has declined ever since the day in 1961 that John F. Kennedy permitted his first conference to be televised live. No longer could information be conveyed on background or off the record. No longer could a president afford to make mistakes, or even small gaffes—as Ronald Reagan learned time after time in his public sessions. Television converted the news conference into a media event, one in which the reporters are little more than part of the setting, mere straight men (and women) for the inevitable presidential punch lines. Now . . . live on our stage . . . the president of the United States. More form, less substance. Always news, but seldom a story. Or, as ABC News correspondent Brit Hume put it in characterizing George Bush's first prime time gathering, "He didn't make much news. But then, this isn't a news event we're talking about. It's an event. It's politics."[34]

Much of the substantive slack in news content created by the televising of news conferences, however, has been taken up by a related device, the press briefing. Though not strictly accurate, let us think of a press briefing as a news conference featuring members of the staff rather than presidents or other officeholders. Ranking officials do sometimes meet with journalists in these settings, but much more common are appearances by lesser officials or press officers of the agency conducting the briefing. Such briefings are daily occurrences in the White House, the Pentagon, the State Department, and many other agencies of the government. They tend to be relatively small and quiet affairs—crisis periods aside—and to produce large volumes of routine news, the sort of thing that fills the inside pages of a newspaper and occasionally spills onto the front page below the fold. Here background and off the record still live, though not as freely as they once did. Here the trial balloon still rises above the horizon from time to time. Press briefings are, by and large, lower-risk affairs than full-scale news conferences—for top officials, at least, if not for those directly on the journalistic firing line—if only because the briefing officer has relatively lower status, and his or her boss can usually be disassociated from any errors or misstatements that are made. Sometimes this means that journalists are able to elicit more information than they otherwise might. But more often, it means that they get less. The briefing officer, after all, probably does not know everything that is going on in the agency, and must, in any event, report on the briefing immediately afterward to a higher authority. This interplay of uneasiness is captured with remarkable clarity in a pair of colloquys that took place in the White House press room, one pertaining to an appearance by White House Chief of Staff John Sununu, and the second concerning the rules for a planned briefing by Rozanne L.

Ridgeway, assistant secretary of state for European Affairs, on a forthcoming summit meeting between President Reagan and Soviet leader Mikhail Gorbachev.

In the first instance, Sununu had complained in an interview on CBS's "Face the Nation" that the Washington press corps would rather have information presented off the record or on background rather than in public so that its members could enhance their status by seeming to have access to secret sources of secret information. The implication was that he would prefer to have all briefings on the record. Reporters clearly took his message to heart (or at least to mind) later in the month when Sununu was to brief them on the president's pending State of the Union Address. The exchange, reported later in the *Washington Post,* went as follows:

> Press Secretary Marlin Fitzwater: This afternoon's briefing is on background. It's attributable to senior administration officials. Not for publication or use. The briefers are Governor Sununu, the president's chief of staff, and General [Brent] Scowcroft, the president's national security adviser.
>
> Governor Sununu will have some opening remarks to give you an overview of the State of the Union address. General Scowcroft will then discuss national security matters. And I ask that you hold your questions until both of them have made presentations, and they'll both stay here to answer your questions together.
>
> The information they give you is for immediate use. And with that we will go ahead and begin the briefing. . . .
>
> Q: Is this on the record, Mr. Sununu?
>
> Q: Why does this have to be on background?
>
> Fitzwater: It's on background because the president's giving his address this evening. This is attributable to senior administration officials. That's the correct way to do it.
>
> Q: What's correct about it? There's nothing here—insight—they can't say on the record, is there?
>
> Fitzwater: The purpose here is to give you information, to flesh out the facts and material. The president's words tonight will speak for themselves.

Q: Well, the governor's accused us of wanting it on background.

Q: Yes, we're not the ones who want this in secret.

Senior Administration Official: I don't mind not briefing.

Q: Come on.

Q: Wait a minute.

Q: Don't be temperamental . . .

Senior Administration Official: I'm not being temperamental. I just don't want to cause a problem.

Q: You accused us of wanting to do everything in secret, governor. Let's do it in the open.

Fitzwater: The briefing is on background. The record is as we stated.

Q: We don't want you to be a faceless . . .

Senior Administration Official: I don't mind giving you an on-the-record interview whenever you ask for one . . .

Q: When?

Q: Now.

Senior Administration Official: . . . but the fact is that you wanted some background for tonight's speech, and that's what we're here to give you. . . .

Q: Who said we wanted background?

Q: Press ahead.

Senior Administration Official: How are we going to do this?

Fitzwater: It's on background.

Senior Administration Official: It's on background . . .[35]

In the second instance, there was agreement that the briefing would be public. The question was one of just how public it would be—specifically whether audio and video coverage would be permitted.

Q: Marlin, have you made a decision on whether Roz is going to be for sound and cameras as well as on the record?

Fitzwater: She will be regular briefing rules—silent film for five minutes . . .

Q: Why is she on the record but not on camera?

Fitzwater: Well, we don't do very much of those kinds of briefings here . . .

Q: The State Department briefs on the record, on camera all the time. You should be able to cope with . . .

Fitzwater: Well, they have more courage than we do . . .

Q: What's your objection to radio and television coverage?

Fitzwater: That it is too high a risk for me . . . that you can't talk on camera, you can't discuss issues, you can't—you end up in very stilted kind of conversation and also I don't believe press spokesmen ought to become television personalities.

Q: . . . Why is the risk greater for people to be on record for radio and television than it is for . . .

Fitzwater: Well, that's a good question, and one we ought to write a book about. But see, I have a lot of very firm theories about the power of television, and about its responsible use, and—and irresponsible use, and one of the problems with doing things on film is that you open yourself up to all sorts of—of problems unique to the power of television.

Q: What's that?

Fitzwater: One is, simply, that you provide film which can be shown over and over again, of any—any aspect of a briefing, that can be used and edited by editors to make all sort [sic] of points that were far from the original intention.

Q: But is it not your experience that quotes can be used over and over again in the print media by editors who, if they wish to distort, can distort them?

Fitzwater: My experience has been that it's far less likely and far less— far less of an impact. . . . The point is, is simply again that in the course of my standing up here for an hour and a half and going through any number of topics and subjects and so forth, there are all kinds of visual images that are—that come up, there are jokes told, there is a lot of laughter and banter between us and so forth, which in a television setting would portray an entirely different kind of image.

Q: Why is that bad—to portray whatever the image actually is?

Fitzwater: Well, what would happen would be that I would indeed tailor the reality of my image to the necessities of television.[36]

In recent years—Marlin Fitzwater to the contrary notwithstanding—even the press briefing has become something of a media event as Cable News Network and C-SPAN, the cable television public affairs network, have begun to provide live coverage of some of these affairs. This has led those seeking a more private channel to a renewed emphasis on informal contacts between public officials and reporters—power breakfasts, news maker sessions with editorial boards (even some of these are now being televised), and the like. From the perspective of the journalist, these meetings can be used to get private insights into the thinking of key policy makers—a latter-day version of inside dope. From the perspective of the public official, they can be used to establish a personal relationship with journalists on the theory that they will at least give the news maker an even break in return.

Finally, in this regard, we ought to mention the ever-present press release. For Immediate Release. Though statistics on such things are hard to come by, more trees may give their lives each year for the production of press releases than for any other paper product produced and consumed in Washington, D.C. The city is literally awash in them. They are issued by every agency and office, every interest group and activist. The White House produces an average of one for every breath the president takes—some days counting inhalation and exhalation as distinct acts—and even that venerable and august body, the United States Supreme Court, which has almost no other organized press function, uses releases to announce its decisions. News organizations employ whole cadres of support staff to winnow, to cull, and, most often, to dispose of the collected wisdom reflected therein.

But not all of the trees die in vain. Some press releases do make the day book or stimulate a story, and some shape the news by giving reporters a particular perspective on events. Many are a handy instrument of balance—the oft-cited views of responsible spokespersons of opposing points of view. And a chosen few—especially, but not exclusively, in the smaller news markets where reporting resources are limited—actually *become* the news. Verbatim. Without attribution of the source. It is, to be sure, cheaper than hiring journalists! A number of years ago, for instance, I was studying the role of communication in several midwestern congressional campaigns. As part of the study, I read all the news releases from each candidate, and every issue of every newspaper in each district. Somewhat to my surprise at the time, I must confess, I discovered that—more often than you might think—it was difficult to tell the two apart except for the fact that one rubbed off on my hands. No wonder so many former journalists are now employed on Capitol Hill and environs as press aides. The inverted pyramid rides again.

Today, in fact, printed press releases have been supplemented with video versions for local television news. Corporate public relations departments and trade associations produce many of these, but even the House and Senate maintain television studios for their respective members to do the same. Some stations edit portions of these releases into their own pieces, while others use them intact—often without disclosing their source. And their acceptance rate is sufficiently high to have spawned a small industry—or, more correctly, a small segment of the larger communication consulting industry—that specializes in placing video news releases on local newscasts.

Beyond these formal points of interaction between reporters and public officials, there lies a wide array of informal contacts as well. The two groups may be adversaries in public, but they are not necessarily that in private—a condition that the smart public official will foster and exploit. For example, shortly after becoming secretary of state in the Bush administration, James Baker hosted a reception for some thirty reporters (and their spouses) who regularly cover State; referred to in-house as the "inner group." Held in the Treaty Room, the lavish affair featured shrimp, roast beef, liquor, and a chance to meet and greet the new Bush elite.[37] Though more extravagant than most such efforts, the Baker reception illustrates a tack on media relations that is commonplace.

In addition to these diverse mechanisms for getting the word out *publicly* (and influencing the choice of vocabulary), prospective news makers have yet another device available for getting the word out privately—the news leak. No discussion of contemporary press strategies would be complete without some attention to what have come to be known since the days of Richard Nixon as "plumbing problems."

Leaks are the great leveler of strategic political communication— anyone can crack a pipe. News makers use leaks for a variety of purposes: to send messages between different parts of the federal bureaucracy, to send messages within a single agency but outside of channels, to bring matters before the public, to alert Congress or the president to some pending problem. Leakers populate the news underground; they are clandestine forces in the information wars that rage in politics. Where politicians typically make news to make a name, leakers make news to make trouble—trouble for a president, a legislator, a political party, a disliked boss, or a distrusted superior. Unlike briefing officers or other public news makers, leakers seek protection in anonymity. Journalists are more than happy to provide it—to protect their sources—because leaked information is more likely than official information to have news value. Someone is, after all, going to some risk to make it known. Impact. Conflict. Drama.

It is a mistake, however, to think that all leakers are outsiders or whistle-blowers. Many so-called leaks originate from the very same folks who bring you press conferences and power breakfasts. Sometimes it is in their interests to get information out—truthful or otherwise—while maintaining their own public distance from it. Henry Kissinger, at the time he was Richard Nixon's National Security Advisor, once became so incensed about leaks from the staff of the National Security Council that he ordered wiretaps on their telephones. When this became known sometime later, reporters suggested that it had actually been Kissinger himself who had been the source for much of the information in question. Kissinger, incidentally, was also an ardent practitioner of the backgrounder. Reporters traveling with him during his days as secretary of state were often treated to policy insights which they were required to attribute to such noted personages as "a source close to the secretary of state," "a high-ranking State Department source," or "a source accompanying the secretary of state." On one occasion, the *Washington Post* became so frustrated with this charade that it accompanied one such story with a picture of the secretary which bore a caption that said, in effect, "A Source Traveling with the Secretary of State." Call for Roto-Rooter.

More recently, John Sununu became the target of leakers when he inserted himself into the final stages of the process that was about to yield a new and more proactive administration position on the issue of global warming. President Bush was scheduled to present a speech on the topic in February 1990, and a draft had cleared such diverse hurdles as the secretaries of State and Energy, the administrator of the Environmental Protection Agency, and the White House Science Advisor, whose collective approval represented the first broad consensus on the subject in the Bush administration. At the last minute, and apparently on his own initiative, Sununu ordered that the speech be significantly toned down. This angered several of those who had acceded to the original draft, and prompted one or more of them to leak the story to the *Washington Post* in an apparent (and unsuccessful) effort to both embarrass and circumvent the chief of staff. Aftershocks of the struggle reverberated through the newspaper's pages for weeks afterward.[38]

Perhaps the most insidious form of leak is the use of rumor or innuendo, a device that has increasingly found its way from the campaign into the governance process as a corollary of the trend toward negativism. Rumors, especially juicy ones, are a genuine temptation to news organizations. They have all the elements of a good story. But most of the time, prudence wins over prurience. If there is no supporting evidence, don't publish. That may not stop an ardent would-be communicator, however. In the absence of evidence, it may be possible to force publication by turning a rumor into a media event.

A good example of how this is accomplished was provided by an incident that took place in the summer of 1989, when it became clear that Thomas Foley would succeed Jim Wright as Speaker of the House of Representatives. Rumors began to circulate that Foley had some unsavory personal habits. When these rumors failed to make print, an aide to Georgia Republican and House Minority Whip Newt Gingrich (Gingrich having been instrumental in Wright's political demise), pointedly asked reporters if they were looking into Foley's private life. "We hear it's little boys," the aide is quoted as having said. Foley was forced to make the rounds of his colleagues, assuring them of his propriety. Still, though, not a word reached the public. What to do?

The solution came from Mark Goodin, communications director for the Republican National Committee and a principal aide to party chairman Lee Atwater. On the day of Foley's swearing-in as Speaker, Goodin released a four-page memorandum to party leaders comparing Foley's voting record to that of New York Congressman Barney Frank, an avowed homosexual. The headline read: "Tom Foley: Out of the Liberal Closet." Now, *this* was news. Atwater initially stood behind the memorandum, Foley was forced to respond publicly to the implications it raised, and Frank went so far as to threaten to release the names of homosexual *Republican* members of Congress if such behavior continued. By creating an unavoidable news event, the Republicans had assured not merely that their rumor would surface, but that it would float.

In the end, Goodin resigned, Atwater apologized, and even President Bush pronounced the incident disgusting—while at the same time reaffirming his confidence in the party chairman. But the message was there—in print and on the air—for all to see.[39] The negative multiplier was at work once more. The lessons of the fall campaign had been learned; the permanent campaign was merely its extension. Willie Horton strikes again!

And finally, when all else fails, there is confrontation. What all of the devices we have considered to this point—even the news leak— have in common is that they assume a general acceptance of the rules of the game. Briefers and leakers alike recognize that journalists have a job to do—indeed, as much as any other citizens, they subscribe to the myth of the free press and the free people—and, though they may resent specific actions of the news media that cause them discomfort, they accept the quasi independence of news organizations from political institutions as legitimate. Their objective is not to undermine the news media, but to use them for personal advantage. If anything, they have an incentive to reinforce the apparent independence of the media so as to preserve for themselves an important instrument of leadership.

But there are people who do not subscribe to this consensus—who simply cannot tolerate the sustained adversarial posture of the media. Usually such people occupy isolated positions in the government, often

below the level of public visibility. But at least once in recent history—during the Nixon administration—they clustered at the top. This
attitude was expressed often by the president himself, as in a 1972
memorandum to political adviser Pat Buchanan, in which he observed

> if you consider the real ideological bent of the *New York Times*, the
> *Washington Post, Time, Newsweek* and the three television networks,
> you will find overwhelmingly that their editorial bias comes down on
> the side of amnesty, pot, abortion, confiscation of wealth (unless it is
> theirs), massive increases in welfare, unilateral disarmament, reduc-
> tion of their defenses, and surrender in Vietnam. . . . The battle ahead
> will . . . be a vicious, brutal one because the left wing media will fight
> much more cleverly than the right wingers have fought. . . . They will
> lie, distort and do anything that is necessary to get into power. They
> never allow their piously held principles to get in the way of their
> overriding drive to gain and wield power.[40]

During the Nixon years and pursuant to a systematic approach to
media relations, journalists were subjected to personal inquiries by the
Federal Bureau of Investigation[41]; news organizations were threatened
with tax and antitrust actions; presumed leakers—notably Daniel Ells-
berg in the famous "Pentagon Papers" case—were subjected to illegal
searches; efforts at prior restraint of the press—against the *New York
Times*, again in the Pentagon Papers episode—were undertaken; and a
general program of harassment and intimidation was set in motion. In
his treatise on political language, Murray Edelman has argued that "it
is the talk and the response to it that measures political potency, not the
amount of force that is exerted. Force signals weakness in politics, as
rape does in sex."[42] In much the same way, President Nixon's confrontational tactics signified a failure of communication strategy.

While Richard Nixon's approach to the media may have demonstrated some distinctly pathological characteristics, the core of his insight is nevertheless valid. Communication can be used to achieve
power, to exercise power, and to hold onto it. And more and more, the
lines separating those functions are being blurred as leadership comes
to be defined in terms of strategies rather than objectives. To what end
is the permanent campaign directed?

Notes

1. Elmer E. Cornwell, Jr., *Presidential Leadership of Public Opinion* (Bloomington: Indiana University Press, 1966), pp. 45–47.

2. Steven R. Weisman, "President Proposes 83 Major Program Cuts; Tells Congress U.S. Faces 'Day of Reckoning,' " *New York Times,* 19 February 1981, p. A1; and "Highlights of Message," *New York Times,* 19 February 1981, p. A1.

3. Martin Tolchin, "Democrats Vow to Weigh Package as They Start Shaping Alternatives," *New York Times,* 19 February 1981.

4. Hedrick Smith, "Reagan Plans a Drive to Regain Momentum on Economic Package," *New York Times,* 14 April, 1981, pp. A1, A14.

5. Edward Cowan, "President Implores Supporters to Help in Passing Tax Bill," *New York Times,* 12 June, 1981, p. A1.

6. Howell Raines, "President Demands Tax Cut and Budget Be Passed by August," *New York Times,* 17 June 1981, p. A1.

7. Hedrick Smith, "Democrats Seek Public's Support to Counter Reagan Tax Proposal," *New York Times,* 7 July 1981, pp. A1, D19.

8. Ibid.

9. "Do the Networks Always Shortchange the 'Loyal Opposition'?" *TV Guide,* 11 March 1978, p. 8.

10. "Lobby Drive," *New York Times,* 20 July 1981, p. D2.

11. "Advertising Thrust," *New York Times,* 21 July 1981, p. D12.

12. Adam Clymer, "G.O.P. Radio Tax-Cut Ads Set," *New York Times,* 24 July 1981, p. D2.

13. Edward Cowan, "25% Cut in Tax Rate Voted," *New York Times,* 30 July 1981, p. A1.

14. David Hoffman, "Bush Seeks to Amend Constitution," *Washington Post,* 28 June 1989, pp. A1, A4.

15. David Hoffman, "President Praises Ruling, Urges Stronger Action," *Washington Post,* 4 July 1989, p. A10.

16. David Hoffman, "Calling Flag Burning Wrong, Bush Urges Speedy Approval of Amendment," *Washington Post,* 1 July 1989, p. A4.

17. Quoted in Mark Hertsgaard, "Did the News Media Go Easy on Reagan?" *Washington Post,* 21 August 1988, p. C1.

18. Paul Taylor, "Consultants Rise via the Low Road," *Washington Post,* 17 January 1989, pp. A1, A14.

19. Ann Devroy, "For White House Political Operation, Focus Will Be Policy, Not Popularity," *Washington Post,* 19 March 1989, p. A8.

20. Michael Isikoff, "Drug Buy Set Up for Bush Speech," *Washington Post,* 22 September 1989, A1, A22.

21. Anthony Lewis, "The Intimidated Press," *New York Review,* 19 January 1989, p. 26.

22. As quoted in "The Stockman Article: Excerpts from Atlantic," *New York Times,* 12 November 1989.

23. Dale Russakoff, "Courting the Media with Metaphors," *Washington Post,* 13 July 1989, p. A21.

24. Ibid.

25. Stephen Hess, "Confessions of a Sound Bite," *Washington Post,* 22 October 1989, p. C5.

26. Janet E. Steele, "Why Do Television's Academic Experts So Often Seem Predictable and Trivial?" *Chronicle of Higher Education,* 3 January 1990, p. B2.

27. Quoted in "The World of Congress," *Newsweek,* 24 April 1989.

28. Quoted in "Reagan to Mix Economics, Politics on TV Tonight," *Wall Street Journal,* 13 October 1982, p. 14.

29. Niccolo Machiavelli, *The Prince* (New York: Mentor Books, 1952), p. 110.

30. John W. C. Johnstone, Edward J. Slawski, and William W. Bowman, *The News People: A Sociological Portrait of American Journalists and Their Work* (Urbana: University of Illinois Press, 1976), p. 230.

31. Cornwell, *Presidential Leadership,* pp. 13–26.

32. Ibid., pp. 147–153.

33. Eleanor Randolph, "Quieting the White House Press with Access," *Washington Post,* 12 March 1989, pp. A6, A7.

34. Eleanor Randolph, "Bush's Prime-Time Debut Comes Up Short," *Washington Post,* 10 June 1989, p. A3.

35. *Washington Post,* 5 February 1990, p. A9.

36. "The Rules According to Fitzwater," *Washington Post,* 23 May 1988, p. A9.

37. "Baker Hosts His New Press Corps," *Washington Post,* 31 January 1989, p. A15.

38. Michael Weisskopf, "Shift on Warming Sought," *Washington Post,* 3 February 1990, pp. A1, A7; "Sununu Defends Changes in Speech," *Washington Post,* 5 February 1990, p. A5; Michael Weisskopf, "Environmentalists Try to Cut Sununu Down to Size," *Washington Post,* 22 February 1990, p. A21.

39. Ann Devroy and Tom Kenworthy, "GOP Aide Quits Over Foley Memo," *Washington Post,* June 8, 1989, pp. A1, A10; and Dan Balz, "The Public Politics of Rumor," *Washington Post,* 8 June 1989, pp. A1, A10.

40. Quoted in Bruce Oudes, ed., *From: The President: Richard Nixon's Secret Files* (New York: Harper & Row, 1989), pp. 475–76.

41. Daniel Schorr, "The FBI and Me," *Columbia Journalism Review,* November/December 1974, pp. 8–14.

42. Murray Edelman, *The Symbolic Uses of Politics* (Urbana: University of Illinois Press, 1964), p. 114.

5 WHAT'S GOOD FOR MOBIL OIL

When Herbert Schmertz retired in April of 1988 as vice president of Mobil Oil Corporation, the company—and the oil industry—lost its most effective advocate. Over a period of some twenty years, Schmertz's doctrine of "creative confrontation"—some might term it "slash and burn public relations" instead—had raised the voice, the visibility, and the political vitality of "Big Oil," and had contributed to a much higher level of public relations sophistication on the part of big business in general. As steward of Mobil's $30 million per year public affairs budget—of which, by his retirement, he was paid a reported $640,000 per year, in all likelihood making him the nation's highest-paid public relations practitioner—Herb Schmertz was a force not merely in American politics, but in American society.[1]

Those twenty years were tough on the oil industry. Oil had always been a source of some controversy—particularly in seemingly annual and highly contentious battles over a tax loophole called the "oil depletion allowance," by which oil companies were permitted to reduce (or even eliminate) their income tax obligations on the basis that oil was a wasting asset (one that could not be replaced). But through the mid-1960s it seemed that the biggest problem Mobil had was Texaco, the biggest Texaco had was Sunoco, and so forth. Gasoline was cheap, by today's standards, and the major oil companies competed with one another aggressively to sell it. They cut prices—I can remember buying a gallon of gasoline in Sweetwater, Texas, one day for 16.9 cents—they offered premiums to induce customers to visit their stations—free glasses or steak knives; double S&H Green Stamps on Wednesdays—and they even promised prompt, courteous, and effective service—you could trust your car to the man who wore the star, the big, bright Texaco star. We didn't know it at the time, of course, but those were heady days indeed.

They came to an end on a beach along the Santa Barbara Channel on the coast of California in 1969. There, on January 30, an off-shore well operated by Union Oil sprang a leak, spreading gooey crude over one of the most photogenic stretches of shoreline in America, and one, not incidentally, located close to the media center of Los Angeles. The televised scenes of dead fish and oil-soaked, dying sea birds are familiar to us now, but they were a rude shock in 1969. And there were more shocks to follow in fairly short order as an epidemic of oil spills and other hazardous materials accidents struck at home and abroad. The world, it seemed, was truly awash in oil, and it did not have anything to do with a glut in the marketplace.

There were two principal products of the Santa Barbara oil spill of 1969. The first was a major-league black eye for the oil industry, which suddenly came to be seen as public enemy number one for what was perceived as its cavalier attitude toward the environment. The second—clearly related to the first—was the rebirth of environmentalism in the United States and an extraordinary increase in the membership, resources, and political clout of a wide range of environmental interest groups. Literally overnight, groups like the Sierra Club, the Wilderness Society, Friends of the Earth, and others burst into newfound national prominence. In an era of controversial movements— civil rights, women's rights, gay rights, consumer rights, antiwar—environmentalism seemed one that almost everyone—everyone except Big Oil, that is—could agree on. But the real threat posed to the oil industry by the environmental movement was less one of scale than of demographics—it attracted support from a wide range of upscale groups, groups who had the education and resources to engage in sustained and effective political action. In effect, the Santa Barbara spill mobilized—energized—the first "yuppie" political movement. And Big Oil had cause for concern.

While part of the industry's response was to pay more attention to the nuts and bolts of environmental protection, it also undertook the first in what was to become a series of image-building public relations campaigns. Suddenly the oil companies discovered what wonderful environmentalists they had been all along, and wanted to share the good news with us. Look, said one of the new wave of television commercials. We have 129 producing oil wells on this tropical island in the Caribbean, and we've landscaped them so nicely that no one even notices. Look, said another, replete with underwater photography that rivaled anything Jacques Cousteau accomplished since. We built this off-shore platform out here in the Gulf of Mexico, and, while it's true that we stirred up a little dust while doing it, the fish came back! How could we have so misjudged the motives and actions of Big Oil?

Next came the oil embargo of 1973 and 1974, when—in protest of American support for Israel during the most recent of a series of wars in the Middle East—the Arab nations cut off supplies of oil to the West. Gasoline was rationed, where it was available at all, and depending on the day of the week, lines of cars with odd- or even-numbered license plates stretched for blocks from any station that was pumping the lifeblood of American mobility. When the tap was reopened, the price had quadrupled, and over the balance of the decade it tripled yet again. The good old days were over.

Well, that wasn't quite true. The good old days were *not* over for the oil companies. They had just begun. Because the oil companies were not just retailers of Exxon Supreme and Mobil One, not just victimized consumers once removed. They were oil *producers*. And as producers, they were receiving the fruits of the embargo and the subsequent price hikes just as if they were Arab oil sheiks. Their profits went through the ceiling. They became the darlings of Wall Street, acquiring and being acquired, investing and divesting, consolidating and diversifying. It was a sight to behold.

And beheld it was—in Washington. There were, it seemed, questions to be asked. *Political* questions. Was it not obscene for these giant corporations to be making so much money at the expense of the poor and—significantly—the middle class, who were struggling to pay their heating bills? Did not "the people" have a claim on these "windfall profits"? And who were these companies, after all, that they could profit from the misfortunes of the American people? Were oil tankers queuing up off-shore, as reported in the media, waiting for oil prices to rise before coming in to discharge their precious cargoes? Oh, they were "American" companies in name, all right—Texaco, Mobil, Exxon, Standard, and the rest—but just how *American* were they? Were they corporate citizens of the whole world first, or were they patriots?

In Washington, questions like that usually get answered, and when they do, the result is not always in the best interests of the objects of public attention. That was surely the case here. A wave of legislation burst upon the shore, every bit as threatening in its way as the wave of Santa Barbara crude that had first set the political juggernaut in motion. It was legislation to tax the profit windfall, to control prices, to protect the United States supply of oil, to encourage alternate sources of energy, and—most frightening of all to Big Oil—to break up the biggest oil companies. Putting a tiger in your tank was the furthest thing from the minds that ran Exxon.

Time and again, the environmentalist, consumerist, pro-American shock troops hit the beach. Time and again, Big Oil was forced to respond. And time and again, the front line formed on the television sets in America's living rooms. "Bringin' home the oil, bringin' home the oil," sang a hearty Irish folk group as the screen showed a Gulf Oil tanker plying the world's oceans to bring precious crude home to America. We're "synergistic," proclaimed Sid Caesar on behalf of Texaco. We're not an evil monopoly, but a whole that is greater than the sum of its parts. Because we explore for the oil, we know where to find it. Because we found it, we know how to refine it. From the pipelines to the refineries, to the stations that we own . . . God Bless America, our home sweet home.

And it was into the thick of this battle for the hearts and minds of the American people and their representatives in Congress that Herbert Schmertz—former labor lawyer and political advance man in the campaigns of John and Robert Kennedy—led the forces of Mobil Oil and, by example, the whole ten-gallon-hat set. In a highly controversial move in the early 1970s that has since become commonplace, Mobil began buying space in news magazines and elite newspapers to express its political views. It produced television advertisements doing the same, and, when the networks declined to run them, citing the requirement under the Federal Communication Commission's "Fairness Doctrine" that they would have to provide equal time to spokespersons with opposing views, Mobil took out newspaper advertisements to complain—and on at least one occasion even offered to pay for the opposing views to be stated. When Schmertz took offense at a critical report, he sometimes sent the journalist responsible a gift-wrapped blowup of the offending piece with those portions he regarded as erroneous circled and corrections noted in the margins. In 1974, Mobil purchased newspaper advertisements to respond to *New York Times* columnist Tom Wicker's characterization of the "pious, self-serving, devious, mealymouthed, self-exculpating, holier-than-thou, positively sickening oil-company advertisements in which these international behemoths depict themselves as paragons of virtue embattled against a greedy and ignorant world." Not guilty, said Mobil. When WNBC-TV in New York ran a series on gasoline prices in 1976, Mobil placed a newspaper advertisement headed "What Ever Happened to Fair Play?" and when CBS ran a feature on oil company profits, Mobil placed an ad, this time headlined "How CBS on October 24, 1979, Prefabricated the News." In 1980, Mobil sued the *Washington Post* for libel, a case that was settled in 1987 in favor of the newspaper. Mobil later distributed antiregulatory cartoons to some 5,000 small newspapers, where they typically ran without attribution to the source, and it hired broadcast journalists to produce "news" videos which it sent to local television stations. In 1983, the *Wall Street Journal* wrote an editorial against Mobil's "campaign of intimidation," and the next year Mobil pulled all of its advertising from that newspaper and refused to send press releases to, or answer questions from, *Journal* reporters—a policy that stayed in place until 1986. For one of the biggest publicly held companies in the United States, this was the equivalent of the Mayor of New York refusing to talk with the *New York Times*.[2]

But if it was Schmertz's confrontational tactics that got him (and Mobil) attention, it was another of his moves that marked the genuine sophistication of his strategy. Herb Schmertz bought the Public Broadcasting Service (PBS). Literally. At the time, the network and its funding agency, the Corporation for Public Broadcasting (CPB), were under heavy fire from the Nixon administration, as suggested in a 1971 memo from Clay T. Whitehead to President Nixon, and in a related message from Charles Colson to Lawrence Higby, all of the aforenamed being members of the White House staff. Whitehead wrote,

> The immediate goal is to eliminate slanted public affairs programming on public television as thoroughly and quickly as possible. The longer range and more fundamental goal is to reverse the current trend of CPB toward becoming a BBC-like fourth network supported by public funds, which inevitably would reflect the taste, politics, and morality of the national artistic and intellectual elite. . . .

There is, and has always been, a deep division within public broadcasting over the extent of national control versus local station control. . . . This provides an opportunity to further our philosophical and political objectives for public broadcasting without appearing to be politically motivated.

We stand to gain substantially from an increase in the relative power of the local stations. They are generally less liberal. . . . Further, a decentralized system would have far less influence and be far less attractive to social activists.

Therefore, we should immediately seek legislation to . . . make a drastic cut in CPB's budget. . . .[3]

"I have reviewed [a draft of] Whitehead's memo to the President," wrote Colson.

. . . The President shouldn't meet with anybody from Corporation for Public Broadcasting under any circumstances. The fight is going to get dirty. . . .[4]

Mobil Oil became public television's first major corporate underwriter in 1970, a year before the Whitehead and Colson memos were written, but at a time when the writing was clearly on the wall. By 1988, Mobil was spending some $10 million annually on PBS programming. The real value of this money—when we view it in strategic communication terms—is not the support it provides to what is now, much more than in Nixon's day, a widely accepted quasi-public broadcasting service, or the programs that it sustains. Rather, it is the audience that Mobil buys with its money. For in a sense, Clay Whitehead was right. The PBS audience may be small—perhaps 2 percent of the total national audience at any given time and 10 percent of the total national television audience in a typical week—but it is very much composed of an elite. The artistic or other characteristics of that elite, however, are less important than their demographic and political characteristics. The PBS audience as a group represents the most up-scale audience available to a television advertiser, and—over the long run—the most politically active and influential as well. If, in American politics, the squeaky wheel gets the grease, this audience shrieks.

You say oil spills got you down, Bunky? Windfall profits pickin' your pocket? Gas lines stealin' your time? Well, buck up, Bunky, 'cause it's time for "Masterpiece Theatre" and your host with the British accent, Alistair Cooke. Brought to you, don't ya know, by the Mobil Oil Corporation. They must not be such bad folks after all. Indeed, shortly after Mobil had contributed $100,000 to the producers of another PBS favorite, "Sesame Street," in 1975 and run a national newspaper advertisement warning that Big Bird, a star of the show, was an endangered species because of a shortage of funds, the chairman of Mobil received a packet of letters from some California schoolchildren and a check representing 1,334 pennies they had raised. "Dear Mobil Oil," said one letter. "Most people are mad at you but we like you. Thank you for helping Big Bird stay on TV. We are glad to help too."[5] Don't think for a moment that there were not some moms and dads reading those letters as well.

◆ ◆ ◆ ◆

Politicians, government leaders, and governments themselves are not the only ones with political interests in our society, and they are not the only practitioners of strategic political communication. Other players—special and public interest groups, trade associations, and corporations—get into the game as well. And some, like Herb Schmertz, are important and accomplished communicators.

It was the late political scientist V. O. Key, Jr., who pointed out in his classic book, *Politics, Parties, and Pressure Groups*, the vulnerability of business as a favored interest in American politics and the importance of using communication to sustain its position of privilege. In effect, said Key, business must create and continually press forward a myth of its own social value. Business people, he observed, are few in number and lack the inherent moral authority of "the sturdy agrarian yeomanry or the horny-handed toiler of the factory and foundry." But what they lack in votes, he went on, business people make up in money and intelligence, resources they must use to advantage. The politics of business, said Key, must include

> aggressive attempts to mold the attitudes of both the general and special publics. To gain public favor business associations and corporations employ in large numbers public-relations experts, those masters of the verbal magic that transmutes private advantage into the public good. . . . [Of] fundamental significance is the continuing propaganda calculated

to shape public attitudes favorably toward the business system as a whole or toward particular types of business.[6]

It was a concern that Herb Schmertz and a host of other business communicators have shared, and advice that they have heeded well.

And there has been good reason for their concern. A 1975 national survey of public opinion, for example, found that 67 percent of the public expressed a "low approval" of big companies, up from 47 percent ten years earlier. Fifty-seven percent thought that the government should limit corporate profits. One American in three thought the oil companies were the worst of the lot when it came to ethics, and three in four thought that they, in particular, made too much profit.[7] By the mid-1980s, only 19 percent of Americans said they had a great deal of confidence in the leaders of business,[8] and a mere 18 percent said that they thought business executives were highly honest and ethical.[9] And no wonder! A 1981 report by the Media Institute, a Washington-based research group, compiled after monitoring of portrayals of business on two hundred prime time television episodes, found that two-thirds of business people were shown in a negative light, that roughly half of the work shown as being done by business people involved illegalities, that the major characters who ran big businesses were presented as criminals, and that few of the portrayals showed business to be either socially useful or economically productive.[10]

The response to this perceived problem from the business community—as the breadth of the Mobil Oil effort suggests—takes many forms. Perhaps the most prominent among these is the placement of so-called "advocacy advertising," advertising that is intended to promote ideas or policies rather than products. Consistent with the idea of selling the myth of American business suggested by Key, some advocacy advertising is intended to promote business in a generic sense. In the mid-1970s, for example, the Advertising Council, a nonprofit organization that produces many of the nation's best-known public service spots, undertook a multi-year educational campaign to overcome what it termed "economic illiteracy," having discovered through research that only 1 percent of the American population could correctly identify all five of the functions in our economy of business, labor, the consumer, the investor, and advertising. With a budget of $150 million and support from the Department of Commerce and several major corporations, the effort was designed "to make the workings of the free enterprise system as familiar to Americans as the batting average of baseball players.'' The level of "literacy" the council sought may have been in question—the educational booklet around which the advertising campaign was centered was written at a ninth-grade level and featured original "Peanuts" cartoons—but the concept was pure V. O. Key.[11]

Other advocacy advertising is intended to improve the fortunes of individual companies. In 1987, for example, American television viewers were presented with the image of a space station drifting slowly upward across their screens. Another American space triumph? No. As the station drifted further, its outer markings passed slowly through the field of view—a red star and the letters "CCCP." Lest anyone miss the message, a NASA–like exchange of voices in the background carried a conversation in Russian. "Shouldn't we be there, too?" asked the message at the end. The advertisement—produced by McDonnell Douglas, a major contractor in the American space program—was deemed too controversial by all three networks, who declined to run it, but it appeared on local stations across the country. In 1989, the company followed with a more subtle spot, one picturing a little girl putting on a space suit and helmet and gazing upward as a space station floats by to the strains of "Twinkle Twinkle Little Star." "There's a big world waiting out there, little one . . . ," says a female narrator. "For an educated America, even the sky's not the limit," intones a man's voice.

For all of their "morning in America" feel—and in the first instance the "*wake up* America" message—these spots are not exercises in altruism. The United States program to build a space station—worth an estimated $1 billion to McDonnell Douglas—has been in trouble. Stretch-outs and budget cutbacks have delayed its development, and the will to proceed is very much in doubt. Perhaps that is why, in addition to airing on CNN and the three major networks' public affairs programs—they accepted this one—the advertisement was also set to run repeatedly in selected local markets: Baltimore, Maryland, home of Senator Barbara A. Mikulski, chair of the appropriations subcommittee that oversees the NASA budget; Flint, Michigan, where it might be seen by Representative Bob Traxler, who chairs the House committee that controls the NASA budget; and such other major media capitals as Baton Rouge, Louisiana, Jackson, Mississippi, and Springfield, Massachusetts. "These are all areas," said company spokesman Tom Williams, "where we wouldn't be disappointed if people contacted their congressmen."[12]

Even smaller fish can jump into the advocacy pond. In January 1989, for instance, a small Louisiana company, Marine Shale Processors, bought local time in Washington, D.C., during the network evening news programs for a $250,000 campaign to promote its toxic-waste disposal systems. Basically, the company claimed to turn toxic sludge into harmless gravel. Most Washington viewers were not likely to buy a toxic-waste disposal system that January, but among the audience were legislators and government environmental regulators who very well might. Targeting.

Advocacy advertising does not come cheap. A one-time, full-page advertisement in the *Washington Post,* for example, cost approximately $37,000 ($45,000 on Sundays) in 1989, while a similar placement in the national edition of the *New York Times* cost about $46,000 ($55,000 on Sundays). In that year, Northrup Corporation spent more than $60,000 for local time in Washington to run a television advertisement touting the company's B–2 bomber in advance of a congressional decision on extending funding for the plane. Since at the time the B–2 had never flown, Northrup promoted it as "America's most thoroughly *tested* new bomber"[13] [emphasis added].

Overall, estimates are that some $50 to $75 million are spent each year on advocacy advertising, and the pace of such efforts has been increasing. *Advocacy Reports*, a newsletter that monitors such ads in four outlets—the *New York Times, New Republic, National Review,* and *Columbia Journalism Review*—reported that the volume of placements grew from 118 pages in 1984 to 204 in 1988, or some 73 percent in four years. In addition to government officials, this advertising can be aimed at journalists—some 14,000 of whom work in the Washington area alone. Or, in the case of advertising designed to stimulate contributions, organizational membership, or political action—as in the 1981 effort to mobilize support for the Reagan tax reform package or the 1988 effort to defeat the nomination of Robert Bork to the Supreme Court, in which the *Washington Post* alone ran $220,000 worth of messages for both sides—it can be aimed at the public in general.[14]

Labor has joined the image making as well. Who could have escaped the catchy strains of "Look for the Union Label," the television anthem of the International Ladies Garment Workers Union, which first aired in 1975 and which, by 1980, elicited recognition and a positive response from four out of five Americans. And the more recent and more pervasive "Made in the USA" campaign still fills the airwaves. In 1984 the Labor Institute of Public Affairs, an AFL-CIO affiliate, began a television series called *America Works,* which aired in a number of cities. Along with it came pro-union messages such as one that featured then–Washington Redskins running back John Riggins in a locker room holding up his NFL Players Association card. "Here's my union card," said Riggins as if it were American Express gold. "I wouldn't go to work without it."[15] And during the presidential primary season in 1987 and 1988, the American Federation of State, County, and Municipal Employees launched a $1.2 million campaign in Iowa, New Hampshire, and other key states designed to influence the campaign agenda. "It's time for new priorities," said the union.[16]

Sometimes advocacy advertising strains the limits of truthfulness. The Tobacco Institute, principal trade association of the cigarette industry, for example, ran a series of advertisements in nineteen newspapers around the country which said that a majority of Americans do not support a ban on cigarette advertising, do not support an increase in cigarette taxes, and do not support smoking bans in restaurants. Based on a nationwide survey conducted by Hamilton, Frederick & Schneiders, a respected Washington polling firm that has since been reorganized, the industry campaign was designed to dispel the notion that smokers' rights was an unpopular, minority issue. "Enough Is Enough!" proclaimed the advertisements. Strictly speaking—*very* strictly—each of the three claims just noted was true. A majority did not support a total ban on cigarette advertising—only 41 percent did. But another 34 percent supported continuation of the present prohibition on advertising these products on radio or television. This the Tobacco Institute neglected to mention. Similarly, a majority did not support an increase in cigarette taxes—only 44 percent did. But another 38 percent thought they should remain at the already high level about which the advertisement went on to complain. This the Tobacco Institute neglected to mention. And a majority did not support a total ban on smoking in restaurants—only 24 percent did. But another 74 percent favored continuation of the segregation of smokers into special smoking sections. This left a mere 2 percent of the public supporting the prosmoking position implied by the advertisement. This, too, the

Tobacco Institute neglected to mention. How do we know all this? Because the *Washington Post* got hold of the original data and shared them with the world, much to the embarrassment of the institute.[17]

In addition to being more forthright than that of the cigarette industry, much of the promotional effort undertaken by business is more subtle as well. Mobil's use of public television is not only a case in point—it represented the point of a wedge that is now well embedded in the financing of PBS and its member stations. Big Oil followed the Mobil lead in a big way. By 1981, fully 72 percent of all of the programming broadcast by PBS during its thirty-two-hour weekly core schedule, roughly the equivalent of prime time, was funded in whole or in significant measure by four oil companies: Exxon, Mobil, Arco, and Gulf. Indeed, the same four companies had been among the largest PBS underwriters every year since 1976.[18] Nor is this corporate largesse proffered only by companies from the oil patch. For example, shortly after a division of Allied Chemical was found to have dumped tons of the pesticide Kepone into the James River at Hopewell, Virginia, threatening the public health of those in the area and downriver, and bringing an immediate end to the region's lucrative fishing industry, Allied appeared as one of the principal underwriters of PBS's "MacNeil Lehrer NewsHour," with its elite audience. And in the wake of its own problems with chemical discharges at Bhopal, India, and Institute, West Virginia, Union Carbide, too, became a PBS underwriter.

Commercial television can also provide a vehicle for corporate image polishing. A campaign begun in 1989 by Philip Morris, for example, put the company's name back into television commercials for the first time since the 1950s, but not to sell cigarettes—at least not directly. Rather, the campaign, reinforced by full-page newspaper advertisements, was a 200th anniversary devotional to the Bill of Rights, a potent symbol of American values with which it could hardly hurt to be associated. Estimated cost of the campaign: $30 million per year for two years.[19] Similarly, Dow Chemical set out to rehabilitate its corporate image, damaged for a generation by the company's association in the public mind with the napalm it manufactured for the American war effort in Vietnam. After nearly twenty years, the company has begun a major television advertising campaign. The message to the children of the 1960s antiwar protestors: By caring about people, "Dow lets you do great things."

In 1981, the Federal Communications Commission took steps to make corporate underwriting of public television even more attractive for would-be sponsors by removing certain restrictions on the nature of their messages. Prior to that time, underwriters could only be identified by name. Under the revised rules, still in effect, the identification could include a summary of the company's line of business as well as its corporate logo or symbol.[20] After this decision, some companies, such as Norfolk Southern, even went so far as to develop film or animated logos that closely resemble commercials.

The importance of enhancing a corporation's image should not be underestimated. Joseph Downer, at the time a vice chairman of Arco, told a *TV Guide* interviewer in 1981 that, as a direct result of the $15 million his company had contributed to public broadcasting over a five-year period, "We gain an image of quality. Our sponsorship of the Wolf Trap concerts resulted in a tremendous response from people in government. And, my God, you walk into the departments, or the Congress, and you're identified as Arco, and there's a feeling of warmth. There's no question but that it's helpful to our lobbying effort." But some, like Fred Friendly, who himself gave more than $200 million to public television as head of the Ford Foundation, suggested an even more subtle motive: "By deciding which shows they will underwrite," Friendly pointed out, "they have also decided what will not be on the air. By funding those programs . . . that are harmless, so far as controversy goes, they are structuring the program schedule of public television."[21] It's enough to make Nixon and Company very proud.

Public interest advertising as well as public television can also serve the needs of corporate political communication. Under pressure in recent years on the issues of alcohol abuse and, especially, drunk driving, the beer industry has undertaken an extensive campaign promoting "responsible" drinking. Anheuser-Busch, which has for several years now conducted a "Know When to Say When" campaign, quadrupled the campaign's budget in 1989 to $30 million, or roughly 5 percent of the company's annual advertising expenditures, and in that same year Adolph Coors began a "Now/Not Now" effort, showing scenes at a friendly tavern ("Now") and at work and behind the wheel ("Not Now"). The impetus for all of this seemingly counterproductive advertising? A report on drunk driving was issued by the surgeon general of the United States criticizing alcohol ads and recommending, among other things, a voluntary ban on advertising of alcohol on college campuses by September 1990 and elimination of all tax deductions for all but the simplest of advertisements listing brand names and prices. That, you can be assured, sent ripples through the beer vats of St. Louis, Missouri, and Golden, Colorado. To make sure the word got around, the Beer Institute, the industry's lobby, followed up on the individual corporate promotions with a $2.5 million campaign of its own, this one pointing with pride to the efforts of brewers to combat excessive drinking.[22]

Another strategy pursued by business—one that we have already touched on briefly and will return to in the next chapter—is the "massaging" of the news by creating and distributing video news clips. This strategy, too, was anticipated by Mobil, and has now become commonplace. Sometimes a report produced by a company, or by its public relations firm, will air in its entirety on a local news program, but without any mention of its source. Audio is provided—indeed, one way to recognize these pieces is by the absence of a statement of affiliation at the end of the "report"—"Jane Doe reporting from San Diego" rather than "Jane Doe, Channel 7 News, reporting"—but it is recorded separately from the video track so that it can be stripped off and replaced with an audio track featuring a reporter from the station that runs the tape, thereby giving that station the appearance of vast news-gathering resources, and the company that created the message the added credibility afforded by the local journalists. It is essentially the same game played by the practitioners of negative political advertising, except that these spots are usually served sunny-side up. To further the deception, the names of persons interviewed are not superimposed on the original tape, so that each local station can use its own graphic style. Some stations run these tapes unedited, while others weave pieces of them into locally produced stories. The commercial touches here are often subtle—a feature on school children learning to take photographs (using Kodak cameras), a reminder to adjust your (large Timex) clock for daylight savings time—but when they are used, they are news.[23]

Finally, corporations and others sometimes use strategic communication techniques for damage control when something goes wrong. In late 1985, for example, when the Environmental Protection Agency (EPA) began to suspect that dioxin—a potent carcinogen—was contaminating discharges from the nation's paper mills, the paper industry saw a crisis on its horizon. By February of 1986, when it became clear to the paper companies that the contamination affected not only their discharges but their products as well, the time for action had arrived. The cap was still securely in place, but word of the problem was sure to leak soon. Would there be enough time to avoid a public relations catastrophe? Under the leadership of the American Paper Institute (API) in Washington, the industry developed a "Dioxin Public Affairs Plan" and budgeted $300,000 to manage official and public perceptions of paper products. The plan included "intelligence gathering" at the EPA, tempering news media interest—"Really, folks, there's no story here!"—minimizing public health concerns, and hiring outside experts to counter expected EPA comments on the risks associated with dioxin. API hired a Washington public relations firm, trained representatives of the individual corporations involved on how to deal with the issue, and conducted a consumer survey. The association conducted its own independent tests of paper products and, in September 1987, when the story could be held no longer, announced the results while playing down any threats to health. The outcome? A panic over paper as might have been expected, but a short-lived one, as the industry had hoped.[24]

The value of strategic communication in controlling political damage has not been lost on the nation's religious establishment either. In April of 1990, for example, the National Conference of Catholic Bishops, frustrated by the church's performance in framing the debate on the abortion issue, contracted with the Washington office of the public relations firm of Hill & Knowlton and with the Wirthlin Group, home of former Reagan polling guru Richard Wirthlin, to turn things around. The objective of the three to five year campaign is to change the terms of debate from a focus on privacy and women's rights to one on the "humanity of the unborn." The price tag: an estimated three to five million dollars, with the majority to be paid by the Knights of Columbus, a Catholic fraternal organization. The initial publicity generated by the contract, however, may not have been what the bishops had in mind. Both clients and some employees reportedly severed their ties with Hill & Knowlton's Washington office, and more than a third of the roughly four hundred New York employees of the firm signed a petition protesting the decision to represent the church which stated, in part, "We should not be representing any group in its advocacy of a position which would restrict the fundamental rights of all of us as Americans."[25]

Even foreign companies find the need for damage control from time to time. In 1987, you may recall, a subsidiary of Japan's Toshiba Corporation was found to have passed highly sensitive American submarine technology to the Soviet Union. There was an immediate expression of outrage in the United States, and a strong move to bar Toshiba from further participation in the American market. The potential cost to the company of such a ban—estimated at some $10 billion per year—was staggering, and its response all but overwhelming. Toshiba itself spent an estimated $9 million over a year and a half to lobby Congress and recoup its image, and its wholly-owned subsidiary, Toshiba America spent millions more. Members of Congress were lobbied intensively by members of the Japanese government and of that country's parliament, by officials of Toshiba and of Toshiba America, by officials of the Reagan administration, and by American distributors of Toshiba products who worried, they said, of potential job losses. Even American companies that might be thought to be in competition with Toshiba lobbied for moderation in the American response, apparently out of a concern that their own supplies of Toshiba-manufactured electronic components would be threatened. "In all the 21 years I have been in public office," commented Republican senator Jake Garn of Utah, the principal sponsor of legislative sanctions, "I've never seen a lobbying campaign so orchestrated at so many levels." "It . . . is a warning that the Japanese are more sophisticated than they had been, and their role is much more significant," noted Ronald Morse of the Library of Congress, an expert on Japanese lobbying. And in the end, Toshiba won the day. Rather than an outright ban on doing business in the United States, Toshiba was slapped with a three-year limit on government purchases of its products—a loss of no more than $100 million per year—and even that was tempered with some loopholes. As Senator John Heinz of Pennsylvania characterized the result, "The message of the Toshiba sanctions fight is that up to a point crime does pay."[26]

But quite apart from crisis management, Japanese business, like American, sees the need to establish acceptance among the American public over the long term, to foster, if you will, a Japanese rendition of the what's-good-for-business-is-good-for-you mythos. Beginning in 1986, Japanese industry has engaged in a systematic campaign of strategic political communication in the United States—including elements of lobbying, politicking, and propagandizing—designed to influence national-level policy by generating pressure from below. The emphasis is on individual voters, local officials, and the news media. Headed by the Electronic Industries Association of Japan, the campaign includes, among other things, conducting debates and seminars around the country, publishing local newsletters and magazines, initiating exchanges with state universities and policy planning groups, establishing contacts with state-level economic development offices and local Chambers of Commerce, contacting the local press, and undertaking student exchange programs. It is, in effect, a corporate foreign policy, and one that may be supported by as much as $100 million per year.[27]

We can see, then, that corporations, industry associations, labor unions, and other groups are just as sophisticated as politicians—often more so—in the use of strategic communication, and that their efforts are very much a part of the information environment in which we live. Indeed, as the efforts of Japanese industry just detailed make clear, even foreign-owned businesses get into the act, sometimes, perhaps, to the detriment of their American counterparts, but sometimes—as Toshiba discovered—with their willing assistance. And if foreign businesses are engaged in campaigns of strategic political communication in the United States, can foreign governments be far behind? As they say on television, folks, stay tuned.

Notes

1. Paula Span, "Chronicles of the PR Warrior," *Washington Post,* 28 April 1988, pp. C1, C15.

2. Ibid.; and Michael J. Connor, "Mobil's Advocacy Ads Lead a Growing Trend, Draw Praise, Criticism," *Wall Street Journal,* 14 May 1975, pp. 1, 23.

3. Bruce Oudes, *From: The President: Richard Nixon's Secret Files* (New York: Harper & Row, 1989), pp. 336–37.

4. Ibid., p. 333.

5. Connor, "Mobil's Advocacy," *Wall Street Journal.*

6. V. O. Key, Jr., *Politics, Parties, and Pressure Groups,* 5th ed. (New York: Thomas Y. Crowell, 1964), pp. 91–92.

7. Connor, "Mobil's Advocacy," *Wall Street Journal.*

8. Elizabeth Hann Hastings and Philip K. Hastings, eds., *Index to International Public Opinion 1984–85* (Westport, Conn.: Greenwood Press, 1984), p. 360.

9. Edmund F. McGarrell and Timothy J. Flanagan, eds., *Sourcebook of Criminal Justice Statistics—1984* (Washington: U.S. Government Printing Office, 1985), p. 213.

10. Reported in "TV's Businessman Is Getting Bum Rap as Tube's Big Boob," *Wall Street Journal*, 20 April 1981, p. 10.

11. Michael J. Connor, "Ad Campaign That Seeks to Explain Workings of Free Enterprise System Stirs Controversy," *Wall Street Journal*, 4 August 1976, p. 32.

12. David Olmos, "Lost in Space? Contractor Supports Space Station with TV Ads," *Philadelphia Inquirer*, 11 May 1989.

13. Paul Farhi, "Weapons Firms Carry Out Ad Blitzes," *Washington Post*, 20 July 1989, pp. F1, F5.

14. Paul Farhi, "Advertising That Aims to Sell Ideas," *Washington Post*, 31 January 1989, pp. C1, C6.

15. Stephen Banker, "Look for the Union Label . . . and Much, Much More," *TV Guide*, 31 March 1984, pp. 30–33.

16. Lloyd Grove, "Groups' Ads Seek to Shape '88 Agenda," *Washington Post*, 14 December 1987, p. A24.

17. Richard Morin, "Tobacco Institute Ads Shaded Truth," *Washington Post*, 26 January 1989, p. A16.

18. John Weisman, "Why Big Oil Loves Public TV," *TV Guide*, 20 June 1981, pp. 4–10.

19. "Philip Morris Returns to TV with Patriotic Ad Campaign," *Washington Post*, 2 November 1989, p. E3.

20. Margaret Garrard Warner, "FCC to Let Public Broadcasting Stations Broaden Identification of Business Donors," *Wall Street Journal*, 24 April 1981, p. 7.

21. Weisman, "Why Big Oil Loves Public TV," *TV Guide*.

22. Paul Farhi, "Brewers' New Ad Pitch: Moderation and Caution," *Washington Post*, 4 July 1989, pp. C1, C3.

23. Jeanne Sadler, "Public Relations Firms Offer 'News' to TV," *Wall Street Journal*, 2 April 1985, p. 6; Michael M. Klepper, "Airing Your Corporate Message on the Evening News," *Wall Street Journal*, 23 February 1987, p. 26; and Herma M. Rosenthal, "Beware of News Clips Massaging Your Opinions," *TV Guide*, 21 April 1984, p. 5.

24. Michael Weisskopf, "They Couldn't Control the Dioxin but the Damage, Maybe," *Washington Post National Weekly Edition*, 9 November 1987, p. 28.

25. Tamar Lewin, "Abortion Divides Firm Hired to Help Fight It," *New York Times*, 18 April 1990, p. A14; Peter Steinfels, "O'Connor Defends Anti-Abortion Aid," *New York Times*, 22 April 1990, p. 30; Peter Steinfels, "Knights Aiding Anti-Abortion Effort," *New York Times*, 13 May 1990, p. 18.

26. Stuart Auerbach, "Toshiba Corp.'s Costly Lobbying," *Washington Post*, 13 October 1988, pp. C1, C4.

27. Pat Choate, "Money Talks: How Foreign Firms Buy U.S. Clout," *Washington Post*, 19 June 1988, pp. C1, C4.

6 NOW YOU SEE IT, NOW YOU DON'T

In September of 1982, Ferdinand Marcos, at the time president of the Philippines, was scheduled to make his second official visit to the United States. The political situation at home was turbulent, and for Marcos, much was at stake. A parliamentary system under a new constitution had been introduced the year before, but anti-Marcos demonstrations, terrorist attacks, charges of human rights violations, and open conflict with the Catholic Church continued unabated. Elections at various levels were held, but opposition leaders generally boycotted the process, and there was election-related violence in the south. Labor leaders, reporters, and opposition leaders were placed under arrest, and there was considerable controversy over Marcos's alleged role in the kidnapping of a young man who had become engaged to his daughter over the president's objections. Then–Vice President George Bush's words during a Manila visit for Marcos's 1981 inaugural ceremony notwithstanding (Bush described Marcos as a "true friend of democracy"), Marcos's image needed some polishing if he was to retain the support of his American patrons. The Philippine government went about this polishing in a big way.

Preparations for the Marcos visit began in the spring of 1982 when the president assigned as his new ambassador to the United States Benjamin Romualdez, who happened to be the brother of his wife Imelda. Romualdez had helped arrange an earlier Marcos visit to the United States, as well as a more recent trip to Saudi Arabia. Three additional diplomats of ambassadorial rank were posted to Washington temporarily just to work on the visit. This group was assisted by approximately two dozen media professionals, eleven of whom were public relations specialists from leading Manila agencies.

During the months leading up to the president's visit, the embassy was refurbished and refurnished, and a steady stream of American military, congressional, and media opinion leaders was wined and dined. A hotel chef and a provincial song-and-dance troupe were brought to Washington for this purpose. In April, a Filipino exhibition was opened at Bloomingdale's department store, with Mrs. Marcos as the featured participant. Outdoor feasts were held for some 3,000 Filipino-Americans in the Washington area and for some 12,000 living in and around San Francisco. In addition, a government-subsidized Filipino restaurant was opened in Washington's Georgetown area in time for the official party to dine there during the visit, and a new English-language newspaper, the *Philippine Monitor*, commenced publication. The newspaper was written by the public relations staff at the embassy in Washington, printed in the Philippines, and flown to the United States regularly on the national airline for distribution.

The embassy's media relations group talked with fully 170 American reporters in advance of the visit, and shortly before Marcos's arrival, hundreds of journalists were presented with press kits in the form of expensive bamboo briefcases filled with promotional materials, among which was a book ostensibly written by Marcos himself in anticipation of his trip. Thousands of posters, T-shirts, and miniature Philippine flags were distributed; Washington was blanketed with signs proclaiming "Long Live Marcos and Reagan"; and hundreds of people were bused from as far away as Norfolk, Virginia, to participate in an unofficial welcoming ceremony at that symbol of American democracy, the Washington Monument. And, lest we think that all of this activity was directed solely at an American audience or that strategic communication is purely an American phenomenon, it is worth noting that the ceremony at the Washington Monument was scheduled during the early hours of the morning, so that it would correspond with prime time on Philippines television.

Altogether, this public relations blitz is estimated to have cost the Philippine government at least five million dollars. Its objective, as stated at the time by an embassy spokesman in an interview with the *Wall Street Journal*, was to counter the "bad image" of Marcos and the Philippines in the American press. "We have lost the public-opinion battle practically by default," he said. "Nobody has made a sustained effort to tell our side of the story."[1]

Clearly, such an effort was made in this instance. The question is: What did the Philippine government get in return?

The answer, according to some research that a colleague and I did on the subject some years ago is: worse than nothing. During and after this ''sustained effort,'' the image of the Philippines and its president that was painted by American news media was systematically and significantly *worse* than it had been during the year before the Marcos visit. One possible explanation for this is that strategic political communication, the manipulation of press and public opinion, does not work. An alternative view, and the one to which I subscribe, is that what the Filipinos did was not, in fact, strategic political communication or, if it was, the strategy was flawed.

◆ ◆ ◆ ◆

We have spent a lot of words up to this point examining the uses of strategic political communication in the domestic politics of the United States. We have seen how communication strategies can be applied to market candidates to voters, and public officials and their policies to the public. Domestic uses of these techniques, however, are only part of the picture, for the same devices are also employed—principally by American strategic communication consultants—by or in behalf of foreign governments to influence the ways they are portrayed in the American press, and the kinds of policies the United States government undertakes toward them.

Registered foreign agents—any person or firm engaging in this sort of activity is required by the Foreign Agents Registration Act of 1938 to register and file annual reports with the Department of Justice—now include many well-known American public relations firms, and some 7,500 individuals, who work in behalf of more than 100 countries.[2] The services they provide range from clipping news stories about their client countries that appear in the American press to lobbying with members of Congress and the executive branch. Many of the firms that are active in domestic politics have foreign clients as well.

Together with political scientist Robert Albritton of Northern Illinois University, I have spent much of the last decade or so examining this phenomenon and measuring the effectiveness of international political public relations efforts. In this chapter, I will share with you some of the results of that research.

The use of strategic communication (and lesser forms of political public relations) by foreign governments—as judged by the number of contracts and client countries—has roughly doubled since the 1970s. The most recent report of the attorney general—listing clients, contractors, and services—numbers several hundred pages, and the total value of the contracts each year runs well into eight figures. The client countries over the years have included a veritable Who's Who of folks with an interest in American foreign policy—the Philippines, of course, but also the Shah's Iran, the Soviet Union, South Africa, Israel, South Korea, Canada, Turkey, and many others. And the list of companies serving their needs has been equally distinguished—Hill & Knowlton, Burson-Marsteller, Edelman International, Ruder and Finn—in short, all of the biggest names in public relations and many of the lesser lights as well. They are joined by a bevy of Washington law firms, trade consultants, and general lobbyists like Arnold and Porter, a law firm whose list of clients includes corporations and governments from around the world.

One of the real powerhouses of the industry—in fact, the name of their office building was "The Power House"—over the decade of the eighties was Gray and Company (the firm was acquired in 1986 for $21 million and merged into Hill & Knowlton Public Affairs Worldwide). The firm was founded by Robert Gray, who worked for Reagan campaign manager William Casey in 1980, helped to run the president's inauguration, then set up shop providing lobbying and public relations services to domestic and foreign clients. Among its many domestic customers during this period were the American Trucking Association, Bendix Corporation, NBC, and the Stroh's Brewing Company. Foreign clients included the embassies of Canada and South Korea, the Japanese electronics industry, and the Republic of Turkey, as well as Haiti, Morocco, Saudi Arabia, and the Cayman Islands. The Cayman Islands? The *Washington Post* reported that, in 1984, the company employed 130 lobbyists and "communicators," and set its prior year's income at $11.4 million. Many employees of this and other firms are former government officials whose principal asset is a simple one—who they know.[3]

More recently, another firm with strong Republican roots, Black, Manafort, Stone, & Kelly, has emerged as the bright star of Washington's public affairs firmament. Two of the firm's six partners, Charles Black and Roger Stone, served as senior campaign strategists with the Bush campaign, while a third, Paul Manafort, organized the Republican National Convention. Lee Atwater, Bush's campaign manager and later chair of the Republican National Committee, also has his roots in the firm. On the Democratic side, Black Manafort offers the services of Peter Kelly, formerly finance chair of the Democratic National Committee, and James Healy, longtime aide to House Ways and Means Committee chair Dan Rostenkowski. Though its revenues are small by Gray & Company standards—$2.1 million in 1986, for example—Black Manafort's client base is strong and growing. In 1989, it included Allied Signal, Donald Trump, Aetna Life and Casualty, Bethlehem Steel, Johnson & Johnson, TWA, Union Pacific, the Mortgage Insurance Companies of America, the Large Public Power Council, the Air Transport Association, and the Edison Electric Institute, as well as the governments of Kenya (for $500,000 per year) and Zaire (for $1 million per year), and the Union for National Action—the Philippines political party of Vice President Salvador Laurel ($950,000 per year). Domestic clients pay the firm fees ranging from $10,000 to $25,000 per month, and projected revenues for 1989 from foreign clients alone exceeded $5 million.[4]

What kinds of services do these companies provide for their clients? One set falls under the general rubric of lobbying. If public affairs firms are hired for who they know—for the access they have to Washington decision makers—then using their access is an important part of what they do. Black Manafort, for instance, has been involved in debt negotiations between clients Peru and Somalia, on the one hand, and the World Bank and International Monetary Fund, on the other; in lobbying for a firm seeking to place lottery terminals on federal property; in extending a helicopter production line for Kaman Aerospace; in seeking permission for Allied Signal to engage in the uranium trade in South Africa; and in winning foreign-trade-zone status for a manufacturing plant jointly owned by Chrysler and Mitsubishi—to name but a few recent ventures.[5]

Perhaps more interesting to us in the present context, however, is a second group of services, those relating to communications with the press and public. Here, a great deal of what is produced—particularly by firms that came to the business from the media rather than the political side—takes the form of the traditional bells and whistles that we commonly associate with the practice of public relations. Truckloads of newsletters, news releases, fact files, glossy photographs, books, pamphlets—multicolored, multifaceted, but totally obvious propaganda—are produced and distributed. The propaganda goes to news organizations, libraries, college professors, and a variety of other target audiences. And when it arrives, most if not all of it finds its way rather quickly—indeed, as if powered by unseen forces—into the nation's sanitary landfills.

When journalists and members of the public think about the public relations activities of foreign governments—if they ever do—this is the stuff they think about, and it is small wonder that they discount its importance or potential influence. As William Safire put it a few years back, "The whole business smacks of rainmaking, and it seems to be about as effective."[6]

What our research suggests, however, is that there is something else going on here—something of far greater significance. For in addition to all the flackery and puffery and pap that they distribute, some of the more sophisticated strategic communication firms also provide their clients with some useful kinds of advice, advice as to how best to package their policies in order to gain approval in the United States, how and when to control access to news and information so that they appear to best advantage in the American press, and how to communicate with and through the American news media. Specifically, these companies teach governments what to say about their policies and activities. They train embassy and other personnel in how to talk to American journalists about such thorny problems as antiregime activity or human rights violations. They help governments to control access to information, potential news makers, and events, and to stage media events. And more generally, they anticipate and employ to their clients' advantage the predictable tendencies of journalistic behavior. In short, they do for their foreign clients very much what they do for their domestic ones.[7]

A case in point was the visit to the United States by Japanese prime minister Yasuhiro Nakasone in early 1985. At the time, as for a long time before and after, the imbalance of trade between the two countries was an issue of some importance. Indeed, anti-Japanese sentiment among Americans was growing, nurtured by resentment over what was perceived as a Japanese pattern of closing markets to American goods, especially agricultural goods for which there was presumed to be considerable demand. In advance of the Nakasone visit, viewers of local newscasts around the country saw reports showing American produce on its way to Japan. Mike Mansfield, United States ambassador to Japan, appeared on the report saying, "Japanese markets aren't as closed as we might think." Timely? You bet. Prominent issues and personalities? You bet. Good film? You bet. News? Well, what the audience was not told was that this report—in whole or in part, depending on the station—had been produced for the Japanese government by Gray and Company.[8] For a professional image-slinger, it was just another notch on the old '45.

Even network news operations can be susceptible to such appealing video packaging. In the same year as the Nakasone visit, for example, Gray and Company scored another coup. CNN ran a feature in which former Washington news anchor Meryl Comer interviewed King Hassan II of Morocco, who advised the United States not to worry about his recently concluded treaty with President Reagan's erstwhile nemesis, Muammar Quaddafi of Libya. "Any harsh reaction from the West," said Comer, "must be tempered with the acknowledgement that Morocco is strategically important to the United States, and that in this part of the world, strong pro-American leaders are hard to find. This is Meryl Comer reporting from the palace in Marrakech." What CNN and local stations that picked up the report did not know was that the piece was prepared and distributed by Gray—which apparently neglected to label it as required by law—and that Comer herself was a vice president of the company.[9]

Added to services like these, those firms that have access to officials of the United States Congress and government—principally the Washington-based lobbying firms—sell it, or, more accurately, rent it out. Advice. Assistance. Access. It is an altogether enticing package for a government with policy needs in the United States and a little cash to burn.

The results? We see them every day:

• Michael Deaver, White House deputy chief-of-staff during the Reagan years and close confidant of the then-president and first lady, sold body and Seoul—for nearly $2 million—to protect and extend the trade and economic interests of the Republic of Korea in the United States, and argued Canada's position on acid rain.[10]

• Christopher Lehman of Black, Manafort, Stone & Kelly—who had served under Robert McFarlane in the Reagan White House as a special assistant to the president for national security affairs and was charged with lining up congressional support for arms sales and aid to the Contras—shepherded Angolan guerrilla leader Jonas Savimbi around Washington in 1986 on a visit. This included two private meetings with Secretary of State George Schulz and his advisers on African policy and a private lunch with a dozen senators hosted by then–majority leader Robert Dole, all designed to develop support for his movement among Congress, officials of the Reagan administration, and the news media, and all part of a $600,000 contract between the UNITA (National Union for the Total Independence of Angola) leader and the well-connected Washington firm. Other assistance provided by Black Manafort, according to press reports at the time, included generating statements of support for Savimbi from the president and members of Congress that might be used to pressure the State Department's African Bureau to back him, encouraging the CIA to reassert itself in southern Africa and to provide covert assistance to Savimbi, and offering to the CBS program "60 Minutes" an exclusive interview with Savimbi scheduled to air at the same time as his visit. Representatives of the firm also coached Savimbi on the strengths and weaknesses of his image in the United States.[11]

• Mark Siegel—former executive director of the Democratic National Committee and later presidential aide in the Carter White House—conducted what he described as a "political campaign" in his orchestration of the 1989 visit to Washington of newly elected Prime Minister Benazir Bhutto of Pakistan. Siegel set out to present the emergence of democracy in Pakistan as a triumph of American political values, and planned a five-day media blitz around this theme. He carefully controlled media access to the prime minister, favoring those he thought most likely to pursue the central theme of cooperation among the world's democracies, and avoiding those he thought might ask other "distracting" questions. In advance of the visit, Bhutto appeared on CBS's "60 Minutes" and PBS's "MacNeil/Lehrer NewsHour," and was interviewed by Connie Chung, then of NBC. During the visit, she was interviewed by Peter Jennings of ABC and appeared on NBC's "Today." Siegel saw these interviews as the equivalent of free media in a campaign—seeking to control them indirectly just as a candidate for office might do—while he treated the focal events of the visit as paid media whose scripting could be more directly managed. These included an appearance before a joint session of Congress: "We sacrificed a part of our lives and bore the pain of confronting tyranny to build a just society. We believe in ourselves, in our cause, in our people and in our country. And when you believe, then there is no mountain too high to scale. That is my message to . . . America . . . and to its people." Delivering of the commencement address at her alma mater, Harvard University—"Democratic nations should forge a consensus around the most powerful political idea in the world today: the right of people to freely choose their government. Having created a bond through evolving such a consensus, democratic nations should then come together in an association designed to help each other and promote what is a universal value: democracy." And at a state dinner at the White House: "I didn't know until tonight that Yale ever produced a charming man, and I'm glad I've met the only one."[12] The result? An increase in American aid to Pakistan at a time when many foreign assistance programs were being reduced, dropping of the American demand that Pakistan pledge not to enrich uranium above 5 percent, and final approval of a long-pending shipment of sixty F–16 aircraft to Bhutto's country.[13]

• Douglas M. Bloomfield, formerly the chief congressional strategist for the extremely influential American Israel Public Affairs Committee, signed on as special consultant to Van Kloberg & Associates Ltd., a lobbying and public relations firm which has represented such clients as Iraq, Romania, and Czechoslovakia. His task? To lobby in support of Zairian president Mobutu Sese Seko—accused by critics of skimming as much as $400 million from Zaire's copper exports for his own account, and amassing a personal fortune estimated at some $5 billion—during his presidential visit to Washington in 1989. The Van Kloberg press kit prepared for Mobutu's visit described him as a "key friend" of the United States, one who has supported many American foreign policy initiatives—Zaire, it noted, joined the American boycott of the 1984 Moscow Olympics—and who was responsible for the just-concluded agreement expected to end the civil war in Angola. The State Department, in contrast, in its 1988 review of human rights around the world, noted "the arbitrary harassment, physical mistreatment and detention of ordinary citizens as well as political opponents," that was commonplace in Mobutu's Zaire. Edward Van Kloberg III pointed to a release of some 300 political prisoners the previous March as a sign of improvement. "There has been movement," he said. "Let's encourage him." Von Kloberg & Associates had a two-year, $300,000 contract with Mobutu, which it won in a close competition with Black, Manafort, Stone & Kelly.[14]

And the list goes on.

We can look at the process from the other side as well—that of the client countries. Some examples:

• Canada. In recent years, the Canadians have taken a comprehensive approach to their image and policy concerns in the United States. In addition to working through Michael Deaver to combat acid rain, which they attribute largely to emissions from utilities in the American Midwest, the Canadians launched a large-scale, and ultimately successful, lobbying effort to extract a free-trade agreement with the United States—an effort which, in the end, proved more difficult to conclude in Ottawa than in Washington. Concerned about tourism as well as trade policy, they commissioned Market Opinion Research—Robert Teeter's Detroit-based firm—to conduct a nationwide poll measuring images of Canada south of the border. What did they discover? That, despite its proximity to the United States—what country, after all, is more proximate?—its cultural affinity, and its status as a major United States trading partner, most Americans did not think about Canada very much, one way or the other.[15]

• South Korea. Korean corporations and industry associations have long been major clients of American public relations and lobbying firms, while the Korean government and a variety of cultural and educational foundations have developed an extensive program of exchange visits similar to the Fulbright Program operated by the United States Information Agency. The Korean approach to protecting its interests in the United States, like that of many foreign countries, is to focus on elite-level contacts. And in selecting consultants, the Koreans tend to favor lobbyists over communicators. One exception to this was the effort to generate maximum favorable publicity in the course of promoting the 1988 Summer Olympics in Seoul, for which Korea selected the public relations firm of Burson-Marsteller. Interestingly enough, the Koreans made this selection through elite channels as well—on the advice of former National Security Advisor Richard V. Allen, whose consulting company assists Korean industries on matters of international trade.[16]

• South Africa. The apartheid regime in South Africa has long pursued public relations campaigns and lobbying efforts in the United States. In 1979, twenty-two agents represented South African interests; five years later, the number had increased to thirty-one, nine of whom represented the government in one way or another. Among them: the Washington and Pittsburgh law firm of Baskin and Sears—Philip Baskin was a fundraiser for 1984 Democratic presidential candidate Walter Mondale, while John Sears served for a time as director of Ronald Reagan's 1980 campaign—which received half a million dollars for its lobbying efforts (and broke up when those efforts were revealed); the Washington law firm of Smathers, Symington, and Herlong—with strong Democratic ties—which the South Africans hired during the Carter administration and retained into the Reagan era at the rate of $300,000 per year; Spencer-Roberts and Associates—a public relations firm headed by longtime Reagan strategist Stuart Spencer—which received $12,500 per month to argue the South African case on Namibia; and the public relations firms of Donald E. deKieffer and Sydney Baron, which, over several years, received approximately $2.5 million to conduct seminars on South Africa for prospective corporate investors. Altogether, in the decade from 1974 through 1984, South African interests paid some $7 million to American lobbyists and consultants. At one point in the 1970s, a scandal arising from South African efforts to buy influence in the United States, which included a secret loan to finance the purchase of the *Washington Star* (now no longer published), forced the resignation of Prime Minister John Vorster.[17]

Again, these are but a few of the more prolonged and noteworthy efforts.

There are two general strategies available to countries seeking to bolster their images and influence in the United States. One of these—the what-you-see-is-what-you-get style of public relations that we have already described, with its fancy books and mass mailings—focuses on raising the visibility of the client, getting more attention from the news media and the public. One of the more unusual promotional efforts of this type was that undertaken by Saudi Arabia at the time of the 1984 Summer Olympics in Los Angeles. The Saudis spent an estimated $2 million producing and airing on network television a series of commercials designed to enhance their national image in the United States. A more common form of promotional effort—familiar to any reader of such newspapers as the *New York Times*, the *Washington Post*, or the *Wall Street Journal*—is the placing of large advertising supplements, typically four to eight pages in length, in the most influential newspapers of the United States and other countries. Such advertising is usually intended to promote industrial development or tourism, but sometimes it is placed simply for the purpose of bragging. One study found that the most active countries placing such advertisements included (in order of magnitude) France, India, the United Kingdom, Mexico, Japan, Greece, Switzerland, Italy, and Spain, with many others trailing behind. Altogether, during the eleven years studied (1970 through 1980), 114 countries purchased such advertising.[18] Extrapolating from the study, we can estimate that the two United States newspapers that were included, the *Times* and the *Wall Street Journal,* carried more than 10,000 advertisements from foreign governments during this period.

The second approach to political public relations available to these countries is a more subtle, low visibility approach much like the one the Bush campaign employed in the period leading up to the 1988 presidential primary season. It takes the form of news management and information control, and is intended less to persuade than to manipulate perceptions. Such a strategy can be very effective—indeed, more effective when applied in foreign affairs than in domestic. This is the case for several reasons.

First, the issues and participants in foreign affairs are remote. Members of the public—and, importantly, journalists—are unlikely to have any direct experience with them. Most, if not all, of what we know about, say, Namibia, we have learned from the media. Few of us have passports with Namibian visas stamped in them. In fact, few of us have passports at all, and that is really the point. With our geographic isolation and limited language skills, Americans are not equipped—by inclination or by ability—to deal with the world on equal terms. Unlike our contacts with the domestic scene, where we have personal benchmarks to temper our media-based judgments—they say the economy is weakening, but my company just got a new contract and I got a nice raise—when it comes to foreign affairs, we are entirely dependent on the cameras, microphones, and word processors of the world press. We know only what they tell us. We are vulnerable.

Second, the media themselves are limited in both their ability to cover foreign affairs and their inclination to devote staff and resources to that purpose. These limits arise from what we already know about the business concerns of news organizations. In the first instance, the costs and logistics of foreign coverage—travel expenses, translating, satellite feeds, to name but a few problem areas—make it very difficult to do the job. In the second, the absence of substantial interest among the American audience in news of the outside world eliminates any incentive for the media to bear these costs. Why spend a lot of money and endure a lot of grief to produce news that the audience cares little about, and will not miss if it is not published? No reason at all. If anything, there are strong *dis*incentives for news organizations to deliver such news. As a result, only an elite few—the networks, the prestige press, the wire services—make any serious effort to gather information abroad, and even those efforts they do put forward are limited. Reporters whose responsibilities include two, three, or ten entire countries—think about trying to present an accurate picture of the United States, Canada, and Mexico from a one-person bureau based in Mexico City. Stringers who work part time for news organizations and rush to the scene of an event after the fact to provide us with the news. Journalists who don't speak the language, know the history, or understand the culture of the country they are portraying. They know only what is happening on the surface, and sometimes precious little of that.[19] We are vulnerable.

Third, in foreign affairs, even public officials can have a hard time gathering information, so even they may be dependent on the media for some portion of their understanding of events. Typically, this would be the case with peripheral policy makers such as members of Congress who are called upon to vote on foreign policy questions but have no special expertise. At the very least, their general impressions of one or another area of the world are likely to be shaped by the news coverage they read or see. But at times, even central players can be dependent on the media. In describing early attempts by the Reagan administration to measure the level of political violence in El Salvador, for example—a task required in order to provide Congress with a certification of progress toward ending that country's civil strife—Thomas Enders, at the time the State Department official in charge of the assessment, said in an interview on PBS's "MacNeil/Lehrer NewsHour" that principal among the indicators he used to measure violence was the number of violent incidents reported in the press.[20] And more recently, the likelihood is that most people in our government and others, even at the highest level, received at least as much information about the June 1989 massacre in Beijing's Tiananmen Square from media reports as from diplomatic or intelligence sources. They know little more than we know. We are vulnerable.

Putting all of this together, it is clear that foreign governments—and other foreign interests—have both a motive to influence American opinion and policy, and an opportunity to do so. The question is: How effectively do they do it? Have strategic communications efforts on behalf of these governments improved their standing among the people, the press, and the policy makers of the United States? Two-thirds of that question are very difficult to answer, though we can hazard some guesses.

With respect to the influence of these efforts on public opinion, there is not much information to go on. There are, from time to time, polls conducted that measure the feelings Americans have about various countries around the world, but these tend to be quite infrequent—again, probably, because of the absence of widespread public interest in such questions and, therefore, of a newspaper or other sponsor willing to foot the bill. As a result, we cannot look at a series of results for any given country and conclude that its public relations campaigning was—or was not—successful. There are some tempting tidbits—for example, a survey conducted by the National Opinion Research Center at the University of Chicago in 1986, the year after Canada began its promotional blitz for "A World Next Door," found that country to have been evaluated positively by fully 97 percent of Americans, far and away the most popular of all countries measured.[21] But, in the absence of frequent earlier observations, it is difficult to ascribe this feeling of good will to any single cause, let alone to the public relations campaign.

With respect to influence on the policy agenda, things get even murkier. There are obvious success stories: Benazir Bhutto's airplanes and other aid, South Korea's surprising exclusion in 1989 from a list of countries targeted for harsh trade policies because of their own protective practices, longtime American support for Ferdinand Marcos in the Philippines, the previously mentioned free trade agreement with Canada. The problem is that it is difficult to know just how many such efforts have been undertaken, and what motivated each one. As a result, there is little basis for determining their rate of success.

With respect to the success of systematic efforts to influence portrayals of foreign countries in the United States press, however, we do have a growing body of evidence. Let us consider that evidence at some length.[22]

If one is to *measure* the success of such undertakings, the first task at hand is to *define* it. What does a successful effort at influence look like? The initial answer is: It depends on the circumstances. We must begin by asking ourselves: What does a given country's news image look like at the time it sets the wheels of strategic communication in motion? In particular, it is useful to differentiate between two aspects of news coverage of the client country—visibility and favorability—and to characterize initial images in these terms. Visibility refers to the amount of coverage a country or government (or anyone else) gets in the press. Favorability is a measure of how positive or negative, on average, its portrayal is. Putting these together yields four different settings, or communication environments, in which countries might be motivated to engage in strategic communication efforts, each of which might lead to a very different communication strategy.

The first setting is that of a country that is very much in the news—and consequently prominent in the public mind—but has a generally negative image. While examples vary in appropriateness depending on how a given country is being portrayed at the time that you happen to be reading this book, the news image of South Africa over the last several years is typical of a high visibility, high negative country. If Canada is the world next door, South Africa often looks as if it belongs on another planet. Racial strife. Rigid press controls. Obstinate leaders. Absurd policies. South Africa truly has it all.

For countries in this situation, it frankly does not make much sense to engage in a promotional blitz that can do little more than call attention to the country and, perhaps, even heap ridicule upon it. Consider your reaction today should you begin to see tourism commercials pegged to the evening news offering the alluring message: "Visit scenic South Africa. A land of ocean breezes. A land of mountain springs. A little bit of home in a far away place." Thinking of a visit? Not likely. And that is the point. For a variety of psychological reasons that we need not delve into, people—including journalists—are not likely to be receptive to messages that are so very different from their existing perceptions of a country about which they are, in fact, receiving a lot of much more negative information. Where the negatives are high to begin with, calling attention to the country—any kind of attention at all—only makes them higher.

What to do? If you are advising South Africa or other countries in this situation, your best suggestion is: get out of the news. If you can't make people and press think better of you, at least you can make them think less of you—or more correctly, less about you. Quiet down. Run for cover. Hide from the press. Bide your time in the hope that, left to its own devices, your visibility will decline, and that as a result, people's defenses against your preferred new image will be lowered. Watch . . . and wait.

In the event, a purposeful strategy of withdrawal from the news is hardly so passive. It is under this circumstance that governments often conclude that they must restrict the access to news makers and events that they afford to journalists, especially to foreign journalists. They cut back on the amount and type of information issued by the government itself. They impose censorship. They create visa problems, satellite transmission problems, staffing problems, and a host of other woes for foreign journalists—moves that play directly to the existing disincentives for news organizations to cover foreign news in the first place. It is the home-court advantage with a vengeance. Sometimes—and South Africa is an extreme case in point—governments outlaw news coverage altogether, or so restrict it as to make the journalists' job all but impossible. They arrest and intimidate journalists, or, more conveniently, their sources; they openly follow them, tap their telephones. They beat—and occasionally murder—perceived media troublemakers, or make clear their intention to do so, as the Chinese army did to photographers in the aftermath of the Tiananmen debacle.[23] No more Mister Nice Guy. It isn't pleasant, or pretty, or smooth. But, bit by bit, they squeeze their way out of the news. Bit by bit, they disappear from public view. We don't hear so much about the troubles now, do we? Indeed, a Canadian government study has found that news coverage of South Africa on American networks declined by two-thirds within a year after December 1986, when very stringent press controls were implemented.[24] Things must be getting better.

One of the more effective applications of such a strategy in recent years was that undertaken by the Argentines during the period of the transition to the Videla military regime in the late 1970s. Death squads roamed the country, thousands of people simply disappeared, political repression and economic chaos reigned supreme. By all objective indicators, matters moved from worse to worse still. And yet, as a result of a systematic and rather hard-nosed policy of news management, Argentina's image in the United States press actually improved during this period. Significantly. The news was still substantially negative, but there was a lot less of it.

That, in fact, describes the second of our four communication settings, one in which coverage is generally negative, but visibility is relatively low. Many countries—probably most of those that employ American consultants—find themselves in this situation. Because of the disinterest of the American audience in foreign news, most countries receive little coverage. Because of the criteria of newsworthiness—with the emphasis on drama and conflict—that which is in fact published tends to be on the negative side. Food riots and military coups d'etat are news. Factory openings are not. Third World countries, in particular, complain a lot about these kinds of decisions, which they see as contributing to their collective image of instability—hardly fitting places for American corporations to foster economic development. They are quite right, of course, but fail to realize that the corporations and politicians with whom they must deal at this end have essentially the same complaint. Ask Union Carbide. Allied Chemical. Bruce Babbitt. Bruce who?

The Philippines during the Marcos years—and certainly in 1982 when the events described above transpired—provide an example of a country with low visibility and high negatives. Did the Marcos government do the right thing? In a word: no. Countries with low visibility and negative images—indeed, the lower their visibility, the more this is true—have an opportunity to engineer for themselves a much more favorable portrayal in the press. This is the case because—given their near invisibility in the media—neither journalists nor members of the public are thinking much about them. To put it bluntly, they are just not very important. As a result, the guards of these two groups are lowered, and they will be unlikely to resist positive messages—so long as those messages are subtle and do not directly call attention to the fact that a persuasive effort is underway. The objective of the strategic communicator in this situation, then, is to improve the favorability of the country's portrayal *without calling attention to the effort and without raising its visibility in the news.* The Philippine effort—with its overt and outsized promotional elements—got it only half right, and the result was not as intended. Not only did the news image of the Philippines worsen, but the public relations blitz actually generated a counter blitz of propaganda by opponents of the Marcos regime. Marcos, in fact, would have been well advised to stay at home.

The third and fourth settings in which communication efforts may be undertaken are quite different in that, in each instance, the client country has, not a negative image, but a positive one. There is no need to change people's minds or to distract them. Rather, the objective is to draw their conscious attention to the good thoughts they are already thinking, and to find ways of reinforcing and extending them. Switzerland—a land of bankers, mountain villages, and yodelers little in the news but favorably portrayed—exemplifies one such setting. Great Britain—ancestral home (in spirit if not reality) to many Americans and much in the news—exemplifies the other. In point of fact, there are negative things to be said about each of these countries. Switzerland has a very restrictive social and political system, while Britain has severe economic and political problems and a government that has moved aggressively in recent years to limit freedom of the press under terms of the "Official Secrets Act"—on the books since the German spy scare of 1911—which prohibits government officials from disclosing, and reporters from *receiving* or publishing, any information not specifically authorized by a higher authority, and provides prison sentences for those who violate its terms.[25] However, aside from an occasional piece on the most violent football fans in the world—those from Liverpool—most of what we see about both countries is cast in a positive light.

It is in situations like these that promotional efforts such as that in behalf of Mr. Marcos, and advertising supplements like those placed by so many countries in the *Times* and the *Wall Street Journal* can be expected to pay dividends. Where images are positive but visibility low, the objective is to build recognition. Where visibility is already high, the objective is to firm up support. Social psychologist William McGuire has likened this to inoculating patients to protect them from disease.[26] Here, however, the disease is wrongheaded thinking, and the vaccine is a large dose of positive reinforcement. Promote. Promote. Promote.

For all of its evident national-ego-gratifying appeal, however, promotion is not the only—nor necessarily the most effective—form of inoculation against slippage in a favorable image. Another device is that of encouraging those with favorable views of a country to espouse them publicly—to go on the record with their support. Over the years, for example, Israel has been a particularly effective practitioner of this technique, especially in applying it to members of Congress. The idea is that once a person has made a public proclamation of support, the psychological cost of changing his or her mind—in the form of the public embarrassment that inevitably accompanies the admission of error—is simply too high to bear. The result? A friend for life. To assess the effectiveness of this device, compare the treatment of Israel in the American press and public opinion during the period of the *Intifada*—the uprising of resident Palestinians—with the treatment of the governments of South Korea, China, or the Philippines when confronted with, and responding to, similar antiregime activities. Please pass the vaccine.

All of that, at least, is the theory. The question that Albritton and I asked in our research was: Does this actually happen? Do countries with high visibility and high negatives that hire American consultants, in effect, succeed in getting out of the news? Do countries with low visibility and high negatives that hire American consultants actually achieve a more positive image as their visibility bottoms out? And so forth. The answer, in a nutshell, is yes. There are some factors that limit the effectiveness of these efforts to manipulate news images, but by and large, they do succeed.

To arrive at that conclusion, we analyzed news coverage of a number of countries in the *New York Times* over a period of years. In each instance, we were able to determine from Department of Justice records that a contract with an American public relations adviser had been signed, and when it took effect. We then measured the amount and favorability of coverage of each client country for several time points during the year immediately before the contract date and the year immediately after. Comparing these two periods—and adjusting for events, trends, and other factors that might have influenced the results—we ascribed any differences we observed in a given country's news image between the precontract and postcontract years to the efforts of the consultants. What we found was a consistent pattern that resembled very closely the situation-specific objectives of strategic communication set forth above. Our conclusion? Systematic efforts at manipulating news images work. And if they work when applied to the *New York Times,* which publishes more foreign news than any other American newspaper, is far less dependent on wire service and other outside sources in gathering that news, and is as well equipped—by virtue of the skill of its journalists—as any American news organization, and better than most, to defend itself against such efforts. If these techniques are effective on the *Times*, they must be even more so when directed at the general run of American news media, which are far more vulnerable.

Sometimes, these manipulative efforts become known to reporters and can be disclaimed, if not offset. The *Times* itself, for example, discovered a few years ago that an anonymous source, whom it had quoted extensively on some charges about Roberto D'Aubuisson's involvement with Salvadoran death squads, had been paid $50,000 by a group of American opponents of the Reagan administration's policy toward El Salvador to come to the United States for the express purpose of making these charges.[27] In addition, at times in the past the *Wall Street Journal* has reportedly maintained a "blacklist" of countries that should not be accepted as clients by American public relations firms.[28] And American media have gone out of their way to report on the efforts of the South African government to restrict the foreign press. But the fact is that much of the news that is "supposed" to get out does—subsequent retractions to the contrary notwithstanding—and much of the news that is "not supposed" to get out does not, never to be missed. It is news, or it is not.

The conduct of strategic communication campaigns by American consultants working for the interests of foreign governments raises a number of thorny issues. Three of these are probably of greatest importance. They center on the revolving door that clearly operates between government service and the consulting firms, the potential for conflict of interest among practitioners, and the question of just who has the right of free speech under the United States Constitution—and how far that right extends.

The revolving door generates enough breeze to cool off even a July afternoon in the nation's capital—no small feat since the site of the city was once a swamp. Extending an example we developed earlier, consider a portion of the roster of employees who worked in a recent year (1985) at Gray and Company. Among them: a former legislative aide to two Democratic senators, a former postmaster general of the United States, a former consumer affairs adviser in the State Department, a former public information officer in the Department of Agriculture, a former press secretary to the Senate Agriculture Committee, a former Democratic Senate aide, a former official of the Federal Communications Commission, a former general counsel to the Federal Communications Commission, a former foreign service officer with the U.S. Information Agency, a former special assistant to President Carter for congressional liaison, and on, and on, and on. Nor was the door open only to former government officials. The Gray and Company staff included comparable numbers of former journalists—from Mutual Broadcasting, NBC News, *Newsweek,* Scripps-Howard News Service, and elsewhere—as well as a smattering of others with interest-group or association experience.[29]

What is interesting here is not so much the revolving door as the open one—the door to some appropriate place in the federal establishment that one or another of these individuals could walk through at any time. To be sure, Gray and Company had its share of household names—Frank Mankiewicz being a case in point—but most of the folks listed on this roster were second or third tier players at best. They were important to Gray and Company not for who they were as individuals, but for who and what they knew as a collectivity. One from column A, two from column B, and one apiece from X, Y, and Z. As a group, they had entrée to almost any office in Washington. And that was why they all lived in The Power House.

The issue of the revolving door, then, is not so much one of whether individuals ought to be permitted to leave government service and turn what they have learned there to a profit in the private sector. Rather, the issue is whether having done so, they have the ability—and the right—to barter their access as well as their knowledge. Do they have the ability? Unquestionably. Do they have the right? That is a more vexing question, and one that, in the end, begs an answer.

Most cities live on commerce in goods and services—money is the measure of success. Washington lives on commerce in information and perception—money counts, but status and contacts count more. Who and what you know *is* who you are. In such a place, the question of right is, quite simply, moot. This is the way it is, therefore it is right. Nothing anyone can do is likely to change it. And if someone did somehow succeed, the government itself—which is, in its way, as dependent on the lobbyists and communicators as they are on it— would likely grind to a halt. Oil the gears and grease the wheels. It's a major public works project. Just read the sign: Your Utilitarian Ethics at Work.

The real question here, some might suggest, is not whether ethical violations occur, but whether a moral vacuum sweeps clean. Is there so much conflict of interest in the ways of Washington that most of those involved fail to notice? On the political side, there is some evidence suggesting the affirmative—the denouement of the inquiries into the finances of Democratic congressional leaders Jim Wright and Tony

Coelho in June of 1989 and the entrepreneurial/authorial machinations of Georgia Republican Newt Gingrich, offering cases in point. On the press side as well, there is a hint of moral blindness. The congressional press gallery went through a purge of members with lobbying and other nonjournalistic interests in 1989, but not without considerable pain, and in the spring of that year the *Washington Post* published sources and amounts of honoraria received recently by leading journalists there and elsewhere—though some pointedly refused to cooperate.[30] And in the consulting business, Michael Deaver's troubles over charges of influence peddling and giving false testimony in a case relating to his alleged improper contacts with former colleagues in the White House adds to the scene.

In all probability, these are isolated cases and not indicative of failings on the part of most persons engaging in political communication and related activities. That we so widely doubt and question the ethics of those engaged in strategic communication—whether public relations or lobbying—and especially those serving as agents of foreign interests, probably has less to do, in the final analysis, with concerns about ethical practice per se than with a suspicion we all harbor that what these communicators are about is itself, in its very essence, just not right. How could Americans try to pull the wool over the eyes of other Americans for the benefit of some oil sheik or tinhorn dictator? This is, at its core, a First Amendment question—a question of tolerance and free speech.

At a general level, most Americans wholeheartedly endorse the First Amendment to the Constitution. Free speech? Free press? Yeah, I'm for that! But abstract principles are one thing, specific applications another, and we are not always as (small "l") liberal in practice as our values suggest. Communists work at the local newspaper? No way! Homosexuals teach in the local schools? You mean *practicing* homosexuals? Recall that Baskin and Sears, one of the law firms representing South Africa, was forced to disband when their activity became known—the instant reason being a threat from the City of Pittsburgh to withdraw its half million dollars in annual business from the partnership. Baskin stayed in Pittsburgh; Sears kept working for the South Africans. South Africa. Now there is an acid test of principle.

Adding to this natural reluctance to extend rights to members of outgroups in our society—those who do not look or think like the majority—is the fact that the folks in question here are actually representing *foreigners*. Well, maybe that is just too much. It is one thing if *we* set about fooling ourselves, but quite another if someone else does it. In that sense, the issue is not "free speech" per se, but *whose* free speech it is we are talking about. Is it the speech of the strategic communicator, an American who, however misguided, is expressing his or her own opinion on foreign policy and happens to be in the employ of a like-minded foreign government? Or is it the speech of the foreign government, filtered through an American proxy in return for a pile of money—money that probably originated in American foreign aid in the first place?

These questions—even in less pejorative form—are not easily answered. The best evidence may be found in the comments and actions of those actually in the business—comments and actions that make it clear that money does play a part in the decision to represent foreign clients, but that almost all practitioners draw lines in the ethical and political dust between themselves and certain regimes or interests. Countries like the Soviet Union or Marxist Angola, for example, do seem to have a more difficult time than others finding representation. "The worst regimes," complained one public relations consultant, "typically come in talking about 'cultural' representation, but sooner or later, they want you to go to that [Capitol] Hill and put out propaganda."[31] Some of these lines, of course, may be false trails—laid down by professionals to provide public relations cover for a decision to avoid a client simply because it might give one's firm a bad name. But most seem to reflect, at the very least, a serious effort to construct a self-satisfying rationale for representing any specific interest. Does that make it right? One person's rationale is another's lame excuse. That is the nature of life in a pluralist society. *Caveat emptor*—let the buyer beware.

Notes

1. This summary is based on the description of the campaign in Jarol B. Manheim and Robert B. Albritton, "Public Relations in the Public Eye: Two Case Studies of the Failure of Public Information Campaigns," *Political Communication and Persuasion* 3 (1986), pp. 265–91. Additional details can be found in Greg Goldin, "The Toughest Accounts," *Mother Jones*, January 1985, p. 29.

2. Attorney General of the United States, *Report on the Foreign Agent Registration Act of 1938* (Washington, D.C.: U.S. Department of Justice, 1985).

3. Phil McCombs, "Inside the Power House," *Washington Post,* 28 June

1984, pp. D1, D9; Phil McCombs, "The Connection Makers," *Washington Post,* 29 June 1984, pp. C1, C6; and Stuart Auerbach, "Foreigners Hiring Reagan's Ex-Aides," *Washington Post,* 16 February 1986, pp. A1, A14, A15.

4. Thomas B. Edsall, "Profit and Presidential Politics," *Washington Post,* August 12, 1989, pp. A1, A6.

5. Ibid.

6. William Safire, "An Excess of Access," *Roanoke Times & World News (VA),* 19 February 1986, p. A7.

7. Jarol B. Manheim and Robert B. Albritton, "Changing National Images: International Public Relations and Media Agenda Setting," *American Political Science Review* 78 (1984), pp. 641–57; and Richard S. Tedlow and John A. Quelch, "Communications for the Nation State," *Public Relations Journal* 37 (1981), pp. 22–25.

8. Jeanne Saddler, "Public Relations Firms Offer 'News' to TV," *Wall Street Journal,* 2 April 1985, p. 6.

9. Mary Battiata, "What's News? Well, There's a Gray Area," *Washington Post National Weekly Edition,* 15 April 1985, p. 11.

10. Safire, "An Excess of Access," *Roanoke Times.*

11. Patrick E. Tyler and David B. Ottaway, "The Selling of Jonas Savimbi," *Washington Post,* 9 February 1986, pp. A1, A8.

12. Information about the Bhutto visit is drawn from a personal interview with Mark Siegel, July 1989; the official texts of the prime minister's statements; and Donnie Radcliffe and Martha Sherrill, "Bhutto, Back at the White House," *Washington Post,* 7 June 1989, pp. C1, C8.

13. For a more complete discussion of the Bhutto visit see Jarol B. Manheim, "Coming to America: Head of State Visits as Public Diplomacy," paper presented at the Annual Meeting of the International Communication Association, Dublin, Ireland, June 1990.

14. David B. Ottoway, "PR Salvos Fill Skies with Flak over Mobutu," *Washington Post,* 28 June 1989, p. A21; and William Claiborne, "Mobutu Refurbishing Image Tainted by Corruption Charge," *Washington Post,* 29 June 1989, pp. A27, A32.

15. Personal discussion with Norman T. London, Academic Relations Officer, and Harry F. Adams, Counsellor, Embassy of Canada, 1986.

16. Jarol B. Manheim, "Political Culture and Political Communication: Implications for U.S.-Korean Relations," paper presented at the Annual Meeting of the American Political Science Association, Washington, D.C., August 1988; Jarol B. Manheim, "Rights of Passage: Elections, Olympics, and the External Communications of the Republic of Korea," paper presented at the World Congress of the International Political Science Association, Washington, D.C., August 1988; and personal interview with Daryl Plunk, vice president, Richard V. Allen Company, 1989.

17. Rick Atkinson, "Law Firm's Split Airs S. African Lobbying," *Washington Post,* 12 March 1984; Goldin, "Toughest Accounts," pp. 28–29; and "Pittsburgh Forces Hand of Pretoria Lobbyists," *Africa News,* 19 March 1984, pp. 6–8.

18. Odekhiren Amaize and Ronald J. Faber, "Advertising by National Governments in Leading United States, Indian and British Newspapers," *Gazette* 32 (1983), pp. 87–101.

19. For some examples see John Weisman, "Ignorants Abroad," *TV Guide,* 28 May 1983, pp. 2–8.

20. The interview was broadcast on January 21, 1983.

21. Reported in "The Depths of Ignominy," *Roanoke Times & World News,* 6 September 1986, p. A11.

22. Portions of the discussion that follows are based on Manheim and Albritton, "Changing National Images," *American Political Science Review.*

23. For other examples, see John Weisman, "Intimidation," *TV Guide,* 23 October 1982, pp. 4–10.

24. Cited in "South Africa's Toughest Censor," *Columbia Journalism Review,* July/August 1988, p. 6.

25. Alan L. Otten, "Some of the News in Great Britain Is a Big Secret," *Wall Street Journal,* 28 December 1979, p. 6.

26. "Inducing Resistance to Persuasion: Some Contemporary Approaches," *Advances in Experimental Social Psychology* 1 (1964), pp. 192–202.

27. "Guerrilla P.R.," *Wall Street Journal,* 22 March 1984, p. 30.

28. Edward Langley, "Nothing but Trouble . . . but So Rewarding," *Public Relations Journal,* June 1981, p. 27.

29. Ann Cooper, "Image Builders," *National Journal,* 14 September 1985, pp. 2058–59. See also Auerbach, "Foreigners Hiring," *Washington Post.*

30. Eleanor Randolph, "Should Journalists Report Their Own Honoraria?" *Washington Post,* 14 April 1989, pp. A1, A8.

31. Patrick E. Tyler, "Hostile Nations Shopping Here for PR Advice," *Washington Post,* 11 January 1986, pp. A1, A17.

7 IN OUR OWN IMAGE

The eastern approach by air to Anchorage, Alaska, is nothing short of breathtaking. It weaves through icy mountain passes so deep that they alter one's sense of scale. Peaks rise above the wing tips of jumbo jets, transforming them in the mind's eye into nothing more than 300-seat Piper Cubs, and it seems that wheels down must be imminent—yet on it goes, mile after frosty mile. Then it is out over open water—the mountains fall behind—and on to a harsh, flat expanse of coastal plain. This time, the plane goes down more than the land comes up to meet it, and a lighted finger of runway beckons seductively in the distance. A last turn, a gentle gliding motion, and the thrust of the engines yields to solid ground. The cabin pours forth its passengers into the terminal.

The airport at Anchorage, for those who have yet to experience it, is a combination of shopping mall and junkyard that captures much about our age and its place. Inside the modern terminal building, gates and waiting areas are strewn in a rectangular pattern around the perimeter of a commercial core offering everything the weary traveler could desire—imported French fashions, native Alaskan crafts and their mass-produced cousins, boxes of smoked salmon, and ten—yes, ten—different varieties of beef jerky. Outside, flung as if by centrifugal force to the outermost fringes of the pavement and stark against the barren local landscape, lie the rusting hulks of past aviation glories—the haunted cabins of dead passenger craft and freighters stripped of their dignity as of their airworthiness—not altogether a sight to inspire confidence.

It was from this outpost of commerce and transportation that the sky-blue Boeing 747 airliner lifted off the runway at 10:00 on a Wednesday morning (local time) in the summer of 1983, carrying 240 passengers and a crew of twenty-nine on the second leg of a flight that had begun the night before from New York's Kennedy Airport. Lumbering westward, the plane crossed the International Dateline into Thursday. At 3:23 in the morning (Japanese time), precisely two and a half hours before its scheduled landing, the crew contacted air traffic controllers at Tokyo's Narita Airport to report their position. Radar showed the plane to be holding an altitude of some 30,000 feet—nearly six miles above the Pacific—though there was some uncertainty as to its precise location. Just another routine reflection of another routine flight. But that was about to change. At 3:30, the Japanese controllers noticed that the altitude of the inbound traffic had dropped to 16,400 feet, and concern spread that the jetliner might have run out of fuel and been forced to ditch in the ocean. Moments later, the radar echoes disappeared altogether. The journey of Korean Air Lines (KAL) flight 007 had ended far short of its intended destination at Seoul's Kimpo Airport, but its saga had only begun.

The northwestern corner of the Pacific Ocean is one of the most remote, hostile, and downright inhospitable areas on this planet. In part, this is a product of its geography—far enough north to be cold and cloudy much of the time, and far enough from everything to be utterly beyond reach. But in part, it is a product of politics. For the nearest landfall along much of the northwestern Pacific is on the coast of the Soviet Union, and the Soviets—who maintain extensive and strategically vital military installations in this corner of their country nearest the United States—take a very dim view of intruders.

In the present instance, it seems, in addition to the air traffic control system in Tokyo, there had been yet another radar tracking the passage of KAL 007 as it coursed through the darkness over the Kamchatka Peninsula, the Sea of Okhotsk, and Sakhalin Island, all hundreds of miles off its assigned course—a radar of the Soviet strategic defense command, which dispatched four SU–15 fighter jets to intercept and investigate the intruder. And this time, there really was a bear in the woods.

The Soviets had already shown their sensitivity to violations of their airspace by Korean Air, having forced down a flight from Paris to Seoul that had strayed over the Soviet Union in April 1978. In that instance, interceptors had fired on the plane, killing two passengers

and wounding ten, and forced the aircraft to make an emergency landing on a frozen lake near Murmansk. As a measure of the desperation
of the current moment, in the first hours after the mysterious disappearance of KAL 007, the Murmansk downing was held forth as evidence enhancing the probability of the most hopeful of the available
scenarios—that this flight, too, had been subjected to a forced landing.
In the event, of course, what transpired was substantially more terrible.

After some days of initial confusion, the events of those few fateful
minutes in the skies over the Soviet's Pacific rim became clear. According to the Soviets, KAL 007 first appeared on radar 500 miles
northeast of a naval base on the Kamchatka Peninsula, where it joined
an American RC–135 spy plane, which they had previously been
tracking. The two flew together for some ten minutes, after which
one—the RC–135—broke away and turned toward Alaska, while the
other turned westward toward a Soviet nuclear installation. The second
plane skirted ground-to-air missile batteries, and the fighters were
scrambled. According to the Soviets, the plane was transmitting brief
coded radio signals of a type usually associated with intelligence missions. It then passed over international waters and on over still more
military facilities on Sakhalin Island. Six more interceptors were dispatched and, again according to the Soviets, tried every possible measure—radio contacts, dipping wings, flashing lights, and eventually
tracer bullets—to force the plane to land. When it failed to respond, the
order was given by the local commander to stop the flight. Two missiles from an SU–15 brought it down.

Some of these facts—particularly those related to the role of the
RC–135 and any implication that the Korean Air flight was on a spy
mission intended to be cloaked as navigational error—have been dis-
puted by the United States and Korea, and none of them were clearly
evident at the outset. What concerns us here, however, is not the events
in the sky over the Soviet Far East, but their political fallout half a
world away in Moscow, and their impact on political communication
Soviet style. That impact was quite noteworthy.

The Soviet Union's first response to the news of the disappearance
of KAL 007 was nothing if not predictable. On September 1, the date
of the disaster, the Reuters News Agency reported that an official of
the Soviet Foreign Ministry had told a Japanese official in Moscow
that the Korean airliner was not on Sakhalin Island—this proved, of
course, to be true—and that the Soviets had no other information about

the flight—which may also have been true given the fact that the decision that led to downing the plane had been undertaken at the local level. From that point forward, events proceeded as follows:

September 1. The Japanese Air Force reported tracking a plane flying near Sakhalin—several hundred miles from the location KAL 007's crew had reported to air controllers in Tokyo—which disappeared from radar screens shortly after being joined by several other planes. A spokesman for Korean Air speculated only that a mid-air explosion might have occurred. Later in the day, officials of the Korean Ministry of Foreign Affairs, citing the United States CIA as their source, said it appeared that the plane had been forced to land. U.S. officials declined comment on the report. The Soviets issued a statement late in the day saying the plane had been sighted flying without navigation lights, and had ignored their efforts to guide it to a landing. There was no reference to any further action on their part.

September 2. The United States announced that the plane had been shot down by a Soviet jet fighter using a heat-seeking missile, this after the interceptor had conducted a visual inspection of the intruder. Governments around the world expressed their dismay through diplomatic channels. A Japanese military spokesman cited radar and other evidence that the plane had been hit by a missile. TASS, the Soviet news service, carried a report that an unidentified aircraft had twice invaded the country's airspace and that fighter jets had tried "to give it assistance in directing it to the nearest airfield." Instead, TASS noted, the plane had continued flying toward the Sea of Japan. Later in the day, the Soviet government accused the United States of complicity in a spying mission using the civilian airliner and, expressing regret over the loss of life in the incident, condemned those who would use such a tragedy for political gain. "There is reason to believe," said the statement, "that those who organized this provocation had deliberately desired a further aggravation of the international situation striving to smear the Soviet Union, to sow hostility to it, and to cast aspersions on the Soviet peace-loving policy."[1] The statement went on to imply that the 747 may have been downed accidentally by the warning shots that were fired in its direction.

September 3. TASS quoted Australian sources as saying that the Soviets might have mistaken the 747 for an American spy plane with a similar radar signature.

September 4. A Soviet general indicated that the pilot who shot down KAL 007 may have mistaken it for an American RC–135, which, he claimed, has a similar profile [in fact, the two aircraft look quite different]. The general emphasized the suspicious behavior of the plane and the protracted efforts to force it down, but stopped short of stating that the Soviets had shot it from the sky. Later in the day, Washington said that the Soviets had, in fact, picked up a second plane on radar some hours earlier which they took to be an RC–135. TASS carried several Western speculations about whether flights like that of KAL 007, or planes like the Boeing 747, are used on spy missions. The Soviet government said it had located some debris off Sakhalin Island, but delayed agreeing to a joint search operation with the United States.

September 5. President Reagan acknowledged that an American reconnaissance plane did fly close to KAL 007, but said that it had landed in Alaska a full hour before the Korean plane was downed.

September 6. Pravda, the official newspaper of the Soviet Communist Party, said that warning shots were fired past KAL 007 only after it changed course and altitude in a way that would bring it over a Soviet air base, and that in addition to *seven* RC–135 spy planes, there were three American naval vessels in the vicinity of the 747's flight at the time of the incident. Rather than acknowledge the downing of the jetliner, the article cited the restraint shown by Soviet defenders in *not* shooting it down. Soviet television said the objective of the flight was to test air defenses in the region. Then, late in the day, after the United States played an actual recording of the Soviet pilot's radio conversations with the ground during the incident at a dramatic session of the United Nations Security Council, the Soviets issued a statement confirming that the fighter pilot was ordered to "stop" KAL 007.

September 9. At a news conference, Marshall Nikolai V. Ogarkov, chief of the Soviet General Staff, acknowledged that the downing of KAL 007 was neither an accident nor an error. Rather, the district commander of the air defense forces in the far eastern region of the country had concluded that the plane was on a spy mission over important facilities, and ordered it shot down. Ogarkov and two other senior officials took questions from Soviet and Western reporters for some two hours, during which their view of events as summarized above was developed.

The news conference, which the Soviets hoped would put an end to continued speculation over their actions and motives and the political cost and discomfort that arose from their seeming unresponsiveness, was an extraordinary event. Conducted by the marshall and by a first deputy foreign minister and the head of the International Information Department of the Central Committee of the Communist Party, it was an unaccustomed exercise in openness and candor—or at the very least it appeared to be so. Ogarkov stood before a large wall map of the area on which he traced the series of events leading to the shooting down of the plane. He and his colleagues explained the delay in acknowledging the denouement of the incident as having resulted from the need to undertake an on-the-scene fact-finding visit, and blamed the loss of life on those who had sent the civilian airliner on its spy mission, rather than on the Soviet defenders, who had made every effort to discourage the plane from its mission.[2] In his efforts to persuade the world of this point, perhaps he was aided, at least at a subliminal level, by the unfortunate designation of the flight—"double-0 seven"—which conjured up images of James Bond spy thrillers, at least among the Anglo-American segment of his audience.

♦ ♦ ♦ ♦

Though the controversy over the downing of KAL 007 continued for some time afterward, the Soviet's news conference served a cathartic purpose—it got a credible account supporting their actions into the sphere of world opinion, and it reduced the pressure that had been mounting on the government for more than a week. Indeed, the fact that such a conference was held at all suggests just how intense that pressure must have been. However reluctant they may have been to take this path, and however out of character it seemed at the time, the Soviets nonetheless appear to have learned something about world opinion from their experience: that a posture of candor and cooperation can pay dividends. From that point forward—though not without hesitation, as in the case of the accident at their Chernobyl nuclear plant, where denials and understatement again characterized their first, reflexive response, but were supplanted with more or less frank admissions of concern and responsibility as the dimensions of the disaster became apparent to the Kremlin leaders—the Soviets adopted a new and more sensitive strategy of dealing with the world's press and public, one that provided if not a free flow, at least a freer flow of information. In this, they anticipated the even more sophisticated policy of *glasnost'* that would later be implemented under the leadership of Mikhail Gorbachev, and perhaps even gave impetus to it. In a sense, the Soviets were at last learning to play an American game—the game of political public relations. In fact, in October of 1985 the Communist Party of the Soviet Union adopted a new guiding manifesto—its first since 1961—that calls on the party to use contemporary techniques of television and of measuring public opinion to stay in touch with the Soviet—and, by extension, other—people.[3] (Perhaps this explains the extraordinary 75-minute call-in program that appeared on Soviet television in November 1989. Answering questions from the public was Major General Anatoli Bondarov, a senior KGB official. The topic: What is the KGB really like? "Are Soviet spies sexual athletes like James Bond?" asked a Leningrad schoolgirl. "I don't think these qualities are really required for agents of any secret service—and certainly not the KGB," Bondarov replied.)[4] And in short order—with Gorbachev's penchant for the grand and very public gesture—they would learn on occasion to beat the Americans at their own game.[5]

In effect, the apparent success (from the Soviet perspective) of the KAL 007 news conference in disseminating the Soviet view of the event and disposing of the problems it created has led to a new style of competition among the major powers—a competition for the hearts and minds of external publics, not through heavy-handed propaganda on the model of the Nazi efforts of the 1930s and 1940s, or through so-called disinformation campaigns, but through a growing appreciation of the role played by public opinion in setting and limiting the policy agenda in democratic political systems, and by the use, or even the manipulation, of established, indigenous media to harness its influence in any particular instance. To be sure, the older methods are still with us. In 1983, for example, the same year as the KAL 007 incident, the *Wall Street Journal* reported on a story that had circulated that spring. Just as he set foot on the moon, the story ran, astronaut Neil Armstrong heard a human voice chanting in a foreign language. Upon returning to earth, he discovered the chant to have been the *azan*, the Moslem call to prayer. Armstrong thereupon converted to Islam, an act for which the National Aeronautics and Space Administration (NASA) fired him. The story appeared seriatim in the press of India, Egypt, Pakistan, and the Philippines, each time requiring a response including telephone press conferences with the astronaut, who repeatedly denied all. That and other embarrassing stories—some of a more serious nature—are attributed by the United States Department of State to the Soviet KGB.[6]

But times—and tactics—are changing. And while the level of sophistication of these new efforts to date can hardly qualify them as "strategic" political communication, they do have in common several of the characteristics we have been exploring. These efforts incorporate media events, carefully crafted images and symbols, and a variety of policies or actions that facilitate or impede (depending on need) journalists in the pursuit of their work. What they lack so far, for the most part, is an underlying strategy of influence, but that may not be far away.

We see these techniques of the new international political communication employed by a variety of different players. In the case of KAL 007, and later Chernobyl and the Gorbachev initiatives on arms control and disarmament, the main player has been a government. Here, the objective is to use news events and the like to communicate messages to another government not directly, but rather, indirectly through its people. The Reagan or Bush administrations may not have been willing to negotiate a reduction in strategic nuclear weapons or conventional forces in Europe, the Soviet reasoning ran in the 1980s, but if we could convince the American people—for example, by unilaterally and very visibly reducing our own forces or armaments—perhaps American public opinion—acting in our behalf—would pressure them to do so. Alternatively, perhaps we could accomplish the same end even more circuitously by appealing to West German public opinion, hoping that this, in turn, would cause the Bonn government to urge our preferences on Washington.

This approach to international exchange is one of a variety of forms of government-to-people communication that has come to be known as "public diplomacy." Other instruments of public diplomacy include cultural exchange programs, international shortwave or satellite television broadcasting, and the full range of governmental public relations and promotional activities we explored in chapter 5. This latest wrinkle in governmental posturing has long been practiced by the West, but in recent years has entered the diplomatic arsenal of the Soviet Union as a major policy tool.

Governments, however, are not the only practitioners of public diplomacy. They are, in fact, sometimes its intended targets rather than its perpetrators. The "People Power" revolution in the Philippines, the student demonstrations in South Korea which we detailed earlier—these and other similar events possess a distinct element of public diplomacy. Increasingly, we see the citizens of one country use the media and public opinion in a second country—typically, but not necessarily, the United States—to pressure their own government and to advance their grievances. Would the Marcos government in the Philippines have departed peacefully—or at all—in the absence of pressure from the United States? One can never be sure of such things, but it does seem unlikely (and will seem more so three chapters hence). This is not to say that such occurrences are no more than mere media events—they are the products and instruments of very real and far more significant political forces than such a characterization would imply. But to say that an upheaval is genuine—even spontaneous—is not the same as saying that it is unguided. To the contrary, the most successful of such events tend to have or to develop some strategic or tactical components. And strategies or tactics aimed at the media—foreign as well as domestic—can play a central role in the effective leadership of such mass movements.

A more recent case in point is provided by the 1989 student and worker demonstrations in Beijing's Tiananmen Square and in Shanghai. Given its evident breadth, the so-called "democracy movement" in the People's Republic of China must have been developing for some time—indeed, it was probably an inevitable by-product of ten years of economic change and increasing exchanges with the West. Many thousands of Chinese students studying in the United States and elsewhere during that period cannot have helped but be influenced in some way by their exposure to Western political ideas as by their introduction to Western technology. Encouraged by party leader Hu Yaobang—who was subsequently deposed for this very reason—and sparked by his death in April, the movement was rapidly broadening its base and gaining visibility. Yet the mass mobilization of Chinese citizens from all walks of life, and their descent upon Beijing's central square, came only a few days before an event sure to bring the world's press to the

Chinese capital—the arrival of Mikhail Gorbachev for the first Sino-Soviet summit meeting in more than two decades. It seems entirely likely that the leaders of the movement saw an opportunity to pressure their government to respond to their demands so as to avoid the embarrassment of spoiling the Gorbachev visit.

That, of course, proved to be something of a miscalculation. Rather than yield to the massed demonstrators, the Chinese government shuttled the Russian visitor through back doors and canceled portions of his itinerary, an outcome that only served to embolden those in the streets and to spread the movement to other cities. Foreign news media reported breathlessly on the inaction of the government—was it patience, virtue, indecision, or a power struggle?—and on the birth of true people's democracy in a Communist state. Were there not English-speaking students and others available to the cameras at all hours to state the objective, and signs *printed in English* proclaiming that "We Shall Overcome"? Was there not a styrofoam Statue of Liberty—Statue of Liberty!—constructed in front of a government building in Shanghai, and a variant on the theme, a Goddess of Democracy, in Tiananmen Square itself?[7] Do you think that did not make the front page of the *New York Times* and every other newspaper, and the lead of every network evening newscast, in the United States? Do you think it failed to shape the perceptions that visiting journalists formed of events? Considering the timing of events and the selection of imagery, it is difficult to conclude that prospective media coverage was not a consideration in the activities of the Chinese democracy movement.

And even as the movement faltered in the face of the overwhelming power of the Chinese state and military authorities, the strategy worked. For it was—and remains—the government that was on the defensive, not the demonstrators of Tiananmen Square. And as a direct result, the governments of the United States and other Western countries that have extended their trade and other ties with China in recent years have been forced to scale back those contacts, and the people of Hong Kong—principal assets of a prize the Chinese have long sought and which is soon to be theirs—have lost all confidence in a future under Chinese rule. Those who are able are now far more likely to leave than to remain. Talk, again, is strength; force is weakness. By their language skills and visual imagery, the students of the new Chinese generation have shown that they understand this better than do the entrenched leaders of the old.

What are the strategies and tactics at work in these and other incidents? We have already outlined a few of these, but let us be a bit more systematic in our review of some of the elements in operation.

Style. The best example of this point is, of course, Mikhail Gorbachev. Not only does Gorbachev understand the value of taking and holding the public relations initiative—as evidenced by his now-lengthy series of very public arms-control proposals—but he understands the news value of working a crowd in the manner of a Western politician. On a visit to Washington some years back, he made news by halting his motorcade and "spontaneously" mixing with the bystanders. In West Germany he did the same, and became for a moment in 1989 the most popular political figure in the country. What makes this such an effective device for the Soviet leader—though probably one of diminishing value over time—is the sharp contrast it represents with the behavior of his predecessors and with the resultant public expectations. Simple as the gesture may be, it is of great symbolic value in the game of public diplomacy. It represents a break with the past, a sign of progressivism. As if to make this very point, one West German tabloid, *Bild-Zeitung*, described Gorbachev's 1989 visit there under a headline which read, in translation, "Gorbachev Has Enormous Erotic Radiance."[8] Just think about that. A Russian leader with sex appeal! In addition, Gorbachev meets with foreign journalists more often than did previous Soviet leaders, and handles himself with grace and ease in such settings. Even as he gathers to himself unprecedented formal powers, he looks and acts—to a point—like a Western politician.

Equally as important as the visual aspects of Gorbachev's style are its verbal aspects. It does not hurt that he is perceived outside his country as a progressive and, in a Soviet context, as something of a democrat. More than that, however, Gorbachev has learned well the lesson of KAL 007. He employs candor and seeming openness to disarm his potential critics, and readily confesses to errors and weaknesses in the Soviet system when that seems appropriate. After an incident in which Soviet pipeline operators had detected but failed to act on a gas leak, only to see sparks from two passing trains ignite a huge gas cloud and kill several hundred people, for instance, he commented that this was yet one more example of poor training and work habits in Soviet industry—a point that was taken at the very least as a reference encompassing the accident at Chernobyl.

Location. Two criteria, in particular, seem to be reflected in the locations selected for key events intended to attract foreign notice. The first is the symbolic value of one or another venue. Tiananmen Square, for instance, more than merely the location of the country's principal government buildings, is the symbolic heart of China. Events that occur there are, by definition, important. The second is the accessibility of a venue to the press. In Seoul, for example, during the demonstrations described in chapter 2, the major events were centered in the downtown area in the immediate vicinity of the hotels where the foreign correspondents were housed. Both the symbolism of the locations and the access they provided to events directly address the criteria of newsworthiness applied by the Western press. The years-long civil war in Sri Lanka is not news in the West—no journalists or network television cameras are there to tell us it is happening. But the beating on camera of a politician in Panama City is grounds for military intervention.

Timing. It is more difficult to draw firm conclusions about the purposeful timing of events designed for foreign news consumption. The number of variables—countries, time zones—is very great, and the sophistication of the communicators somewhat uncertain. In at least one instance, however—the demonstrations in Seoul—there was clearly one external public (and government) that those involved hoped to reach—that of the United States. The fact that demonstrations started daily at a more or less fixed hour and ended just as regularly (a) before darkness set in, and (b) in time to permit satellite feeds of the resulting video footage and its editing in New York for the same day's evening newscasts, may or may not have been coincidental. But purposeful or not, it was surely effective.

Drama and conflict. Events like those we have been describing tend to have an inherent drama that makes them newsworthy. Where the events are orchestrated by opponents of a regime to try to bring outside pressure on those in power, this apparent drama is generated by the contrast between the idealism and seeming naivete of the challengers on the one hand, and the repressive efforts of the authorities on the other. The result is a version of the morality play—democratic popular movement versus oppressive regime—that we have seen in recent years in reporting from China, Korea, Panama, the Philippines, and elsewhere. The backdrops and names of the cast change, but the plot line, and even major segments of the scripted dialogue, are constant.

Fill in the blanks. And the impression of conflict that the story creates is only enhanced as the popular forces speak openly to and through the foreign media while the government does its best to shut them down—even, as in the case of China in 1989, to the extent of threatening photographers at gunpoint and expelling journalists who violate government decrees.

As is the case in their domestic coverage, the media are sometimes vulnerable to manipulation when covering foreign affairs precisely because of their penchant for maximum drama. On one day in the midst of the coverage of events in China in 1989, for example, all of the major American media reported two stories which they took to be indicative of potential troubles atop the Chinese government. One suggested that Prime Minister Li Peng had been shot in the leg during an assassination attempt, though not seriously wounded. The other suggested that senior leader Deng Xiaoping was dead or near death in a Beijing hospital. Neither Li nor Deng had been seen in public for several days at the time these stories surfaced. Both were generally reported as unsubstantiated, but the frequency with which they were repeated, and the common accompanying qualifier that many accounts of events were difficult to verify under the chaotic conditions extant in Beijing, gave them some credibility. Later, as we know, both stories proved false.

What is interesting about these two rumors—and that is all they were—is their common origin. This became clear in an interview on the "MacNeil/Lehrer NewsHour" of June 8, 1989, with Jing Huang, a Chinese citizen studying at Harvard University, who had traveled to Beijing as an interpreter for two American social scientists studying nonviolent student movements. Part way into the interview, Jim Lehrer asked Huang what he read into the fact that Deng Xiaoping had not then been seen in public for quite some time. There ensued the following exchange:

Huang: Ah. . . . Yes, I think it might be true that Deng Xiaoping has been out, because several days ago my friend and I created a rumor that Li Peng got shot by his bodyguard, and just two days later . . .

Lehrer: You *created* the rumor?

Huang: Yes, exactly. Just two days later the spokesman of [the] State

Council said Li Peng's okay and now he appeared. But the rumor—we also created rumor about Deng Xiaoping—partly by us and partly by some other people—said Deng Xiaoping has been sick, or had been killed, or so on, so forth. But so far there is no response from government where he is. According to my information, some military leaders and some provincial party secretaries have made many many calls to Deng Xiaoping's office. Usually, at least Deng Xiaoping's secretary should answer the phone, but in the past few days—I should [say], in the past two weeks—nobody answered the phone in his office. That's why I believe he has been out. At least at this moment.

Lehrer: He's not runnin' the show right now.

Huang: No.

Lehrer: No. This idea of starting rumors. [Hint of a smile] We reported both stories that you just said you were involved in starting rumors on. Back here in this country, this program and other programs actually reported those as developments. Ah . . . are you taking credit for that?

Huang: Ah . . . yes. Because sometimes people also learn to play games. . . .

Huang went on to make clear the way in which he and others had floated rumors—something on the order of trial balloons—through the foreign media and elsewhere, to force a governmental response, from which they hoped to gauge the state of affairs within the Chinese leadership. Lee Atwater himself could not have been more effective.

Not all of these media-directed actions and strategies have the desired effect, however, at least in the long term. A case in point is provided by the 1981 decision of the Korean government to host the 1988 Summer Olympics.[9] After the assassination of President Park Chung Hee in 1979, South Korea experienced a period of political instability that culminated in a violent confrontation in the city of Kwangju between student demonstrators and military forces under the command of General Chun Doo Hwan. In the aftermath of this clash, which left between 200 and 2,000 persons dead and a bitter residue that still flavors Korean politics today, Chun formed a new de facto government and in September of 1980 was sworn in as Korea's president.

The new administration faced three difficult problems. First, substantial expansion of the Korean economy was producing a higher standard of living for many citizens, but was also a source of significant social dislocation as a traditional, agricultural society was rapidly converted into a modern, industrial one. Second, the improving economic conditions were generating rising political expectations as well, and there was no consensus among the Korean elite as to what form political development should take. In the wake of Kwangju, however, the legitimacy of the government was widely questioned, especially by the young. Finally, the regime in neighboring North Korea continued a series of threats and hostile actions that commanded attention. The decision to host the Olympics was directed at each of these three concerns.

First, the decision was intended to associate the new government in the public mind with the country's growing economic prosperity. It was a form of credit claiming. Second, the government anticipated that their selection as Olympic hosts would produce a surge of national pride among Koreans, and that this spirit of boosterism would create an opportunity of several years' duration for the government to build its own support. And third, the government believed that by focusing world attention on the Korean Peninsula for the better part of a decade, it could insure itself against overt hostile acts from the North while, at the same time, renewing flagging world awareness of the threat it perceived itself to be facing.

While some of these objectives clearly were achieved, hosting the Olympics was primarily a catalyst for change in Korean political life. Rather than a force to legitimize the Chun government, the Olympics became a force for its removal. In the summer of 1987, and for the better part of a year following, the government found itself between a proverbial rock—the student demonstrators—and a hard place of its own creation—the opening date of the Olympic Games. The coming of the games made Korea newsworthy: it brought the world's press to Seoul. And the presence of the press and the negative image of Korea it conveyed to the world as the now-familiar morality play unfolded— conferring legitimacy on students and opposition leaders and draining it from the government—ultimately forced the ruling party to make significant concessions. The only way to maintain stability, it seemed, was to permit change; so the huge clocks posted around Seoul to count down the days to the Olympics numbered instead the days of the old political order. Even the style of leadership adopted since 1987 by

Chun's successor as president, Roh Tae Woo—with its proactive sensitivity to public opinion and its Gorbachev-like penchant for unexpectedly progressive moves—is a product of this mix. The World to Seoul and Seoul to the World.

A more mundane example of the same phenomenon—a sort of media management boomerang effect—is provided by one incident following the "unpleasantness" in Beijing in which the Chinese government pirated some ABC news footage of a man claiming to have seen many bodies in Tiananmen Square after the army swept through and brutally suppressed the demonstrations. This was contrary to the government line, and shortly after the leadership reasserted its control, Chinese television—in a post-Maoist version, perhaps, of "America's Most Wanted"—broadcast the ABC footage with an on-screen appeal to identify and turn in the man as an enemy of the state. Within one hour he was in police custody, having been fingered by a woman who had watched the program and who recognized him on the street. He was then pictured—somewhat the worse for wear—publicly recanting his description and apologizing for his error.[10]

At the same time that governments and people around the world are learning to deal with Western media on their own terms, American experts are exporting their approach to domestic political communication at an increasing rate. A recent issue of *Campaigns and Elections*, a magazine devoted to campaign consulting and related endeavors, surveyed the extent of these exports, which it found evidenced in such diverse places as Australia, Switzerland, the Federal Republic of Germany, France, Israel, Japan, Canada, Mexico, Chile, and even the Soviet Union, where interest-group politics and political advertising seem to be taking root. In addition, many American consultants provide services to candidates in election campaigns in other countries, especially in Latin America and, most recently, in Eastern Europe. While this may be good for the balance of trade, it does not always serve the larger interests of American foreign policy. Les Francis, an American consultant who traveled to Bolivia as part of a team of observers during that country's 1989 national elections, tells, for example, of an American consultant to one of the Bolivian presidential candidates who adopted a negative style, denigrating the other leading candidates in the race. While such a strategy *may* have been appropriate for use at home, where a stable democracy has operated for many years, its probable effect in Bolivia, where the institutions of democracy are especially fragile, could have been much different—undermining confidence in a new and largely untested political system.

As much as these observations may reveal about the Soviets, the Chinese, the Koreans, and others, they reveal still more about the media and people of the United States. For the common theme running through virtually all of the reports of these events in American media, and the perceptions of and responses to them among the American people—the theme reflected in the title to this chapter—is how much the world is coming to think, to act, to *be* like the United States. Electronic convergence may be taking over where the much-touted "harmonic convergence" of 1988 fell short. Since both media and audience subscribe to this particular myth, it is one of potentially great potency.

The myth of electronic convergence—that television, and communication generally, helps us all to realize how much we have in common—gains its support through two possible lines of argument. First, there is the impression among Americans that the world is reshaping itself in our image. This decidedly ethnocentric interpretation is reinforced by actual events—it was, after all, the Statue of Liberty and her cousin that were central symbols of the action in China—and by the tendency of American journalists to see overseas events through American eyes. We were prepared, we *wanted*, to accept Mikhail Gorbachev, upon his rise from obscurity to power, as a Western man—to believe reports that this little-known fellow was a jazz lover, scotch drinker, and a pragmatist—because our doing so made him fit more closely with *our* collective image of what a responsible world leader of the modern era should be. We clung to these descriptors—probably still do—despite a State Department conclusion at the time that this image of the new Soviet leader was itself a product of a KGB disinformation campaign.

More to the point, perhaps, is the remarkable turn of events in the domestic politics of the Soviet Union, Poland, the former East Germany, and the rest of the Eastern Bloc—a turn that has seen dissidents elected to a new Soviet legislature, the Polish *Solidarity* labor movement overwhelm the Communist party in free elections, and the two Germanys reunified. Each of these events has a significant domestic impetus, and each resultant political structure will reflect far more of its own history and circumstance than it will any external model. But Americans nevertheless revel in the notion that the goal in each in-

stance is a system more like our own, and that things are, quite literally, moving our way. It is very flattering to consider the new direction
in world affairs as a turn toward us—spelled U.S.—and flattery goes a
long way in politics.

The second line of argument is a bit different, though no less self-
centered. It draws on the notion that reality is merely a social construction—that it is only what people believe it to be. If that is true, then
events are significant only as they give people cues as to what they
mean, and there can be as many different interpretations—actually,
different realities—as there are groups of people with different perspectives who receive these cues from events. Putting it another way,
the argument is that we simply impose our own image on events,
whatever they may be. By assigning meaning to the words and images
that bring us news of events, we—or our journalists in our behalf—
create our very own view of political reality. Democracy. Democracy.
Democracy. What the students in Tiananmen were asking for was, in
fact, *not* democracy as Americans usually conceive of it. They wanted
an end to favoritism among the party elite and, significantly, the children of the elite, with whom they would soon be competing for positions, and a dialogue *within* the Chinese Communist party. But after
two or three weeks of network news coverage, Americans could be
forgiven if they concluded that the end of the one-party Communist
state was nigh. Words—as we saw in chapter 1—have great power; it
takes a while for their meanings to catch up.

In this regard, it is instructive to compare news coverage of two
very similar events of recent years—the downing of KAL 007, which
we have already examined in some detail, and the shooting down by
American forces in the Persian Gulf of an Iran Air jetliner in 1988. In
the latter instance, faulty radar interpretation on the part of the Americans led to fears that the airliner was a military craft undertaking a
suicide attack on the American fleet in the gulf. A surface-to-air missile brought the plane down with a loss of some 290 lives. The interesting aspect of these two incidents in the present context is the difference
in their respective portrayals in the American press. As pointed out by
political scientist Robert Entman, newspaper headlines and the covers
of weekly news magazines were filled, in the first instance, with words
and symbols denoting evil intent. "Wanton Act," decried the *New
York Times,* quoting government sources, while *Time* and *Newsweek*
ran pictures of a 747 along with the words "Murder" and "Shooting

to Kill.'' The language was active: why did Moscow do this brutal thing? In the second instance, *Time* actually had a cover with a picture of the planet Mars on it, and both news weeklies emphasized the theme of trying to find an explanation, and devoted much journalistic soul-searching to how such an awful ''mistake'' could possibly have happened. The language was passive: why has this tragic thing happened? By Entman's count, the KAL incident led the news for nine days—we have already seen how it was finally removed by the Soviets—and Iran Air for a mere two.[11] We build our own reality, and we populate it (or have in recent years) with evil Russians, irrational Iranians, and honest, hard-working Americans. Small wonder that our mental construction of society itself colors our perspective on events.

And that, in the final analysis, is what links the emerging style of international political communication to the argument that underlies the balance of this book. For these increasingly commonplace tactics and ploys—and any larger strategy they may reflect—derive their ultimate power, at least inadvertently, from the central notion of strategic political communication: that journalists and their audiences display consistent and predictable patterns in their respective behaviors, and that those patterns can be used to advantage by persons who understand them and are in a position to create settings in which they will be employed. One way or another, the world truly is molded in our own image—at least as far as we ourselves are concerned.

Notes

1. ''Tass Statement on Incident,'' *New York Times*, 3 September 1983, p. A1.

2. John F. Burns, ''Soviet Says Order to Down Jet Came at a Local Level,'' *New York Times,* 10 September 1983, pp. A1, A4.

3. Gary Lee, ''Gorbachev in Prime Time Is the Season's Hottest New Show,'' *Washington Post National Weekly Edition,* 11 November 1985, p. 16.

4. Michael Dobbs, ''The Spies Who Love You: KGB Call-In Show Portrays Soviet Agents as Just Plain Folks,'' *Washington Post,* 3 November 1989, p. A37. In 1990, the KGB formed a public relations unit which began a wide-ranging campaign—including tours of KGB Headquarters and the notorious Lubyanka Prison—to change the agency's image. See Michael Dobbs, ''Open House at the KGB,'' *Washington Post,* 8 January 1990, p. A29.

5. Charles Paul Freund, ''Put-downs in Place of Policy,'' *Washington Post,* 23 May 1989, p. A13.

6. John J. Fialka, ''Tales of Imagination in the Foreign Press Give U.S. Headaches,'' *Wall Street Journal,* 15 December 1983, pp. 1, 21.

7. See Jim Hoagland, ''Marshall Law Backfires in Beijing,'' *Washington Post*, 25 May 1989, p. A53, for a discussion of indirect American influences on events in China.

8. Charles Paul Freund, ''Russo-Erotic Chic: How the Reds Changed Their Image from Stolid to Suggestive,'' *Washington Post*, 18 June 1989, p. C1.

9. The discussion on this point is based on Jarol B. Manheim, ''Rites of Passage: The 1988 Seoul Olympics as Public Diplomacy,'' *Western Political Quarterly*, June 1990, pp. 279–95, and, in turn, on a series of some two dozen interviews with officials of the Korean government and the Seoul Local Olympic Organizing Committee during 1987 and 1988.

10. This incident is set in context by Dick Polman in ''In China, TV Becomes a Weapon of Crackdown,'' *Philadelphia Inquirer*, 14 June 1989, pp. 1D, 5D.

11. Lecture presented at The George Washington University, April 1989.

8 THEY'RE RIOTING IN AFRICA

Some years ago, a CBS news correspondent whose identity I do not recall told on the air of having received word that he was to be reassigned from the network's bureau in Riyadh, Saudi Arabia, to New York. Here is the story as I remember it:

Among the small groups of Western correspondents assigned to places like Riyadh, news of such transfers is hardly secret, and it rapidly becomes public knowledge among those with a need to know. So it came as no surprise to the correspondent that, shortly after his notice of transfer arrived, he was approached by someone claiming to represent the Palestine Liberation Organization, who asked him whether, on his way to New York, he would be interested in stopping overnight in Beirut, Lebanon—at the time headquarters of the PLO and not nearly as chaotic as it is today—for a personal meeting with PLO Chairman Yassir Arafat. As any journalist presented with such an opportunity to interview a leading world figure would, he accepted the invitation.

On the appointed day, he landed in Beirut and checked into his hotel. Sure enough, at the agreed hour there came a knock on his door. Upon opening it, he was greeted by two men who, with apologies, blindfolded him. They led him out of the hotel, helped him into a vehicle, and drove in circles through the streets of Beirut for what the correspondent estimated to have been about two hours. They then stopped the vehicle, helped him out, led him into a building and up some stairs, halted, and knocked on a door. The door was opened, he was led inside, and the blindfold was removed. And there, across the room, was Yassir Arafat, who immediately arose, crossed the room, and greeted him warmly. The two men sat down on the sofa and began a wide-ranging conversation.

About ten minutes into the interview, the telephone rang. One of those present answered, speaking in hushed and hurried tones. He then hung up, rushed across the room, and whispered something to Arafat. The chairman turned to the journalist and said, "Hurry! We must get down on the floor. There are Israeli terrorists in the neighborhood." Just as the two reached the floor, the sound of automatic weapons and exploding grenades could be heard in the street. One of the men in the apartment took a handgun, positioned himself at a window, and began firing into the street below.

After two or three minutes, the firing stopped and things got very quiet. Then the telephone rang and one of Arafat's aides reached up very carefully to retrieve it. He spoke briefly into the receiver, then to the PLO chairman. Arafat, in turn, told a much-relieved correspondent that the danger had passed. The pair returned to the sofa and continued their conversation for two or three hours, after which the correspondent was again blindfolded and driven on a circuitous route to his hotel. He returned to New York filled with new insights into the PLO's political views and, no doubt, with a greater appreciation for its perspective on the Israeli role in the Middle East conflict.

But the story does not end there. Some weeks later, this same correspondent was seated in a bar in Paris, when he happened to overhear a conversation at a nearby table in which a French journalist recently returned from the Middle East was sharing with his colleagues a most unusual experience. It seems that he had been invited by the PLO to stop in Beirut on his way back to Paris for reassignment, and to meet with Yassir Arafat. He had been blindfolded and driven through the streets to the meeting, and right in the middle of his conversation with the PLO leader, Israeli terrorists had struck. . . .

What is unusual about this story is not that a successful manipulation of the Western media was achieved, but that it was eventually uncovered as such. Had the CBS correspondent not been in that particular bar, at that particular table, at that particular time, and had he not been conversant in French (recall that language skills are not widespread among U.S. journalists), the staging of this media event would have passed unnoticed. After all, as news the story was irresistible. It was prearranged. It was timely. It focused on a prominent personality. It involved conflict, even violence. It provided what, for American television, would be a unique twist on the morality play by reversing the then-customary roles of the villain and the victim. And it played on the desire of journalists to be interpreters of events.

In effect, what the PLO had done was to take advantage of the professional norms, the decision-making tendencies, and some of the weaknesses of the Western news media—points of vulnerability we identified in chapter 2—to gain a degree of control over how the organization and its goals would be portrayed. And while their effort may have been more elaborate than most, it was, in essence, no different from the attempts at media manipulation we have already seen to be practiced by corporations, foreign governments, leaders of political movements, political candidates, domestic governmental leaders, and others. For the present, however, let us focus our attention on one aspect of this rather unique PLO press conference, the use it made of violence as an instrument of communication.

◆ ◆ ◆ ◆

One of the most striking facts about political violence in recent years—domestic as well as international—is its ability to attract coverage in the news media. Not only have violent events been afforded extensive and prominent treatment on television and in print, but, with some regularity, the media themselves have become parties to the action. In some instances, this involvement has taken the form of conveying terrorist demands to the government or the public; in others, putting pressure on the government to respond to such demands; and in still others, seeming to play the role of intermediary in any negotiations that may ensue. This demonstrated affinity of the media for stories built around violent imagery gives rise to several interesting questions. among them:

• Why should those engaged in violent acts concern themselves with the media?

• Why should the media play so central and *cooperative* a role in the unfolding of violent episodes?

• What is the effect of news coverage of political violence on public perceptions and government actions?

There is an emergent school of thought among those who specialize in the study of terrorism—perhaps best captured by Alex P. Schmid and Janny deGraaf in their book *Violence as Communication*[1]—that sees terrorism and other forms of political violence as a form of communication in which the very nature of the act—its sheer atrocity, its location, and the identity of its victims—serves to generate the power of the message. Put another way, those who engage in such acts often settle on the type of violence they will undertake, its geographic and other settings, and the selection of victims with an eye toward the newsworthiness of each. If the objective is to send a message to the United States government, for example, what better way is there than to hijack an American aircraft, assault an American embassy or other facility, or harm Americans—even single them out from other nationalities for special attention. In each instance, the perpetrators can reasonably expect that American media will cover the story in some (lurid) detail. They will cover it first because it is violent and will appeal to their audience at an emotional level, second because it involves persons with whom their audience can readily identify, and third because, in all likelihood, it fits with an ongoing story line already familiar to their audience—the saga of vandals assaulting civilization.

In effect, then, when covering stories of political violence, the media serve as vicarious witnesses. They have the task of disseminating the word of what has occurred and what it means—that is, of constructing society's understanding of the event—to a larger public or, from the perpetrators' perspective, to some governmental or corporate enemy whose behavior the perpetrators wish to punish or change. In the process, the media not only provide points of access to public opinion and points of pressure on political leaders for those who resort to violence, but—by the very act of conferring newsworthy status on such persons—they lend some modicum of credibility, legitimacy, or, at the very least, stature to them.

Consider, for example, the seizing of American hostages by Shiite Moslem extremists in Lebanon during the 1980s. Though some ransom demands may have been made—as apparently they also were for some persons of other nationalities taken during this period—these were not kidnappings for profit. They were messages sent by relatively weak and divided clusters of political and religious partisans locked in a lengthy and bitter civil war and in a still longer confrontation with neighboring Israel, and messages sent to a remote, and for all practical purposes, unreachable foe. Go away, they said. *Lasciate ogni speranza, voi ch'entrate.* All hope abandon, ye who enter here. And consider how the story has played in the American media. Moslem fanatics. Families of the victims. Lebanese anarchy. Families of the victims. Syrian or Iranian intervention. Families of the victims. There has been very little news, per se, aside from an occasional pot-stirring video from the kidnappers, but the potency and audience appeal of the imagery—and especially the personalizing of the tragedy through the focus on the hostage's families—has assured that there has been a story throughout. And that story has maintained a level of public awareness and concern that is still felt in the White House, where even the removal of a yellow ribbon from the door of the Oval Office during the changeover from the Reagan to the Bush administration caused a furor among the hostage-story constituency. The ribbon was quickly replaced, and no doubt serves (as intended) as a constant reminder to the president of the fate of some half dozen lost souls.

Schmid and deGraaf have identified a number of uses to which those engaged in political violence can put their ability in order to attract media attention. Some of these include communicating messages to a mass audience, far larger than might be present at any specific incident; polarizing public opinion, forcing people away from centrist or moderate views and toward the extremes; making converts or attracting popular support for their cause; conveying specific threats, demands, or bargaining messages; arousing public sympathy for their victims in order to pressure a government to make concessions or meet their demands, the hostages in Lebanon being a case in point; establishing credibility or legitimizing their actions, either, as noted, by the mere attraction of news coverage per se or by the broadcasting of demands or ideological manifestos; or, in their wildest dreams, inciting public opposition to a government.[2] In effect, each of these objectives serves to extend the reach of those employing political violence from the immediate theater of action to the full length and breadth of society. Each is a potential source of power. As retired Air Force general and former Secretary of State Alexander Haig has summed it up, "Terrorism often constitutes a cheap form of low-intensity warfare. It is a cost-effective way of attacking another country."[3]

In addition to generating their own news, terrorists and others engaged in violent acts receive information from the media about such matters as countermeasures that are being taken against them or public reactions to their deeds. I recall, for example, one of the earliest airliner hijackings in the 1960s—when taking unscheduled visits to Cuba was becoming quite the rage—in which a plane was on the ground at El Paso, Texas, with a hijacker aboard holding the crew and seeking an island vacation. Both the FBI and the remote truck from a local television station were on hand. After several hours of "negotiations," and in full view of the television cameras scanning across the tarmac, FBI agents began an assault on the plane by approaching from the tail, out of view of the cockpit, where the hijacker was presumed to be holding forth. Closer they came, and closer. It was better than any script Efrem Zimbalist, Jr., ever performed. News in the making. Live at five. Serious stuff. Then, suddenly, the screen went blank, and after a moment of silence, a rather embarrassed announcer noted that it had probably not been a good idea to provide live television coverage of the FBI assault since this particular airline was, at the time, advertising that it had just put television sets aboard its planes for the entertainment of its passengers. Cuba, I hear, was very nice that time of year.

Sometimes the feedback effects of news coverage can be even more sinister. Israeli sources tell, for instance, of one incident in which an airline hijacking to Kuwait dragged on for some days. In a dispatch from the scene, a BBC reporter indicated that the will of the hijackers appeared to be weakening. Unfortunately, the hijackers themselves were monitoring the BBC broadcast and heard the report. In a demonstration of their continuing resolve, they immediately killed several of their captives and tossed their bodies from the plane.

Though we tend to think of terrorists—or freedom fighters, depending, as we noted in chapter 1, on one's perspective—as the principal perpetrators of political violence, others make similar use of the media.[4] Large-scale, organized, antiregime movements—such as UNITA in Angola, Moslem rebels in the southern Philippines, or the forces that overthrew the white minority regime in Southern Rhodesia, now Zimbabwe, during the 1970s—are examples. Movements of this kind raise sizable armies, sometimes led or assisted by mercenaries, and mount sustained resistance against established governments. Antiregime violence of this type—essentially on the scale of civil war or close to it—is similar to terrorist violence in several ways. First, of course, it is, by definition, violent, and for that reason it is likely to attract the attention of the media. Second, it is antiestablishment in character, and in all likelihood must contend with stronger and better-organized forces. And third, like terrorist violence, it is intended to destabilize a regime, to undercut its policies, and to undermine public confidence in it, all as a means for bringing about its overthrow.

Beyond these similarities, however, large-scale, organized, anti-regime violence differs from terrorism in important ways which—if they do anything—significantly enhance its perpetrators' ability to attract and influence news coverage of their activities.

For one thing, antiregime movements often have a base of popular support among the indigenous populations of areas in which they operate, support that terrorists are often denied. The Vietcong was able to operate with great effect over many years in South Vietnam—and could sustain itself against propaganda wars as well as bullets—precisely because it had this type of support. A contemporary example of a group with indigenous support might be the African National Congress in South Africa, while a group evidently lacking popular backing would be the Contras, the organized resistance to the former Sandinista regime in Nicaragua. Beyond establishing credibility, the existence of indigenous support boosts the confidence of both the leaders and followers of such movements, and may enhance their willingness to talk with journalists or to provide them with access to events, facilities, or key personnel.

Second, and potentially of equal significance, these movements often have the tacit—or even the overt—support of other governments, sometimes those of neighboring states, which are willing to provide them with both sanctuary and legitimacy. The so-called "frontline states" performed this function for the revolutionary forces that eventually brought about majority rule in Zimbabwe, while the controversial support of the governments of the United States and Honduras did the same for the Contras. It was precisely this kind of support that UNITA leader Jonas Savimbi was hoping to generate during his 1986 visit to the United States, as described in chapter 6.

Third—and at least partially as a product of the first two points—many antiregime movements possess some level of popular support among foreign publics upon which they can build. It is clear, for example, that public disdain for the current regime in South Africa has led both the United States government and American corporations to alter the ways they do business in and with that nation. In contrast, it seems likely that the African National Congress could—if it chose the route of armed resistance—reasonably expect initial popular support in the United States, at least until the South African government succeeded in labeling the Congress as a Communist-led or -inspired organization.

So important can external popular support be in freeing (or causing) foreign policy makers in second countries to support an antiregime movement, that these outside governments will sometimes try to convince their own people to allow them to render such movements some assistance. That seems to be the lesson of at least one of the Reagan administration's efforts undertaken in behalf of the Contras between 1983 and 1986. During this period, according to a report of the General Accounting Office and some related materials, the State Department's Office of Public Diplomacy for Latin America and the Caribbean (LPD) set as its objective "to gain sufficient bipartisan support in Congress to permit approval of increased assistance, economic and military, to Central America and to preclude crippling restrictions on actions in support of U.S. policy objectives in the region." They accomplished this by, in effect, hiring contractors to produce research reports on Central America, then informally replacing this contractual obligation with requests to produce propaganda for domestic consumption—for example, an editorial entitled "Morality and the Central America Issue" and an essay entitled "The Managua Connection: The Sandinistas and Middle Eastern Terrorists." Both the distribution of government-generated propaganda materials within the United States and the lobbying of Congress by officials of the government, especially where they do so by spending government money to generate citizen contacts, are expressly proscribed by law. In addition, LPD issued a secret, single-source contract—that is, there was no advertisement of the job or bidding for it—to International Business Communications, a firm with close ties to the administration which had earlier provided public relations services to the Contras and funneled money to them. Someone in authority clearly thought this was an activity worthy of some attention.[5]

Antiregime movements have the potential to engage in long-term, large-scale actions that maintain pressure on the target government, while at the same time retaining the ability to create—almost at will—the type of dramatic events that are likely to attract media attention. They can, in short, do everything that terrorists can do—and more. As a result, the strains placed on the target government by an ongoing and organized violent opposition can be considerably greater than those resulting from more or less isolated acts of terror, and can render that government relatively more susceptible to a war of words and images. The long-term pressure softens up the government so that the occasional sharp blows sting all the more.

Finally, organized antiregime movements are much more likely than terrorists to have in place—or be able to create—an infrastructure that can cultivate and service journalists over a long period of time, the sort of activity exemplified in the Arafat story with which we opened. In effect, in addition to the dramatic impact of their activities, the leaders of such organizations have an opportunity to conduct more or less routine relations with the media in ways similar to those employed by more conventional political leaders.

Some antiregime movements actually go so far as to organize extensive public relations efforts abroad that resemble in every way those conducted by governments. During 1988, for example, the Mozambique National Resistance, or Renamo, confronted with dwindling international support for its efforts to overthrow the Marxist government of the former Portuguese colony on Africa's east coast, conducted a press tour that included a low altitude flight across government-held territory in a small plane, landing in a narrow clearing. "Welcome to Free Mozambique," said Afonso Marceta Dhlakama, president of Renamo. "Please hurry—the plane must leave at once for its own safety." In a series of interviews—one lasting nearly eight hours—Dhlakama then proceeded to deny that his movement had been established by the former white regime in Southern Rhodesia to destabilize Mozambique or been subsidized by South Africa for the same purpose, and that his forces were responsible for reported mutilations of civilians—including cutting off the ears and noses of those suspected of aiding the government. On the positive side, he claimed to control some 85 percent of Mozambique's territory, though the circumstances of their arrival gave the visiting journalists some pause on this point.[6]

In addition to terrorist groups and antiregime movements, even governments can resort to political violence as a means of communicating, either with other governments or with their own people. An example of government-to-government communication through violence is provided by the Iranian regime during the seizure of the American embassy in Tehran and the holding there for more than a year of many American hostages. As we have already seen, this was quite a media event in the United States—for the obvious reasons—as the tally of days of captivity led newscasts for months. While the role of the Iranian government in orchestrating the events of those days came rapidly to be realized, what was less widely noted at the time—and when noted, was effectively ignored—was the extent to which the government was also orchestrating news coverage of those same events.

Bill Curtis, who was in Tehran for CBS News at the time, has attributed great sophistication to the government's propagandists, noting, for instance, that the slogans on the walls of the embassy compound and on many of the signs carried by demonstrators were in English—Farsi, not English, is the native language of Iran—that the major government ministries had next-day delivery of the *New York Times,* complete with critiques of individual reporters provided by observers in the United States; and that direct-dial telephone service with the United States provided them, again through observers stationed here, with immediate reports on television news coverage of the scene, network by network and journalist by journalist.[7] This picture is rounded out by stories told at the time by other journalists of daily assistance provided by the "Iranian students" holding the embassy: assistance in identifying the best camera locations and angles for the coming day's "spontaneous" activities and in moving equipment to those spots.

American journalists in Iran, it is clear, were not an endangered species, but they were carefully nurtured. Indeed, even the designation of the principal players as "students" might, in the light of other examples we have examined, be seen as an effort by the Iranians to gain legitimacy for the perpetrators of the outrage with the American audience using a derivative of the theme of youthful rebellion against oppressive authority. Otherwise, why did they not refer to themselves as "soldiers of the revolution," or some equivalent term?

Journalists do sometimes recognize that they are being manipulated by governments, though the results are perhaps not as salutary as one might expect. CBS's Dan Rather, quoted in a story in *USA Today* after having been summoned from his Baghdad hotel room one midnight—unshaven, running a fever, and without even a fresh shirt—for an interview with Iraqi President Saddam Hussein in which he was forced to use an Iraqi camera crew rather than his own, observed that the Iraqi leader had media-savvy aides who "can talk ratings, know who's on radio and TV, and know the difference between *USA Today,* the *Los Angeles Times,* and the *New York Times.* They know who the editors are and how they play stories." They even knew enough about the CBS anchor so that the president talked with Rather about the journalist's interest in fly fishing.[8] Rather clearly realized—and his experience demonstrated—that the Iraqis were playing the news management game. This recognition did not, however, prevent his network from running a full-page advertisement *in the same issue of the newspaper* (and in other major papers) listing CBS News's Persian Gulf "scoops" under the banner headline, "IF YOU WERE WATCHING CBS NEWS, YOU WERE THE FIRST TO KNOW."[9] But what, precisely, did you know? And more importantly, was it CBS or the Iraqis who chose to tell you?

An example of government-to-people communication through violence per se is provided by the Chinese government in the days after the Peoples Army cleared Tiananmen Square of demonstrators in the summer of 1989. During this period, the government used its monopoly control of all domestic media to impose its interpretation of events on the population—ironically, to deny that violence had been employed. Yet, central among the images transmitted in those days were those of many "counterrevolutionaries" who had clearly been beaten while in police custody. Here, rather than denying the use of force in its penal system, as is the normal practice of governments and would have been consistent with their larger claim, the Chinese leadership was actually highlighting it, and in the process generating among those who might harbor antiregime feelings a fear of the *implied* use of force. One of the interesting aspects of this campaign of intimidation in the context of our consideration of strategic communication, incidentally, was that in its latter stages, governmental news reports appeared almost exclusively in local rather than national media. In this way, the regime hoped to reach its own people without attracting international attention and further alienating foreign governments and businesses.[10]

For all of their differences of skill and sophistication, motive and opportunity, scale and resources, each of these types of political violence—whether initiated by terrorists, an antiregime movement, or a government—traces its potency, its magnetic attraction for news coverage, to the same root source, and one that should, by now, be familiar: an ability on the part of the perpetrators to identify and use to advantage the established patterns of behavior of journalists and news organizations. Put most simply, political violence is, by its inherently dramatic nature, news, and its value as news is amplified as additional criteria of newsworthiness, beyond mere drama, are met. The higher the drama, the more outrageous the violence, the more prominent or more highly symbolic the target, the more accessible the events, and so forth, the more extensive the news coverage will be. And all of these factors—drama, target selection, location, timing, and the like—are at the discretion of the perpetrators.

The peculiar vulnerability of the news media—at least those in the United States—to manipulation of this sort traces to three basic causes. These, too, should now have a familiar ring about them.

First, as we have already noted, in selecting items for the news, journalists have an understandable tendency to pick stories with high dramatic content, especially those that contain violence. Indeed, the more graphic the violence, the more attractive the story is. At work here is a confluence of two major journalistic forces—a story of evident importance, and a story of evident audience appeal. And this is one where the journalists and the M.B.A.'s can usually agree. During the week in 1989 in which Chinese authorities brutally put down the demonstrations in and around Tiananmen Square, for example, the ratings of ABC's "Nightline" program, which focused on China, rose *41 percent* over the previous week. And three weeks into the Persian Gulf crisis of 1990, the network evening news programs had added a total of six million viewers to their sagging August audiences, while "Nightline" had added two million of its own.[11] Violence, then, plays to—and its perpetrators benefit from—the primary selection biases of news organizations.

Second, in gathering information to build into the news, the media are limited by the degree of access they have to events and news makers. Where political violence is concerned, those limitations can be especially stringent, and may amount to an almost complete dependency for the raw material of news on the news makers themselves—on the perpetrators. Casting disclaimers left and right, journalists may still find themselves passing along messages shaped by terrorists or others simply because the story is important enough to demand coverage, and because potentially "tainted" information is the only kind they can get.

Sometimes, of course—and this, too, is illustrated by the story of Yassir Arafat—it is difficult, even impossible, to know that information is tainted. I recall hearing a story—though I cannot vouch for its validity—of a journalist who had covered the hijacking of an American plane that set down in one of the Arab countries and sat on the ground for several days. Hour after hour, a small corps of reporters and technicians braved sun and sand to maintain a vigil—just waiting for some action. Eventually, the cost and boredom of the assignment, which was yielding little information and less film, grew sufficiently high that all made plans to depart the scene. In the early morning hours of their scheduled departure day, this journalist was awakened by his cameraman, who told him that they must rush to the airport—there was to be some action. Rush they did, and they evidently got there just in time. In fact, the very instant their camera was in position and ready, the hijackers blew up the plane. Film at eleven. Exclusive. Kablooey! The film went in the can and off to network headquarters as quickly as possible, and the correspondent and cameraman prepared once again to leave. How did you know that something like that was going to happen at such an odd hour, asked the reporter. Well actually, came the reply, I am one of the hijackers. Is it news, or is it Memorex?

And third, the news media—this time collectively rather than individually—may be relatively more vulnerable in these circumstances than they might otherwise be because of their tendency to reflect one another's content. This is the case, as we suggested earlier in a different context, because news gathering—especially abroad, where much of the world's political violence occurs—is centralized in a few wire services, broadcast networks, and syndication services; because news organizations compete for the same audience using the same criteria of newsworthiness in selecting their content; because journalists are encouraged to practice pack journalism, all covering the very same events, often with the same emphasis or perspective; because, in order to protect themselves from legal liability and political threats, news organizations seek safety in numbers and find danger in isolation; and because most media outlets are dependent in the very same degree on the very same sources for the information that they fashion into news. The resultant homogeneity may deprive media and audience alike of important alternative perspectives or interpretations.

The net result? All of these considerations combine to produce a confluence of interests between the news media and those who engage in acts of political violence. Political violence is the stuff of front pages. Audiences want to learn about these events, and journalists feel a sense of obligation to tell them. As a result, the media are naturally— and by most lights, correctly—inclined to afford them extensive and prominent coverage. It does no good to pretend that these things do not happen—indeed, doing so may only lead the perpetrators to raise the level of atrocity to a point where it can no longer be ignored. In providing such coverage, however, the media give to the forces of violence that which they most covet: exposure and implicit legitimacy. It is truly a Hobson's choice. But in the selfsame act, the forces of violence give to the media that which *they* most covet: dramatic events that attract and hold the attention of large audiences. This makes the choice considerably easier. Acting independently and in their respective self-interests, then, the news media and the forces of violence aid one another, perhaps at the expense of established political leaders, third-party governments, social stability, or the public interest.

What is a government or a news organization to do? How can the institutions of a society insulate or defend themselves against such blatant—and, in the case of the media, such tempting—manipulation? There are, in fact, several defensive strategies available, though none of them is particularly satisfactory.

The most obvious solution available to a government is censorship—the requirement that reports of violence or other events deemed by those in authority to be injurious to their interests be submitted for governmental approval prior to dissemination, with the clear prospect that dissemination might be restricted or prohibited—and its more subtle, or at least less direct, variant, outlawing news coverage of certain events or excluding journalists altogether. Recent history offers many examples of such governmental defenses at work—the Israeli government's placing areas of unrest off limits to journalists during the *Intifada*, the Palestinian uprising in the occupied territories, and the prohibition on making photographs or video recordings of demonstrations and violence in China during the Beijing Spring are two that come readily to mind.

Perhaps the most remarkable effort devoted to keeping the bad news from being news is that undertaken over the last decade or so by the government of South Africa, which confronts a disorganized but potentially overwhelming antiregime movement. Faced in the early 1980s with the second in what seemed to be developing into an emerging series of violent confrontations with blacks sparked in the township of Soweto, and subjected as a direct result to immense political and economic pressures from the outside, South Africa's leadership—determined not to yield on the larger policy questions—decided to thumb its figurative nose at world opinion. In a series of progressively more stringent legal restrictions, the Pretoria government has literally forced its way off the front pages of the world's newspapers and television screens by outlawing a wide range of news-gathering practices, and by threatening journalists with expulsion or—even worse—with arrest and imprisonment. To protect itself from media-wielding revolutionaries, the country has developed into very much of a closed society.

Short of censorship and other exclusionary tactics, when dealing with external publics, governments can also employ a device we explored in chapter 6—political public relations and news management. The study of the strategies and effectiveness of such efforts that I described in that chapter, for example, included two countries which, at the time studied—the mid-1970s—faced antiregime violence. The first was South Africa; the second was known then as Southern Rhodesia. Since we have already dealt somewhat with the former, let us focus here on the latter.

At the time it acquired the services of a public relations consultant, the government of Southern Rhodesia was in the midst of a long-running struggle to retain white minority rule, a struggle which could only be sustained with the support of—or, at worst, in the absence of active opposition from—major world powers, including the United States. During the year after it hired a consultant, the Rhodesian government opened an information office in Washington, conducted a press tour of a rural village that had recently been attacked by opposition guerrillas, focused world attention on the "kidnapping" of black children by Botswana-based rebels and on raids by the rebels on Catholic missions, and—in a notion reminiscent of the failed American "strategic hamlet" program in Vietnam—promoted the development of "protected villages" for the black population. In addition—perhaps in an effort to appeal to the elite of the antebellum American South, which the Rhodesian regime apparently believed still to exist and hold power in the United States—the government floated a rumor that white women all across the country were contemplating suicide at the mere thought of majority rule. While these bells and whistles were sounding, however, the government also undertook a rather more sophisticated approach to its problem by starting to manage the news.

One of the problems that the Rhodesians faced in their news portrayal—at least in the United States—was the predominance of violent images. Indeed, and as one might well expect under the circumstances, if there was one factor that contributed most to the high negatives they were experiencing, it was the reporting on political violence. Realistically, the government was not in a position to restrict that reporting—if journalists were excluded from entering the country directly, they could always find a way in from one of the frontline states, and in that case might be less available for, or interested in, hearing the government's views. So the regime of Ian Smith did the next best thing—it controlled its own releases more carefully. Much in the way that an industry can install scrubbers on a chimney to eliminate pollutants before they enter the atmosphere, the government cleansed its own rhetoric of references that might enhance the impression that Southern Rhodesia was a violent place. One example, in particular, makes very clear how this was done.

Prior to the hiring of its public relations consultant, the government had been in the practice of releasing a biweekly report on casualties from the continuing civil conflict. Ten police, seven civilians including one woman and two children, and seventy-three guerrillas died in violent clashes last week. The objective, one supposes, was to generate sympathy for the effort the brave (white) Rhodesians were making. But more to the point, the regularity of this report virtually assured that it made the day book of every journalist or news organization covering that area, and its contents appeared in the press like clockwork. One thing that we discovered in our later research, in fact, was that these reports had a multiplier effect. Just like negative advertising in domestic political campaigns, each report generated more than its weight—in fact, more than twice its weight—in news, commentaries, editorials, or letters to the editor, all replete with references to the Rhodesian violence. Immediately upon the signing of the public relations contract— and presumably, therefore, on the advice of the consultant—the government ceased to issue these reports. Indeed, it appears never to have issued another over the several subsequent years that it survived. The result was a significant drop in references to violence in portrayals of Southern Rhodesia in the United States press. Both the impetus to such reports and the multiplier effect were eliminated in a single stroke—an *in*action. Things *must* have been getting better.[12]

The overall results from our studies of news from Southern Africa, however, were less sanguine—at least from the perspectives of the two minority regimes. Although, in both instances, we did find that public relations and news management efforts improved the news images of the countries in question somewhat, both images were controlled primarily by the presence, level, and intensity of the political violence they were experiencing. The initiative was clearly with the forces arrayed in opposition to each regime.

One other device deserves mention here, if for no other reason than the fact that it is frequently suggested during those periods when political violence—especially domestic political violence—reaches relatively high levels. It is a device available not to governments, but to the media. That device is *self*-censorship.

Proposals for media self-censorship are especially intriguing because they go to the very heart of the conflict between commercial and journalistic values. Historically, as noted, such proposals have been considered seriously only when domestic violence has become a critical problem, so let us consider them principally in that context. In such circumstances, is it possible that political violence might not be news?

Set against the established newsworthiness of domestic political violence is the fact that news organizations, as commercial enterprises, are not only part of the established political and economic orders of our society, but—as we noted earlier—are principal beneficiaries of the status quo. Quite aside from their near-term financial interests then, and all the more so as the perceived threat to society increases, the media have a clear-cut institutional stake in combating social instability and thwarting fundamental social change. In addition, editors—no doubt more than reporters—might become persuaded that a larger public interest is served by withholding news than by disseminating it. Though the impetus was rather different from the one we are addressing here, it may be instructive to recall in this regard that, during the years of World War II, when the survival of the nation was in jeopardy, the media did voluntarily cooperate to restrict publication of outcomes of engagements, troop movements, and other sensitive information. And more recently, the media have withheld information whose release might threaten national security or human lives. During the Iran hostage crisis, for example, the whereabouts of six Americans who had eluded the Iranians, though known, were not revealed by the press, and the fact that one hostage held in a 1985 hijacking of a TWA airliner in Lebanon was an employee of the National Security Agency was similarly concealed.

These decisions, however, appear to be reached on an ad hoc basis, and their direction is not consistent. In 1983, for instance, one network reported that the United States had intercepted coded radio traffic between Syria and Iran associated with a bombing of the American embassy in Beirut that took sixty lives, and was using the messages to track the perpetrators. Almost at once after the report, the traffic

stopped, greatly hampering the counterterrorist effort. It was the same
group that later attacked the American barracks in Beirut, killing 241
marines.[13] And in 1979, at the outset of the seizure of the embassy
compound in Tehran, NBC broadcast the first interview with one of
the hostages. To obtain it, the network agreed to broadcast as well an
unedited statement by one of the Iranian militants.[14]

For those who have grown to maturity recently, the character and
impact of fundamental social upheaval may be difficult to fathom, but
for those who lived through the 1960s and early 1970s, it is not so hard
to understand how individuals and institutions might be pressed to
act—for reasons of self-defense—in ways that appear inimical to their
normal interests and behaviors. And we do have at least one documented instance where such fears did lead to self-censorship of the
press. This occurred in 1919, an especially interesting year in the present context.

By any standard—even that of 1968—1919 was a tough year in
American history. It was a year of disillusionment, as tens of thousands
of men returned to the work force in the aftermath of the Great War,
displacing as they did tens of thousands of women who had entered the
work force during the war to offset their absence. It was a year of
severe economic dislocations, as many were unable to find work, and
everyone who had it seemed all at once to be on strike. It was a year of
an energy crisis—just as the country had successfully industrialized,
the government announced that known reserves of oil would be completely used up within ten years. It was a year of public alcoholism—
another product of the war—sufficiently widespread to prompt a
short-lived amendment to the United States Constitution. It was the
year of the Red Summer, as fear spread that the Bolshevik revolution
which had overwhelmed czarist Russia would sweep westward
through Europe and the United States. It was a year of foreign adven-
turism, with an American-led Allied Expeditionary Force chasing after
the Red Army half a world away because some godless Russians had
declared war on the American way of life. It was the year in which the
Communist party of the United States was formed for the expressed
purpose of stimulating industrial unrest and destroying the capitalist
system. It was the year when the *Chicago Tribune,* in reporting on
labor unrest on the west coast, proclaimed that "it is only a middling
step from Petrograd to Seattle." It was the year in which the president
of the United States suffered from a debilitating stroke, and in which

speculation ran rampant as to who, if anyone, was in charge at the White House. It was a year of anarchy and violence, which saw one bomb destroy a portion of the home of the attorney general of the United States, and others dispatched unsuccessfully against some two dozen national leaders of commerce and government. It was a year of social change, which saw a second, and longer-lived constitutional amendment grant women the vote—the political price they extracted for service on the home front during the war.[15] It was—was nothing sacred?—the year of the Black Sox scandal, which rocked major league baseball. It was far and away the worst of times, Dickensian or otherwise. It surely must have seemed as if the whole fabric of society was coming unraveled. Say it ain't so, Joe.

And added to all of these troubles, as if they were not enough, 1919 was a year of widespread racial unrest. Between April 14 and the first of October, race riots occurred in twenty-two cities around the country: Chicago, Washington, Knoxville, St. Louis, Memphis, Birmingham, and sixteen sister cities tasted racial violence. During the same period, seventy-four blacks were lynched in the United States. The causes of this violence are not hard to discern. Housing was tight because of the reduction in new starts during the war. Competition for jobs was intense, not merely because veterans were returning to a slowed-down civilian economy in large numbers, but because massive migration from the rural areas to the cities in the years just before 1919 had dramatically increased the urban black labor force as well. Added to the general pressures on society and the xenophobia triggered by the red scare, these factors produced an incendiary mix—a mix that exploded into the closest thing to a nationwide race war that this country was to see before the 1960s.

One of the more significant outbreaks of racial unrest occurred in Chicago, where it had been preceded by two years of violence that had included twenty-seven bombings of black-owned homes. Unlike the riots of the 1960s, which were largely restricted to blacks rioting in black neighborhoods, the 1919 clashes included forays by whites into black neighborhoods and, on a much smaller scale, the reverse. The most common dynamic was for a small group of whites to invade a predominantly black area, then to be encouraged by larger groups of nonparticipating spectators to escalate the violence and mayhem. Many, mostly blacks, were killed and injured, and property loss was substantial.

All of this is of interest here principally because of the role and response of the local news media. Aside from their contribution to the conflagration by publishing inflammatory reports of atrocities committed by blacks against whites—often against women and children—and because the rioting lasted over a period of several days, news accounts had the effect of recruiting white participants from other parts of the city and from out of town to come and swell the ranks of the attackers. In addition, news accounts of rioting in one city seemed to give ideas to aggrieved persons in other cities, so that media coverage contributed not only to the depth of the problem, but to its breadth. Bigotry and population pressures lit the fires; the news media fanned the flames. But as the severity and generality of the problem worsened and was added to the other extant problems of the day, a consensus emerged among the news organizations that, by and large, this was not a good thing. As a result—and this is the reason we have gone through this rather lengthy account—there developed in many areas a formal or informal "operational code." This was a code of self-censorship under which news of rioting would be embargoed, at least during the period of the actual riot, to limit the spread of the contagion. Such agreements, in fact, became commonplace, and "no news"—or at least, "old news"—became the order of the day, though only, it seems, with respect to race-based confrontations. The practice lasted until the advent of television news, which, perhaps coincidentally, roughly coincided with the revitalization of the civil rights movement and with the racial confrontations of the 1950s and 1960s.[16]

What, then, are we to conclude about the use of violence as an instrument of strategic political communication? In the simplest terms, that it works well, and that there may be little we can do about it unless we are prepared to take steps that may fundamentally alter the character of our society. And that option—fundamental change—may represent a strategic objective of far more importance to the perpetrators than any communication strategy they could employ.

Notes

1. Alex P. Schmid and Janny deGraaf, *Violence as Communication* (Beverly Hills, Calif.: Sage, 1982).

2. Ibid., pp. 53–54.

3. Quoted in John Weisman, "TV and Terrorism," *TV Guide*, 23 February 1985, p. 3.

4. Portions of the following discussion are based on Jarol B. Manheim and

Robert B. Albritton, "Insurgent Violence versus Image Management: The Struggle for National Images in Southern Africa," *British Journal of Political Science* 17 (1987), pp. 201–18.

5. United States General Accounting Office, *State's Administration of Certain Public Diplomacy Contracts* (Washington, D.C.: 1987); and Stephen Engleberg, "Contra Aid Battle Is Stymied, but Disputes Linger," *New York Times,* 18 October 1988.

6. William Claiborne, "Mozambican Guerrillas Launch Attack on the PR Front," *Washington Post,* 31 July 1988, pp. A1, A28.

7. Bill Curtis, *On Assignment with Bill Curtis* (Chicago: Rand McNally, 1983), p. 134, and in an interview on *Morning Edition,* National Public Radio, 13 December 1983.

8. Peter Johnson, "Behind the Scenes of CBS' Saddam Score," *USA Today,* 31 August 1990, p. 1D.

9. *USA Today,* 31 August 1990, p. 5A.

10. Jay Mathews, "Chinese Arrests Grow in Provinces," *Washington Post,* 27 July 1989, p. A25.

11. Tom Shales, "China: The Networks' Closing Chapter," *Washington Post,* 21 June 1989, pp. G1, G9; James Walker, untitled report on ABC's "Nightline," 28 August 1990.

12. Robert B. Albritton and Jarol B. Manheim, "News of Rhodesia: The Impact of a Public Relations Campaign," *Journalism Quarterly* 60 (1983), pp. 622–28.

13. Katherine Graham, "Terrorists Need the Press, But So Does a Free Society," *Washington Post National Weekly Edition,* 5 May 1986, pp. 24–25.

14. John E. Cooney, "News Departments of the TV Networks Join Ratings Battle," *Wall Street Journal,* 2 January 1980, p. 1.

15. Jarol B. Manheim, *Déjà Vu: American Political Problems in Historical Perspective* (New York: St. Martin's, 1976), pp. 47–48, 215–20.

16. Morris Janowitz, "Patterns of Collective Racial Violence," in Hugh Davis Graham and Ted Robert Gurr, eds., *The History of Violence in America* (New York: Bantam Books, 1969), pp. 412–43, passim.

9 POLITICS LEFT AND RIGHT

Seldom has the stylized confrontation between politicians and journalists been rendered in as pure a form as the spectacle that confronted the seventeen million viewers of the "CBS Evening News" on Monday, January 23, 1988. Pitching for the hosts on their home field at Black Rock—the unofficial name of the CBS headquarters building in New York, derived from its architecture—was their ace, Dan Rather. The visitors were represented by then–presidential candidate George Bush.

The visitors were coming to the end of an especially tough road trip. They'd been battered early in the season by Owen Bieber, president of the United Auto Workers union, after an error-prone season's debut in the Soviet Union; they were dodging high hard ones tossed during the congressional hearings looking into the diversion of funds from the sale of missiles to so-called "Iranian moderates" to support a secret, and arguably illegal, war effort in Nicaragua; and they were being tarred with the label "wimp" by press and stalwart fans alike. They came into Black Rock badly needing a win.

Rather offered a tempting target. Heir to the Cronkite legacy, he was an accomplished journalist in his own right, with a reputation for a hard nose and a streak of feistiness. His run-ins with former president Richard Nixon during the Watergate period were legendary. Rather could be counted on to ask tough questions, and to stand his ground. For an effort by Bush to counter the wimp image, he was the perfect foil.

Indeed, reports had reached the Bush staff that, in the tradition of two heavy hitters from Texas, Rather might be gunning for the vice president, trying to get him on the defensive. More than that, Bush's advisers had a pretty good idea that Iran-Contra would be the ground on which the CBS anchor would choose to fight (far from making a secret of this, in fact, the network was actively promoting it), and Roger Ailes had offered suggestions on how to deal with the issue. It was Ailes, too, who reminded the vice president of Rather's brief walkout from the newscast the previous year in a fit of pique when a portion of the program was preempted for a sporting event, thereby creating seven minutes of dead air on the network, a point Bush ultimately used during the interview to throw his antagonist off balance.

And Rather, too, had a game plan, an agenda. Bush, after all, had been playing dodge-'em with the press for nearly two years, and in context, his statements on the Iran-Contra affair strained credulity. The negotiations required to bring the two men together had been difficult. In particular, unlike any of the other 1988 hopefuls to appear on Rather's program, Bush had insisted on a live interview. Historically, the implication of such an insistence was that the subject of the interview did not trust the journalist in question to edit a taped exchange fairly. To Rather, Bush's insistence on a live dialogue must have presaged a contentious session.

Rather spent the better part of that Monday huddling with the program's executive producer, Tom Bettag, and with other members of the staff. Together, they tried to anticipate different ways the vice president might react to pointed questioning, and how Rather should respond if, as they expected, Bush became aggressive. In effect, they rehearsed a variety of possible scenarios.

As Rather was opening the broadcast of the program from the anchor desk in New York, Bush crossed a hall in the Capitol from a small staff room to his own office in Room 214 on the Senate side of the building. There he settled into his chair and was miked by the network audio technician. Both men were in their corners, awaiting the bell.[1]

The exchange between Bush and Rather was preceded by a five-minute background report that focused on Bush's role in the Iran-Contra controversy. As the interview began, the vice president was seated at a desk with a monitor to his right, an ash tray and a large gavel directly in front of him, and a picture of Ronald Reagan on his left which had been turned so that it was in full view of the camera. An American flag was displayed upper left. Rather began the questioning as the camera zoomed in on Bush. The text of what followed is pre-

sented below in parallel columns, each line across the page representing a moment in time, to make clear, within the limits of the print
medium, the argumentative nature of this session.

Mr. Vice President, thank you
for being with us tonight. Donald Gregg still serves as your
trusted adviser. He was deeply
involved in running arms to the
Contras [the forces opposing
the government of Nicaragua]
and he didn't inform you. Now,
when President Reagan's
trusted adviser, Admiral
Poindexter, failed to inform
him, the president fired him.
Why is Mr. Gregg still inside
the White House and still a
trusted adviser?

Because I have confidence in
him and because this matter,
Dan, as you well know and
your editors know, has been
looked at by the ten-million-
dollar study by the Senate and
the House. It's been looked at
by the Tower Commission. The
Rodriguez testimony that you
put on here, I just think it's outrageous, because he was totally
vindicated, swore under oath
that he never talked to me about
the Contras, and, yet, this report
you're making, which you told
me, or your people did—you
have a Mr. Cohen that works
for you—was going to be a political profile. Now, if this is a
political profile for an election,

I have a very different opinion as to what one should be. But Don Gregg wor—works for me because I don't think he's done anything wrong. And I think if he had, this exhaustive examination that went into—was gone into—by the Senate and by the House would have showed it, and you've impugned the—my integrity—by suggesting, with one of your little boards here, that I didn't tell the truth about what—what Felix Rodriguez— you didn't accuse [pointing finger at camera] me of it, but you made that suggestion, and other people were in the meeting, including Mr. Nick Brady, and he has said that my version is correct. And so, I find this to be a rehash and a little bit—if you'll excuse me—a misrepresented— tation on the part of CBS, who said you're doing political profiles on all the candidates, and then you come up with something that had been exhaustively looked into.

Mr. Vice President, what we agreed or didn't agree to, I think you will agree for the moment, can be dealt with in another way. Let's talk about the record. You say that we've misrepresented your record. Let's talk about the record. If we've misrepresented your record in any way, here's a chance to set it straight. Now, for exa—

Let's talk about the full record. Yeah.

Right. Can I just set it straight on one [points finger at camera] count, because you implied

Where—where did we imply that, Mr. Vice President? [Quizzical expression.]

Mr. Vice Pres—

Well, Mr. Vice President— we want to talk about the record on this— because it—

the—the framework here is that one-third—one-third of the Republicans in this poll, one-third of the Republicans, and one-fourth of the people who say that, you know, they rather like you, believe you're hiding something. Now, if you are, here's a—here's a chance to get it out.

from that little thing—[smiles] I—I have a little monitor sitting on the side, here—that I didn't tell the truth. Now, this has all been looked into. This is a re-hash. Well, just here, on this board, where you had the idea that Bush says that he, didn't tell—didn't tell—d—Contra—didn't hear about the Contra's supply from Felix Rodriguez. Felix Redriguez testified under oath. He has been public, and you could have at least run a little picture of him saying that, "I never told the Vice President about the Contras." I'm asking for fair play, and I thought I was here to talk about my views on education, or on gettin' this deficit down.
Yes?

Well, let's—
Well, let's talk about the full record. That's what I want to talk about, Dan.

Yeah.

I am hiding something. You know what I'm hiding? What I told the president. That's the only thing. And I've answered every question put be-

POLITICS LEFT AND RIGHT 189

I do have one.
I—I have one.
You have said that if you had
known—you've said that if you
had known this was an arms-for-
hostages-swap
that you would have opposed it.
You also said that—

that you did not know that
you—
That wasn't a question, it was a
statement.

Let me ask the question, if I
may, first.

That's the president, Mr. Vice
President.

But—
That wasn't a question, Mr.
Vice President.

Mr. Vice President, you set
the—you set the rules for this—
this talk here. I didn't mean to

fore me. Now, if you have a
question, what is it?
Please.
Please fire away.

Yes.

Exactly. Now, let me—let me
ask [points finger at camera]—
may I answer that—directly?

Yes, it was a statement and I'll
answer it.

The president created this program, has testified—or stated
publicly he did not think it was
arms for hostages, and it was
only later that—
And that's me—'Cause I went
along with it because—you
know why, Dan? Because I—

worried when I saw Mr.—Mr.
Buckley—heard about Mr.
Buckley being tortured to death,
later admitted is the CIA chief.
So, if I erred, I erred on the side
of trying to get those hostages
out of there. And the whole
story has been told to the Congress.

step on your line, there, but you insisted that this be live, and you know that we have a limited amount of time.

Exactly, and that's why I— that's why I want to get my share in here on something other than what you want to talk about.
Please.

The president—the president has spoken for himself. I'm asking you to speak for yourself, which you have not been willing to do in the past. And, if I— if I may suggest, this is what leads people to say, quote, "Either George Bush was irrelevant or he was ineffective. He said himself he was out of the loop." Now let me give you an example—You said, "Ask a question."

Uh, may I explain "out of the loop"?
May I explain "out of the loop"? No operational role. Go ahead.

Now, you've said that, if you'd known it was an arms-for-hostage swap, you would have opposed it. You said the first thing you knew it was an arms-for-hostages swap was in December of 1986. Correct?

Exactly.

When the whole thing became briefed to me by Senator Durenberger and the proximity of arms to hostages much closer than we thought on these hearings that were—
Yes

But, Mr. Vice President, you went to Israel in July of 1986, and a member of your own staff, Mr. Craig Fuller, has verified, and so did the only other man there, Mr. Nir, Mr. Amiran Nir, who's the Israeli's top anti-

terrorist man.
Those two men were in a meeting with you and Mr. Nir not
once, but three times, three
times, underscored with you
that this was a straight-out arms-
for-hostages swap. Now, how
do yo—how do you reconci—
I have, sir.
How can you reconcile that you
were there, Mr. Nir underscored
three separate occasions that it
was an arms-for-hostages swap,
and told you you were dealing
with the most radical elements
in Iran. You were dealing
straight away with
the Ayatollah Khomeini.

Yes.

What *they* were doing.
Read the memo. Read the
memo.
What *they* were doing.

I was told what they were doing
and not what we were doing,
and that's the big difference,
and, Dan, I expressed my concerns and reservations about
that. That has been testified to
under oath by Mr. Poindexter.
And it's been confirmed that I
had reservations and spoke up
by Don Regan. In fact, he said
the other day that I expressed
'em to the president.
I don't discuss what I talk to the
president 'cause there's a principle involved—It has nothing to
do with Iran-Contra. It's a principle of confidentiality between
the president and the vice president.
Yes.

That's correct.

But, Mr., Mr. Vice President,
Mr. Vice President—
the president himself has said
he wants all the facts out. He

gave up such things as even his own diary. Every principal, including Secretary Schulz. He gave up some of it.

He did not give up his own diary. His diary, his brief. Well, Dan, let's be careful here because you're saying a political profile [raising his voice]. I will be careful. But I want to get my side of this out.

Yes. sir, I want you to be careful, Mr. Vice President, because the problem here, here is that you repeatedly sat in the meetings. You sat in a meeting in which Secretary Schulz, in the most forceful way, raise—registered his objections, and then you said you never heard anybody register objection—

I wasn't there, if it was the most forceful way. If it was the most forceful way—I've heard George Schulz be, be, very, very forceful; and, if I were there and he was very, very forceful at that meeting, I would have remembered that. I don't remember that. And that is what I'm saying.

Then how do you explain that you can't remember it and the other people at the meeting say he was apoplectic?

Well, then, maybe I wasn't there at that point.

You weren't th—you weren't in the meeting?

I'm not suggesting. I'm just saying I don't remember it.

I don't want to be argumentative, Mr. Vice President.

No [laughing]—no, sir, I don't

You do, Dan [laughing]. This is not a great night, 'cause I want to talk about why I want to be president, why those 41 percent of the people are sup-

And Mr. Vice President, these questions are designed—

Well, Mr—
Mr. Vice President—

Mr. Vice President, I think you'll agree that your qualifications for president and what kind of leadership you'd bring the country, what kind of government you'd have, and what kind of people you'd have around him is much more important than what you just referred to. I'd be happy to—

Well.

And I'm trying to set the record straight, Mr. Vice President.

I—I want you to talk about the record. You sat in a meeting with George Schulz. [Voice rising.] He got apoplectic when he found out that you were—you and the president were being party to sending missiles to the

porting me. And I don't think it's fair [repeatedly pointing finger at camera] to judge a whole career, it's not fair to judge my whole career by a rehash on Iran. How would you like it if I judged your career by those seven minutes when you walked off the set in New York? [Pause] Would you like that? I have respect for you, but I don't have respect for what you're doing here tonight.

Exactly.

Well, I want to be judged on the whole record.

And you're not giving an opportunity.

You invited me to come here to talk about, I thought, the whole record.

Yes, and I've given you an answer. [Smiles.]

[Voice rising.] He didn't get apoplectic. You have to ask Don

Ayatollah Iran—the Ayatollah of Iran! Can you explain how you were supposed to be the— you are, you are an anti-terrorist expert. We—Iran was officially a terrorist state. You went around telling. You—you— But Mr. Vice President, the question is —but you—you made us hypocrites in the face of the world. How could you— how could you sign on to such a policy? And the question is: what does that tell us about your record?

Regan—ask—ask—

I've already explained that, Dan. I wanted those hostages— I wanted Mr. Buckley out of there. Before he was killed, which he has been killed.

That was bad.
Well, had the same reason the president signed onto it. The same reason the president signed onto it. When a CIA agent is being tortured to death, maybe you err on the side of human life. But everybody's ad- mitted mistakes. I've admitted mistakes. And you want to dwell on 'em, and I want to talk about the values we believe in and the experience and the in- tegrity that goes with all of this, and what's—I'm going to do about education, and you're— there's nothing new here. I thought this was a news pro- gram. What is new?

Well, I had hoped, Mr. Vice President, you would tell us to whom you expressed your reser- vations—when you expressed them, and what your reserva- tions were.
What were the reservations?

Yes, I did.

Poindexter testified under oath.

His testi—reservation about getting the control of an opera- tion in the hands of a foreign

And you weren't concerned about sending missiles to the Ayatollah Khomeini?

power. Don Regan stated the other day, and I never heard a word of it on CBS, that the vice president, in the presence of the president, spoke up about his concern about the whole cover of an operation being blown and secret—and people that you're dealing with putting their lives in jeopardy.
And I felt that always on every covert, every covert action.

You weren't—

The president has explained that. The committee looked at that, and so there's nothing new on this.

Mr. Vice President, I appreciate you joining us tonight. I appreciate the straightforward way in which you've engaged in this exchange. Yet clearly some unanswered questions remain.

Fire on another one.

Are you willing—are you willing to go to a news conference before the Iowa caucuses, answer questions from all com— all comers.
I gather that the answer is "no."
Thank you very much for being with us, Mr. Vice President. [Smiles.] We'll be back with more news in a moment.

I've been at 86 news conferences since March—86 of 'em since March . . .

The elements of this little drama are by now familiar. For the candidate, who was carefully briefed in advance of his appearance by his media advisers (and who was coached with improvised cue cards written on a yellow legal pad by Roger Ailes, who stood next to the camera), it represented an opportunity to use Rather's customary adversarial posture in order to establish his own machismo. Thus, the episode was brought to near-confrontation by the implied distrust of the live interview and by Bush's goading Rather about a personally embarrassing action, his seven-minute walk-off. Indeed, not only would a confrontation in which he appeared clearly to be in control counter Bush's "wimp" image, it would appeal explicitly to the more conservative elements of the Republican party, where he particularly needed to strengthen his support. These conservatives had a general distrust of what they regarded as the Eastern-elite-liberal media, and a special dislike for CBS and Dan Rather in particular. By bearding the lion in his very den, Bush had everything to gain.[2]

For the journalist, it was an opportunity to pursue the sacred trust and, not incidentally, to wrap himself in the banner of the free press myth. Rather, we must recall, was free to select any topic he pleased for the interview, and to move from one to the next as seemed productive. That he saw this interview as an opportunity to nail down—at long last—what the vice president knew and when he knew it, is evident from the lead-in to the interview, the opening question, and the single-minded determination with which he pursued the Iran-Contra issue. This was, at all times, a matter of choice. As the colloquy made clear, the format may have been Bush's, but the agenda was Rather's.

Two purposeful decisions were at work here, and their product was high drama. The vice president got his confrontation, the anchorman got his. The candidate satisfied his constituency, the journalist his. While Mr. Bush may have protested that the information developed was not *new*, by every page in Dan Rather's book it was most assuredly *news*. Bad Day at Black Rock? Hardly. In the end, there were no losers on that January day. Rather and his colleagues professed, after some discussion, to be satisfied with their performance, while Bush, describing Rather in less than flattering terms, was heard to observe, "The bastard didn't lay a glove on me."[3] And that—from the perspective of the communication strategist—is the point. If both parties attain their respective goals, all the incentives point in the direction of continuing to play the game. Bush, by the way, was still flush with victory the following June, when, in an appearance on ABC's "Night-line," he kept referring to host Ted Koppel as "Dan." "It's Freud-ian," offered the vice president. "Next time," deadpanned Koppel, "call me Barbara."[4]

Be that as it may, it seems fair to ask, what did voters—the Ameri-can people in whose presumed interest such pageantry is ostensibly staged—learn from this heated little exchange? It is tempting, espe-cially on a close reading of the transcript above, to say they learned nothing. There is, in fact, little of substance in that text. But, then, substance was never the point. The real lessons of the Bush-Rather "debate" were that George Bush, in the role of a prospective presi-dent, was not afraid to demonstrate some backbone, and that Dan Rather, in the role of everyjournalist, would not be intimidated by authority. Both men enhanced their respective images.

◆ ◆ ◆ ◆

More and more, political debate in the United States reflects this em-phasis on image over substance. We have already explored at some length the reasons this is so. But most of that exploration has focused on the area we might think of as lying "upstream" in the rhetorical flow, near the headwaters of the political process—a region populated by politicians, strategists, journalists, and others who produce policies or accounts of policies for later consumption by the mass public. De-mocracy, however, by the very structure of the word, implies that *demos*—the people, those who live within the political system but "downstream"—will exercise the ultimate judgment on policy and personnel alike. And if any one word comes to mind for the way we have characterized "the people" to this point in our narrative, that word is "victims." The people, it appears, are the *objects* of political action, not its protagonists, the instruments of leadership rather than its beneficiaries. In this chapter, we will explore that issue more directly. We will examine whether, in a complex industrialized society like that of the United States, the people are able to meet their responsibilities, and whether, in an age of strategic political communication, it is even reasonable to expect that they do so. In particular, we will look at whether the growing use of manipulative communication has had an adverse impact on the free exercise of the prerogatives of citizenship.

The traditional way in which observers have approached this issue is from the perspective of one ideology or another. Liberals, conservatives, socialists, communists, and others have differing ideas about the nature of citizenship, the relation of the citizen to the state, and the civic duties that attach to those who reside within a given political system. These ideas tend to be more prescriptive than descriptive, and in some ways more idealistic than they are analytical. And, whatever their ideological assumptions, they focus more on the level of principle and policy than on process. *What*, they ask, do people think about politics? Are you concerned about the drug problem? About crime in the streets? What policies do you support for combating both? What is the appropriate role of government in doing so?

But, if our concern is to understand the role of strategic communication in politics, that may well be the wrong question, if only because it is not the question that is of primary concern to the strategic communicators themselves. They are interested instead in understanding not what but *how* people think about politics, and how they *feel* about it. Are you *afraid* of drug addicts and criminals in your neighborhood? Are you *comfortable* with the leadership the president is providing in attacking this problem? Is it important to you that George Bush is a wimp? That Dan Rather is biased, or Sam Donaldson rude? To communication strategists, the views of ideologues (or others) may be important, but their ideology per se is not. Substantively, the left-right continuum of the political spectrum is all but irrelevant. But a rather different left-right continuum—that of neurophysiology—is of central concern. Did he say neurophysiology? He did.

One interesting way of thinking about how and why strategic political communication can be so effective is, in fact, suggested by recent advances in neurophysiology, the study of the structure and function of the brain. Lawrence Burns once described the human brain as "a gelatinous three-pound lump of fat, connective tissue, spinal fluid, veins, and nerve cells—the last generating some twenty-five watts of total power."[5] Doesn't sound very promising does it? But over the last twenty years or so, scientists studying this rather unattractive organ have begun to unlock many of the secrets of human behavior. And more to the point, some of this research has found evidence of a phenomenon that the scientists call "hemispheric lateralization." That sounds like some sort of foreign policy doctrine that Henry Kissinger once thought up—"Ve vill adopt the doctrine of hemispheric lateralization to govern relations between the two sides in the Cold

War''; or, perhaps, like the Strangelovian notion of "MAD," or Mutually Assured Destruction—the idea that if both the Soviets and the Americans knew with certainty that they could blow one another to puppy chow, neither would be tempted to try it.

Hemispheric lateralization, however, is nothing quite so sinister or so frightening. What it means, in essence, is that the human brain seems to be divided into two sides—conveniently known as the left and the right—which differ systematically in their functions. The left brain is better at verbal and quantitative skills, and at deductive, rational, and analytical reasoning; the right brain is better at generalizing from complex patterns, and at creative, holistic, and intuitive reasoning. The left brain prizes the camera, the lighting, the script, and the director. The right brain prizes the movie. The question we might ask, then, is whether political activity is left-brain centered, with a consequent emphasis on logic and reason, or right-brain centered, with an emphasis on form and feeling.[6]

The thrust of strategic political communication efforts in recent years has been—in effect, and, arguably, in intent—to *assure* that for most people politics is and remains a right–brain-centered activity. That is the lesson of the Bush-Rather debate, of the Bush candidacy generally in 1988, and of most of the other contests, media events, strategies, and tactics we have described in these pages. Paint with pastels. Suggest, but don't say. Convey feeling more than logic, wholes rather than parts. It is this holistic, soft-edged message that we see in many campaign spots. It is this obscuring of detail and sanding of rough edges that underlies many political public relations strategies. In this sense, the era of strategic communication may be to politics what the impressionist period was to art.

Even when they take on a harsher tone, today's designer messages have a distinctive right-brain appeal. Consider, for example, a full-page advertisement for the National Rifle Association that ran in the *Washington Post* in June 1989—an advertisement that was refused by both *Time* and *Newsweek*. Headed ". . . The Right of the People to Keep and Bear Arms . . ." the page featured a large photograph of a bloodied Chinese demonstrator near the Great Hall of the People in Beijing surrounded by helmeted soldiers of the Peoples Liberation Army. "The students of Beijing did not have a Second Amendment right to defend themselves when the soldiers came," the text tells us. "All they had was the hope and dream of liberty. Because tyranny cannot tolerate armed citizens, these brave young Chinese could only hurl words and hold out empty hands against an army. . . . America's founding fathers understood that an armed people are a free people. . . . Free to rise up against tyranny. That's why the individual armed citizen remains one of democracy's strongest symbols.''[7] A very powerful visual image, and a very powerful message. But let's move over for a moment to the *left* brain. Just what is the NRA suggesting? That students with handguns should have fired on the tanks of the Chinese army? That the army, rather than put down such a display, would have been intimidated into condoning it? And even more to the point, what is the lesson for Americans? That students or others should go into the streets *armed with guns* when they feel the need to protest? What are the odds that the National Rifle Association endorsed that position in, say, Chicago in 1968? I can guess, can you? Clearly, this was *not* a left-brain message.

Not only do strategic communicators cast their appeals according to this biological one-sidedness, they even select their tools and tactics on the same basis. More often than not, television is the medium of choice. Typically, we attribute the popularity of television as a political tool to the tremendous reach of the medium, to the sense of immediacy its messages impart, and to its ability to convey rich visual imagery. All of these characteristics it does have. But television has another characteristic as well, one that may be especially appealing to strategic political communicators—not as a news medium, and not as an advertising medium, but as a medium per se, as a means of conveying information. Watching television, it turns out, may resemble no other human activity so much as it does being asleep.

Social psychologist Herbert Krugman and other researchers have, for about a quarter of a century now, been conducting studies comparing the ways in which people process information they receive from television with the ways in which they process what they receive from print.[8] These researchers have measured such factors as galvanic skin response and eye-blink rates—measures we encountered earlier in our discussion of testing the effectiveness of various messages—as well as the brain wave patterns generated by experimental subjects, each of these when people were engaged either in reading or in watching television. What they have discovered should not be a surprise. Reading, this research suggests, is a psychologically involving activity. It requires more or less full attention, but more importantly, it requires that the reader *contribute* to the message by giving it meaning. The task when we read is to receive abstract visual data—typically systematic patterns of black ink (collectively known as the letters of the alphabet) organized into irregular clusters (words) and set against a white background—and to interpret these by assigning them meaning based on our culture, past experience, and training. In the process, we ask questions about the message, and *we* supply the answers, often by conjuring up a visual image of the action being described. This relatively high level of psychological involvement is reflected in the patterns of skin temperature changes, eye blinking, and brain waves that characterize persons while they are reading. In addition, when reading, it is the reader himself or herself who controls the pace of communication—fast or slow—and the reader who retains the ability to select material for review—I'm going to skip this, but let me look at that again.

Television viewing, in contrast, is a psychologically passive activity. It requires less than full attention—sometimes much less—and, rather than requiring that the viewer contribute to the message, it may actually *prevent* this from happening. In television viewing, it is the medium that controls the pace, the medium that provides the texture, the medium that selects the questions that are asked, and the medium that provides the answers. It is the medium that determines what information we will review again (and again and again), and what information will go by so quickly that we are left only to wonder. "Let's take another look at the replay of that touchdown from a different angle. . . ." "One small step for man. . . ." In viewing television, rather than receiving too little data and being required, as it were, to fill in the blanks, we receive too much information and are required to let most of it rush past as we follow the main theme of the action. Here, the physiological data point to passivity, to an absence of psychological involvement in the processing of information from the medium.[9]

It was on Saturday that the strike turned nasty. As the picketing miners surged toward the gate, the strikebreakers in the old Ford pickup panicked. They had run this line before, and they feared for their lives, feared that the plant guards could not protect them. A shot rang out, and then another. The first body hit the ground at precisely 3:11 in the afternoon, and before it was over . . .

No, this was not a typesetting error, a misplaced paragraph from another book, or even a sneaky promotion for the writer's next opus. It was instead a little illustration to help make the point, a stylistic anomaly intended to call your attention to the nature of what you are doing right this moment. In reading the preceding paragraph, chances are that you conjured up a mental image of the event being described. How many miners there were. What the gate looked like. What color the Ford pickup was. What uniforms, if any, the guards wore, and how they were armed. Who fired the shot. Who and how many fell. Even, perhaps, whether it was rainy or sunny, warm or cold, dusty or muddy. There is *nothing* in the paragraph that answers *any* of those questions—or even identifies them *as* questions. But as you read, you filled in the image from your own repertoire of stereotypes. That is what is meant by active participation in receiving the information.

Now—and this is the best we can do since this book is not accompanied by a video—consider how this story would have played on, say, the CBS "Evening News" with Dan Rather. While a breathless Leslie Stahl stood next to a blood-stained patch of ground narrating, a tape would roll showing the highlights of the action—preselected according to the criteria of drama and conflict we have noted earlier. Brown-uniformed security guards with Uzis firing on scruffy-looking miners as a black 1965 Ford half-ton pickup with three occupants crashes through the gate and speeds away. Pan the six bodies lying in the dust outside the battered gate. Here with me now is the guard who fired the first shot. I seen 'em comin' at me and I knew that. . . . Back to you, Dan. Thank you, Leslie. In California, today, a circus elephant escaped from its handlers and ran headlong into an ice cream truck. Our Bruce Morton is on the scene and files this report. . . .

Here, the information is part of a larger pastiche whose whole sets the context of understanding—it is presented as news per se rather than as information *about* something—and there are no blanks. The questions that were raised by print are not inherently part of communicating the message via television. They are not questions at all. We know—if we care to—who, how, and how many. But—and this is the point—more often than not, we do not care to know this. What we want from the television portrayal of an event is not the detail, but a general sense of what has occurred, and we *can get* that general sense *without* the detail—something that is not possible with print, at least not with printed messages of phrase length or greater. So we sit back and watch the events unfold. The medium does the work. We let it. And that is the passivity that is reflected in the physiological measures of television viewing.

What this suggests—and what strategic communicators have long known—is that certain kinds of messages are best conveyed using print, and other kinds of messages are best conveyed using television. More particularly, if you want to get across substantive ideas, policy specifics, supporting rationales, television is not the place to do it. But if you want to convey feelings, holistic images, and general impressions, it most surely is. As Republican media consultant Robert Goodman has put it, ''Both advertising and television news are very controlling. They don't let you decide for yourself what to think. They tell you how to feel. The network news is theatrically produced to provide that feeling, which is exactly what [campaign consultants] try to do.''[10] This, for example, was precisely the strategy that the Bush camp employed at the St. Louis rally with which we opened this book. They published the ideas, specifics, and underlying rationales in a book which—it is reasonable to guess—they assumed no one would ever read. They then portrayed the *existence* of this book, stacked high on the podium, to make the holistic point that Bush *had* issue positions. This, together with the other parts of the event's packaging, played very well indeed on television. And that incident, as well as any, makes clear the very systematic way in which political communication strategists are directing more and more of their emphasis toward television, and through it toward the right brains of the American people.[11] In the 1990s, *this* will be the politics of the ''New Right.''

As this right-brain strategy comes to dominate political communication in the United States—and in many ways it already has—we can expect it to have serious consequences for the nature of political life in our society. These consequences follow naturally from the character of the information being communicated, information that is rich in texture but poor in detail, rich in images but poor in ideas, rich in feelings but requiring—*permitting*—no rational thought. Holistic, right-brain communication masks the true complexity of political reality behind a veneer of simplicity. And as the flow of complex information reaching the people declines, and the principal channel by which they receive it shifts from print to television, with its far less substantial psychological demands, the perceived need to perform sophisticated intellectual operations on political information—and later, the ability to do so—will atrophy. Eventually, even people's appreciation of the fact that politics *is* complex will decline. More and more people in the society will lack politically relevant skills, with the result that the political system itself, with—*because of*—its democratic trappings, will become more readily subject to manipulation by persons whose principal claim to power is not their intellectual prowess or even their good sense, but their command of the instruments of strategic communication.[12] Such persons will make the vital decisions that determine the fate of life on this planet. And we will not even notice—or, perhaps, we have not.

This is clearly a wide-ranging speculation, and certainly not an optimistic one. But it is one for which, if we cast our net broadly and make a few leaps of faith that exceed the scientific method, there is emerging some supporting evidence. Two items are particularly noteworthy in this regard. The first has to do with a loss of skill, the second with a loss of confidence.

The loss of skill is evidenced in the decline that has occurred since the mid-1960s in the performance of high school students on the standardized Scholastic Aptitude Test (SAT) and American College Testing (ACT) Program. Through the 1950s and early 1960s, for example, average SAT scores, which measure the aggregate verbal and quantitative skills of those taking the examinations, rose or held steady. Beginning in 1965, however, these scores began a secular decline. Nationwide averages on the verbal portion of the test, for instance, fell from 466 in 1967 (the tests are scored on a scale ranging from 200—tree stump level—to 800—fully flowering genius) to a low of 424 in 1981, before recovering marginally. That amounts to a decline (adjusting for the 200-point base score) of some 16 percent. On the math portion of the test, the average fell during the same period from 492 to 466, for an adjusted decline of 9 percent. Perhaps more to the point, during a roughly comparable time period, 1970 to 1983, scores on the social studies portion of the ACT examination declined from 19.7 to 17.1, or some thirteen percent.[13] And recall that the citizenship skills measured in 1988 by the National Assessment of Educational Progress were minimal. What that latter testing also determined, and what is of special interest in the present context, is that the civic knowledge that *was* extant among high school seniors within one year of voting age was overwhelmingly factual rather than conceptual, absent background or understanding—indeed, very much in the mold of the news accounts that dominate today's journalism.[14]

The interesting thing about these figures in context is that the starting point of the decline corresponds with the point in time at which our first television generation—those in our society who grew up throughout their childhoods with a television in their homes and who cannot remember when it arrived—reached the age of high school graduation. It was in the early 1950s that television became widely available, and within a decade that it was a fixture in nearly every household in the United States. Add fifteen to eighteen years to that, and you have a tempting explanation of the decline in verbal and mathematical—and, importantly, social studies—skills. The temptation becomes overwhelming when you add as well the realization that the average American high school graduate will, at the time of graduation, have spent 11,000 hours in the classroom and *15,000 hours* in front of a television set; that between 1967 and 1988 the percentage of those between the ages of eighteen and twenty-four who read the newspaper daily dropped from 71 to 55; and that the overall time the average American spends reading each week fell by a third during roughly the same period.[15]

The mid-1960s also mark another significant change in a potential indicator of the quality of political life in the United States—the confidence that Americans have in their political and social institutions. For many years, the Harris Poll has regularly asked a national sample of Americans to report the level of confidence that they feel in the leaders of such institutions as medicine, the military, higher education, major corporations, the Supreme Court, Congress, the executive branch of government, organized religion, the press, organized labor, and the like. Until 1966, the results of these surveys were stable, and reflected relatively high levels of confidence. Seventy-three percent of those polled in that year, for example, said that they had a great deal of confidence in the leaders of medicine, 61 percent in those of the military and higher education, and even Congress and the executive branch—never greatly trusted in the best of times—held the high confidence of more than 40 percent of the respondents. Within ten years, however, by 1976, every one of these institutions had fallen in esteem to roughly half its initial standing—or worse. The military fell from 61 percent to 23, major corporations from 55 percent to 16, the Supreme Court from 50 percent to 22, the executive branch from 41 percent to 11, and Congress from 42 percent confidence to 9—nine![16] And despite some slight movement in the years since, all of these institutions (and others) remain at fundamentally lower levels of public confidence to this day.

As we might expect, and as becomes especially clear when one looks more closely at the changes in specific results year by year, the decline in confidence is largely attributable to two historic events of primary importance—the Vietnam War and the Watergate scandal. Vietnam and Watergate—the two best real-life *television* dramas of the decade. Vietnam was the livingroom war—enemy ear counts piling up like so much roast beef at the dinner table—the war that was lost the day that Walter Cronkite declared it beyond victory. And Watergate was the soap opera to end them all—Watergate, The Movie—starring Sam Ervin, John Dean, Richard Nixon, G. Gordon Liddy, John and Martha Mitchell, and a cast of thousands, lurid tales of the lust for power. The *New York Times* may have been a central critic of the Vietnam War and the *Washington Post* a protagonist in the unfolding of the third-rate burglary that shaped what they *knew*, but it was television that brought both stories to the American people, and television that shaped what they *felt*. And what they felt was revulsion, disillusionment—in the word of the day, malaise.

But if it is easy to see what brought about the decline of confidence in American institutions during this period, it is more difficult to understand what has sustained the measures at such low levels in the fifteen years since. Here, too, though, television is a potential culprit. Note if you will the coincidence between the period of declining confidence in institutions and the introduction of image- and emotion-directed news styles by the news doctors. For it was also in the mid-1960s—at precisely the time when it was taking over from newspapers as the preferred source of news of national affairs for most Americans[17]—that television journalism began to separate itself from print journalism, to adopt a distinctive style intended to play to the perceived strengths of its own medium. That new style—the media's own version of strategic communication—played not on thought, but on feeling. We earlier described it as a "feel-good" approach to the news, but that was something of an oversimplification. The news itself was developed to convey feeling *per se*, whether good or bad, while the news *program*—the anchors, the graphics, and the like—was developed to make sure that the feeling the audience was left with at the end of the whole news *experience* was a good one. Indeed, the impetus for the eyewitness and similar news formats was the very fact that events were inherently worrisome. When they blended a greater emphasis on communicating emotion with an increased tendency to focus on drama and conflict, it is a small wonder that television journalists may have produced in their audiences the continuing crisis in confidence that the Harris Poll data reflect.

In this context, it is easy to understand the outpouring of antigovernment, and especially anti-Congress, sentiment reflected in such events as the 1988–89 effort of Congress to give itself and various officials of the executive branch a pay raise. The issue of the pay raise had been building for quite some time. Congress had shown an inability to pass a raise despite mounting evidence that low salaries were discouraging able people from entering government service and despite economic pressures on the members themselves, whose jobs required that they maintain two households. Conservatives, particularly on the Republican side, had used the pay issue as a target of opportunity to whip up anti-Washington sentiment—an effort at which they were easily successful. So Congress decided, with presidential concurrence, to establish an independent commission to recommend massive raises that it could then accept without so much as a vote. The commission recommended, in December 1988, that raises of 51 percent be granted, and President Reagan endorsed the proposal. It was in the bag.

Unfortunately for Congress, the bag its pay raise was in was of the Lipton Tea variety. A Gallup survey at the time showed that 82 percent of the American people opposed the raise, and many resented the fact that it might be achieved without a recorded vote. The catalyst in forcing a congressional vote, however—one whose outcome, like the many before, was predetermined—was an informal group of some twenty radio talk show hosts across the country who began an antiraise mass movement. Roy Fox of WXYT radio in Detroit is credited with starting what came to be known as the ''tea bag revolution''—listeners were encouraged to send to their representatives in Washington tea bags with the message, part George Bush and part American Revolution, ''Read my tea bag, no pay raise''—which quickly spread to other stations. Not all of these efforts were primarily political. Mark Williams of XTRA radio in San Diego conceded, for example, that ''these crusades are designed to involve people in the radio station. . . . They boost ratings''; but they were decidedly effective. Forced to a vote, the pay raise failed.[18]

One of those who emerged to lead this brief but effective taxpayer revolt, incidentally, was consumer advocate Ralph Nader. Nader appeared on the ''Pat Sajak Show'' to organize opposition to the raise. He asked viewers to call his office the next day to register their views, and gave out a telephone number for them to use. Unfortunately for Nader, the number he gave out was that of Campbell-Raupe, a Washington lobbying firm that supported the raise. After the first few calls, Campbell-Raupe began to answer their phone with a verse:

> If Congressman's pay is your gripe,
> Then the number you've dialed isn't right.
> 'Cause they work hard for you all the day and night,
> It's Ralph Nader who isn't so bright.[19]

More revealing still, however—and more troubling—is the approach that we have taken in responding to these problems once we have recognized them. If our students are not doing as well in school and on standardized tests, we "dumb down" the text books they use—lower their reading levels and strip out the most challenging content.[20] Or, almost more insidiously, we "teach to the test"—designing instructional materials and school testing procedures not in ways that will best prepare students to use what they learn in later life, but in ways that will best prepare students *to take the standardized tests.* Thus in some school systems, even in the earliest grades, students are taught to think in terms of distinct, mutually exclusive categories such as those they will encounter on the SATs, rather than in less structured and more creative ways. Closed-ended, multiple choice thinking replaces writing and conceptualizing, with results that have dismayed corporate recruiters in their pursuit of entry-level white-collar workers.[21]

And if our citizens do not have much confidence in their governmental and other institutions, well, let's make them feel better about such things. Jimmy Carter recognized the problem and had a plan to solve it: get the President closer to the people. The plan—put together by advisers Greg Schneiders and Barry Jagoda—included such elements as a televised "fireside chat," with the president clad in a sweater to show that he had turned down the thermostat in the White House to aid in combating the energy crisis of those years; a telethon from the Oval Office, with Carter taking telephone calls for two hours from some forty-two callers; town meetings modeled after those conducted by his predecessor, Gerald Ford, but including members of his cabinet; spending nights on the road or weekends with American families rather than in hotels; inviting ordinary citizens to White House functions; establishing a toll-free telephone number which citizens could call with policy suggestions; inviting the press to sit in his cabinet meetings; and even engaging in televised conversations with such prominent intellectuals as Saul Bellow.[22] These actions and plans moved cartoonist Gary Trudeau *(Doonesbury)* to create for Carter a fictional cabinet officer, the Secretary of Symbolism. Ultimately, however, Carter was not helped by making the White House a home, and he was reduced in the end to trying to cajole the American people out of their malaise. Even that failed when his presidency was taken hostage by the Ayatollah.

Ronald Reagan had a plan as well—quite a different one from Carter's. Where Carter had set about to demystify the White House and to make the president one of the people, the Reagans set about restoring what they saw as the dignity of the place and the job. They reintroduced pomp into White House circumstances, elegance into the presidency, and formality into all White House functions. Down home in Beverly Hills. Reagan also set about systematically restoring the authority of the president, a motive that undoubtedly contributed— along with the creating of a diversion from the deaths of American marines in Lebanon a mere three days earlier—to his decision to invade Grenada. Still, the polls held steady. People trusted Ronald Reagan—"revered" might be the better word—but not the institutions over which he presided.

The most significant shift in the balance from left to right that we have experienced in American politics over the last two decades, then, has less to do with conservative and liberal ideologies than with styles of presenting and receiving political information. During this period, we have seen the development and maturation of a new and highly sophisticated approach to politics, one dominated by communication strategies that employ, reinforce, and reward the lowest common denominator of citizens' political skills—one that threatens our society with the political equivalent of illiteracy. It has proven to be a pervasive phenomenon, infiltrating not only the recruitment and selection of our leaders, but their performance once in office, and affecting not only our domestic policy processes, but our foreign policy as well. We are like the victims in a Karl Malden commercial for American Express—our wallets have just been stolen and our vacation plans are in tatters. What will we do? What will we do? For that matter, what *can* we do?

Notes

1. Tom Shales, "CBS and the Heat of the Aftermath," *Washington Post,* 27 January 1988, pp. D1, D4.

2. David Hoffman, "Seeking to Keep Lead, Bush Carefully Calculates Words, Maneuvers," *Washington Post,* 4 February 1988, p. A18; and from a forthcoming book by Bob Schieffer and Gary Paul Gates as cited in *Washington Post,* 4 July 1989, p. D3.

3. Shales, "CBS," *Washington Post.*

4. Lloyd Grove, "In Turnaround, Bush Courts National Media," *Washington Post,* 13 June 1988, p. A6.

5. Lawrence Burns, "Anatomy of a Brain," *Harper's* 251 (1975), p. 6.

6. William Kitchen, "Hemispheric Lateralization and Political Communication," paper presented at the Annual Meeting of the American Political Science Association, Denver, Colo., September 1982.

7. *Washington Post,* 29 June 1989, p. C12.

8. The following offer a taste of this research: Herbert E. Krugman, "The Impact of Television Advertising: Learning Without Involvement," *Public Opinion Quarterly* 29 (1965), pp. 349–56; Herbert E. Krugman, "The Measurement of Advertising Involvement," *Public Opinion Quarterly* 30 (1966), pp. 583–96; Herbert E. Krugman, "Brain Wave Measures of Media Involvement," *Journal of Advertising Research* 11 (1971), pp. 3–10; and Herbert E. Krugman and Eugene L. Hartley, "Passive Learning from Television," *Public Opinion Quarterly* 34 (1970), pp. 184–90.

9. On a related point, the nature and consequences of this new kind of "experience," see Daniel J. Boorstin, "The Road to Diplopia," *TV Guide,* 14 October 1978, pp. 13–14.

10. Lloyd Grove, "TV News, Ad Images Melding," *Washington Post,* 20 October 1988, p. A25.

11. On the general point here see Douglass Cater, "The Intellectual in Videoland," *Saturday Review,* 31 May 1975, pp. 12–16; and Dorothy G. Singer and Jerome L. Singer, "Is Human Imagination Going Down the Tube?" *Chronicle of Higher Education,* 23 April 1979, p. 56.

12. Jarol B. Manheim, "Can Democracy Survive Television?" *Journal of Communication* 26 (1976), pp. 84–90.

13. United States Department of Commerce, Bureau of the Census, *Statistical Abstract of the United States 1987* (Washington, D.C.: 1987), p. 135.

14. Kenneth J. Cooper, "Test Suggests Students Lack Grasp of Civics," *Washington Post,* 3 April 1990, p. A5.

15. " 'OD'ing on the Tube," *Science News,* 9 July 1977, p. 25; and Robert J. Samuelson, "Does Anyone Read Anymore?" *Washington Post,* 2 May 1990, p. A23.

16. Portions of this series are published annually in Elizabeth Hann Hastings and Philip K. Hastings, eds., *Index to International Public Opinion* (New York: Greenwood Press). See, for example, p. 360 of the 1984–85 edition.

17. Television Information Office, *America's Watching* (Washington, D.C.: National Association of Broadcasters, 1989), p. 14.

18. Susan F. Rasky, "Fury Over Lawmakers' Raise Finds an Outlet on the Radio," *New York Times,* 6 February 1989, pp. A1, A12.

19. "Nader's Crossed Line," *New York Times,* 3 February 1989, p. A12.

20. Lawrence Feinberg, "Textbooks 'Themeless, Dull,' " *Washington Post,* 23 April 1988, p. A10.

21. For related arguments see Arnold Packer, "Our Schools Aren't Teaching What Tomorrow's Workers Need to Know," *Washington Post,* 19 July 1989, p. F3; and Cindy Skrzycki, "The Company as Educator: Firms Teach Workers to Read, Write," *Washington Post,* 22 September 1989, p. G1.

22. Dennis Farney, "Carter's TV Chat to Mark the Start of 'People Program,' " *Wall Street Journal,* 31 January 1977, p. 6; "President May Let Press Sit In on Cabinet Sessions," *Wall Street Journal,* 1 February 1977, p. 12; and "Dial-a-President," *Newsweek,* 14 March 1977, pp. 14–16.

10 ... SOME OF THE TIME

Bill Garrett, former editor of *National Geographic*, tells of a telephone call he received one morning in 1986. At the other end of the line was photographer Steve McCurry, whom he had recently dispatched to Manila for a planned photo essay on the Philippines.

"Bill," said the photographer, "you'll never guess where I am."

Garrett was not especially disposed to try.

"I am in Imelda Marcos's bedroom."

Garrett confesses that, at this point, a number of interesting questions flashed through his mind. With some trepidation, he settled on one.

"Does Ferdinand know you're there?" he asked.

"No," came the rejoinder. "I'm sitting here on Imelda Marcos's bed. The Marcoses have just left the palace and there is a big crowd outside, but for the moment there are just a few of us in here. . . . It's very interesting."

McCurry, it turned out, together with two other photographers, had found his way past the barricades outside the presidential palace, through a rear entrance, through the palace gardens, and into the palace itself. On the streets outside, rival masses of demonstrators were shouting their support of Marcos or Corazon Aquino, respectively, both of whom had been sworn in as president of the Philippines in competing ceremonies earlier that day. Rocks and tear gas filled the air. Inside, an eerie calm prevailed. Ferdinand, Imelda, and all of their principal retainers had left, and no one yet knew it.

Once inside the palace, McCurry came first to a chapel where he saw the Marcoses' servants praying—presumably for protection from the angry crowds outside—then to a banquet hall scattered with debris—trash, syringes, photographs, and clothing. Amid this detritus of the departed first family was an open attache case filled with pesos which was attended by two men, armed with M–16 rifles, who were stuffing money down their pants as quickly as they could. From the banquet hall, he walked out onto the adjacent riverbank, which was littered with burned and half-burned documents, then back inside and upstairs.

McCurry wandered through Ferdinand's bedroom, which he says "looked more like a hospital ward," complete with a hospital-style bed and an oxygen supply. There was also a large wardrobe filled with Marcos's campaign shirts. From the bedroom he went into the presidential study, where he saw a set of security reports about the condition of the country's television stations (which ones had been captured and which were still under Marcos's control), then on into Imelda's bedroom, which, he recounts, was noteworthy for its big sunken bathtub and large wardrobe. Shortly after he phoned his editor (it was actually picture editor Ellie Rogers he called—he forwarded the call to Garrett), people from the streets entered the palace and began looting the rooms. At 11:00, soldiers loyal to Corazon Aquino came into the building and evicted the uninvited guests.

Of particular interest to us are two documents McCurry saw on President Marcos's desk. The first was a telexed document from the U.S. State Department—he couldn't tell whether it had been sent to Marcos or intercepted by him—outlining the political situation in the Philippines. Marcos (or someone on his staff) had circled and underlined portions of the report. Things, it suggested, did not look good. The second, lying right beside it, was a memorandum from the president's media adviser telling him how to present himself on television so as to emphasize through his image the fact that he was still in control. It appeared that these two documents, in juxtaposition, were the last read by Marcos before he left.[1]

◆ ◆ ◆ ◆

The election of February 9, 1986, in the Philippines was an important one. Voters were offered the choice between retaining Ferdinand Marcos, who had held power in Manila for some two decades and whose regime was widely regarded as corrupt and self-serving, or replacing him with Corazon Aquino, the politically inexperienced widow of a former leader of the opposition to Marcos. But it was the event that led, circuitously, to the vote on February 9—the assassination of that former opposition leader, Benigno Aquino, on the tarmac at Manila's airport—that proved to be the true watershed of recent Philippine politics.

In August of 1983, Aquino returned to the Philippines from a self-imposed exile in the United States despite threats from the Marcos government to punish any airline that sold him a ticket. He was accompanied by correspondent Ken Kashiwahara of ABC News—who happened to be married to his sister—and a half-dozen or so other journalists, all of whom were prevented by Filipino soldiers from leaving the plane with him or photographing the scene. As Aquino began his descent from the plane, he was shot dead. To quell the uproar that followed, President Marcos went on television to deny that his government was in a state of crisis and to describe the murder of Aquino—whom he had regularly painted as a leftist—as an internal "Communist rub-out." Though an "assassin" with ties to Philippine Marxists was himself killed at the scene, all subsequent indications suggested that the murder was an action of the Philippine military, presumably acting at the behest of the president. It was, without doubt, the biggest mistake of Ferdinand Marcos's career.

The assassination of Benigno Aquino ignited a firestorm of opposition within the Philippines, and assured that Marcos would lose the support of his principal patron, the government of the United States. (This marked a major change in the American view. Only a few years earlier, at a state dinner in Manila, President Nixon had promised Marcos a seat on the very first passenger voyage to the moon![2]) It led to the unification, at least temporarily, of a fractured cluster of anti-Marcos political parties, and to the entry into the presidential race of Aquino's widow. And it led to the discrediting of the official election results themselves the instant that the government proclaimed Marcos the victor. In the Philippines, in February of 1986, that dog would not hunt.

Marcos's victory claims set off what soon came to be known as the "People Power Revolution," one in which flowers replaced bullets in the rifle barrels of the Philippine army as the people of the nation literally filled the streets, convincing the troops that the Marcos government had lost its legitimacy, and making any sort of military ma-

neuvering impossible. For the outside world, it was a battle of images—the authoritarian and corrupt Marcos versus the worthy Filipino
people. The Saigon boys were in Manila, and the myth of the op-
pressed people combating an unjust government was experiencing one
of its finest hours.

Aquino and her supporters dominated the extensive coverage of the
event provided abroad by the world press. Aquino was the amateur
reformer, the Jimmy Stewart of Filipino politics (Mrs. Aquino Goes to
Manila) come eyeball-to-eyeball with a smug and uncaring elite. It
was, in short, every journalist's dream of a fairytale revolution. For the
Filipinos, it was a battle of images versus reality, one in which words
were weapons. The president took full advantage of the government-
controlled media, especially television, to state his case and repeatedly
appeal to his partisans—of whom, it must be noted in fairness, there
were many—for their continued support. With the aid of his media
advisers and loyalists in the military, Marcos held out against enormous pressures. And in the end—which came on February 25, just two
weeks after the election—it was a battle that Marcos was destined to
lose. As the notes on the desk make clear, there are times when images—and in this instance, perhaps, self-delusions—simply must yield
to reality. And so it was that Ferdinand and Imelda Marcos slunk off in
the night, taking with them literally all the wealth they could carry, to
begin their own exile in the United States.

What can people—individually, in groups, or as a society—do to
confront, to defend themselves against, or even merely to cope with,
the increasing flow of political imagery and its consequences? Are
there, in fact, limits to the potential influence of strategic communication on political life?

Obviously, Ferdinand Marcos discovered at least one such limit.
Marcos put his trust in two things. He trusted television—from his
prime time appearance at the Washington Monument to the very last
hours of his regime, he relied on the power of that medium to secure
his hold on power. As a measure of his trust, Marcos held total control
of Philippine television. Of the five television stations in the country,
the government—which is to say Marcos—owned one, the Marcos
family itself owned three, and a Marcos crony controlled one.[3] Public
television, Philippine style. And he trusted guns—from the airport tarmac to the troops he hoped would sustain him against the "People
Power Revolution." But in the end, both failed him. Television failed

him because it was replaced by direct experience, and because it was overwhelmed by inexorable historic forces. The Filipino people *experienced* the shock of the Aquino assassination, the grief and anger that followed, the bitter and dangerous campaign, and the evident unfairness of the official result. After twenty years of economic and political stagnation and growing corruption, they were eager for fundamental change. Guns failed him because television failed him. The people filled the streets, placing flowers in the rifle barrels and garlands on the soldiers. They placed their bodies in the line of march. Confronted with such forces, manipulative communication may not be an effective weapon.

Even short of revolution, thank goodness, citizen action can be used to counter—or at least to reduce the evident rewards of—the excesses of strategic political communication. When Lee Atwater, at the time newly named chairman of the Republican National Committee and seen by Howard University's president as a point of entry to Republican political and economic support, was named to the board of trustees of Howard University in January of 1989, students at the nation's flagship traditionally black university were incensed. To them, Atwater was the person most responsible for what they perceived as the overtly racist appeal of the 1988 Republican presidential campaign. They responded by shutting down the school until Atwater resigned. Shortly afterward, James Cheek, the university's president of some twenty years followed suit.

But how often does citizen action rise to such levels? One central premise of strategic communication, of course, is that the public is generally not very interested in politics and does not want to get involved. Receiving political messages is a *substitute* for political action, in this view, and not a spur to it. And there is ample evidence supporting that notion. Indeed, such events as revolutions and mass demonstrations are rare, and it is probably a good thing that they are. That said, however, what protections against abuse of the power of strategic communication, short of mass action, do people have? Several possibilities suggest themselves, though in the end, none may provide an adequate defense.

One circumstance that might limit the potential effectiveness of strategic communication arises when some other person or group, whether out of antagonism or indifference, conspires against the communication efforts. One of the implicit assumptions we have been working with to this point, at least outside the competitive context of an election campaign, is that the communication environment—the setting that any given communicator is dealing with—is somehow neutral or benign. Sure there is a "marketplace of ideas," but yours—like all the others to be found there—has free entry. No one out there is actively trying the undermine the message, counter the image. But that, of course, is not necessarily the case. Sometimes one set of images is confronted by another, generated by opposing forces, and sometimes efforts to create images are, quite simply, sabotaged. In recent years, John Tower learned the first lesson; the government of Iraq learned the second.

John Tower, you will recall, wanted more than anything in life to be secretary of defense. He was given his chance by President Bush, even though it was clear from the outset that the Tower nomination would be a hard sell in a Senate filled with former colleagues who had, during Tower's years in that body—and especially as chair of the Committee on Armed Services—taken an intense personal dislike to the former senator from Texas, based, it is said, on his very cavalier manner. Bush delayed for months while the FBI investigated Tower's personal life, and he gave the nominee every chance to withdraw. Still Tower wanted that job, and the president felt he owed him the nomination. So it was that John Tower came before a jury of his peers. In the Senate hearings and debate, and in the media coverage of them, Tower and his supporters tried to portray the feisty Texan as the man singly best qualified by knowledge and experience to head the Department of Defense. But his opponents painted a different image, using a palette colored with public drunkenness, greed, and potential conflicts of interest. Tower, they implied, was a sot and a scum-sucking sleazeball. Back and forth it went for week after agonizing week as the closeness of the impending vote became clear. I won't touch a drop if I get the job, said Tower, indirectly lending credence to one of the principal charges against him. The only reminder of Scotland in the Pentagon will be my attitude toward defense spending. Scholar and statesman, proclaimed Dole of Kansas. Unsteady hand on the nuclear trigger, implied Nunn of Georgia. Tested and proven, said Hatch of Utah. Drunk and disorderly, said Hollings of South Carolina. In most political card games, drunk and dangerous will trump knowledgeable and experienced, and that is precisely what happened to John Tower. By the time the last mud had been slung, he could not have served effectively as secretary of defense even had he been unanimously confirmed—and that he was not.

The Iraqis learned a different but related lesson in the fall of 1988, as they attempted to refute charges that they were engaged in a campaign of genocide against the Kurds, an intensely independent ethnic group that inhabits the mountainous area where Iraq, Turkey, and Iran come together. Immediately following the cease-fire in its war with Iran, the Iraqi army undertook a major offensive against Kurdish mountain strongholds, driving a reported 80,000 refugees across the borders into the neighboring states. The Kurds claimed that their villages had been attacked with chemical weapons—weapons the Iraqis were known to have used against Iran in the earlier conflict. In order to disprove these charges, Iraq's Ministry of Information arranged a visit to the remote outpost of Zakhu, where, it promised, journalists could photograph and interview 1,000 Kurds as they returned from camps across the Turkish border. It was to be a media event that even Cecil B. DeMille might view with pride. Dozens of foreign reporters were airlifted to Zakhu, only to discover that "technical difficulties" at the border had prevented the promised crossing. The "photo opportunity" had been canceled. The Kurds, in declining at the last minute to participate, had simply used the opportunity to embarrass the Iraqis. Indeed, from the government's point of view, things went rapidly from bad to worse. At a second site, Dahuk, some 200 Kurds who had ostensibly just returned from Turkey said on being questioned by reporters that they had, in fact, never left Iraq. As if that were not enough, reporters beginning a helicopter tour from a military air base passed an army truck whose driver and passengers were all wearing gas masks—presumably for the chemical warfare that was not taking place. And in the end, the Ministry of Information confiscated dozens of videocassettes from foreign television crews *on its own press tour* to review footage of several dozen burned and leveled villages over which the government helicopters had passed.[4] All in all, not what one might describe as a productive day.

A clash of images, then, or a clash of wills over what the images will contain, can easily sidetrack a strategic communication effort, and the world is filled with persons and groups motivated to do so. As a result, there may be some protection afforded to society when the natural diversity of interests is reinforced by a broad distribution of image-making skills or sensibilities.

The Iraqi example just noted also suggests a second factor that can limit the effectiveness of strategic communication—the fact that not all would-be strategists are equally skilled—or, for that matter, well skilled. We have generally assumed to this point that those who practice the art of strategic communication know what they are doing, and are able to carry it off. But that is not always the case, and, as the Iraqis learned to their dismay, their failures can be costly. An example closer to home is provided by the Natural Resources Defense Council (NRDC) and its 1989 effort to generate and manage a crisis over the use of Alar—a pesticide of demonstrated utility but dubious safety—on apples.

Having concluded a study showing that, because they ate so many apples and drank so much apple juice, children were exposed to concentrated amounts of Alar, which posed what the group saw as a substantial health risk, the NRDC—an established and respected environmental group—hired a public relations adviser, David Fenton of Fenton Communications, to help it get maximum impact from the announcement of its findings. The plan: offer the story to CBS's "60 Minutes" on an exclusive basis. Simple. Straightforward. Effective. On a Sunday evening in February, Ed Bradley told an estimated fifty million people of the danger. NRDC followed up the next morning with a news conference where the group distributed copies of its report. Unfortunately for the NRDC, the strategy of exclusivity worked all too well.

For one thing, the Environmental Protection Agency, which, as might have been expected, was inundated with calls from anxious mothers, could not respond for nearly a week because the agency did not—as is customary—receive a copy of the study in advance. Result? One angry agency. In addition, reporters who regularly cover the NRDC and are generally sympathetic to its viewpoint, had to explain to their editors why they did not have the report, and had to write their own stories as mere follow-ups to the CBS broadcast. Result? Several angry journalists. Third, when *Newsweek* got hold of a draft of the report and planned a story in advance of the "60 Minutes" broadcast, NRDC had actress Meryl Streep contact Katherine Graham, chairman of the board of The Washington Post Company, which publishes *Newsweek,* and then its editor-in-chief, Richard M. Smith, to try to kill the story. When that failed, the organization contacted all of the scientists and others who were reviewing its research, advised them of

Newsweek's intention to write a story on the study, and asked them not to discuss the contents of the report, even in the most general terms, with reporters. Result? One angry news weekly. And finally, as the broadcast date neared, NRDC itself provided drafts and executive summaries of the report to the *Washington Post,* the *New York Times,* and the Associated Press, and NRDC executive director John Adams telephoned CBS producer David Gelber to say, effectively, that he was breaking the agreement on exclusivity. Result? Even CBS—in whose interest all of these other parties had been alienated—even CBS was angry.[5] If you think it is not nice to fool Mother Nature, just watch out for Mike Wallace. Still, it appears that Fenton himself never got the message. In a lengthy memo he later circulated to interested parties, he celebrated the stir over Alar. "Usually," he wrote, "it takes a significant natural disaster to create this much sustained news attention for an environmental problem. We believe this experience proves there are other ways to raise public awareness for the purpose of moving Congress and policymakers."[6]

Even those we have come to expect to demonstrate great competence in news management sometimes slip up. President Bush, for example, once scheduled a visit to the Amish country of Pennsylvania, where he hoped to demonstrate the vulnerability of even the most traditional cultures to the threat posed by drugs. The centerpiece of the trip was a highly telegenic meeting between the president and Amish leaders clad in their customary black garb. *Great* pictures. Unfortunately for Mr. Bush, however, the religious tradition of the Amish banned television cameras from the event. *No* pictures. Similarly, during his 1989 visit to China, Bush's staff scheduled him for a photo opportunity in Tiananmen Square. His car drove into the square and stopped at a predetermined point where he could be shown with a giant poster of Mao Zedong as background. *Terrific* visuals. But, alas, the event was scheduled at an hour that ruled out network coverage at home. *No* visibility. Even Ferdinand Marcos, who, you will recall, scheduled his 1982 Washington welcome for prime time in Manila, remembered that little detail. And when Bush decided to join the international effort to control chlorofluorocarbons—a major change in environmental policy—he made the announcement in the middle of an unrelated ceremony, and it made scarcely a ripple in the news. New Right (both ideologically and neurophysiologically) House Minority Whip Newt Gingrich's comment on such lost opportunities was right to the point. "This," he said, "is a print administration, not a television administration."[7] His is a view that might help to explain the replacement, less than a year into the Bush administration, of Steven Studdert, the aide charged with orchestrating the president's public appearances, by Las Vegas advertising executive Sig Rogich, described by 1984 Reagan campaign head Ed Rollins as "first rate on television, first rate on image."[8] Indeed, Rogich's importance to the president was amply demonstrated in February 1990, as the presidential entourage prepared to depart on Air Force One for a much-ballyhooed drug summit in Colombia. While Attorney General Dick Thornburgh, Drug Enforcement Administration head John C. Lawn, and Assistant Secretary of State for International Narcotics Matters Melvyn Levitsky were left off the passenger manifest, Rogich went along for the ride.[9]

A third potentially limiting factor in the conduct of strategic communication campaigns is blatancy—the extent to which efforts at manipulation themselves become public. Most of the time, most people—journalists and public alike—pay little direct attention to communication strategies, and as a result, do not see themselves as victims of attempted manipulation. But once in a while, a communication effort surfaces, and when that happens, all bets are off. In our study of international political public relations, Robert Albritton and I found a classic example of this phenomenon during the reign of Shah Mohammed Reza Pahlavi in Iran.[10]

In March of 1975, Iran's news image in the United States—in the terms of our study, which I described earlier—was positive, but low in visibility. Over the past year, there had been a good deal of discussion in the press about the country's efforts at modernization and economic development, its cooperative relations with American banks and defense contractors, its emerging importance as a regional power—the "policeman of the Gulf"—and its military ties to the United States. There was limited discussion of corruption, harsh treatment of political prisoners, and human rights violations, but this was generally in the background. The objective of strategic communication in such circumstances would typically be for the government in question to take steps to raise its visibility and reinforce its positive image, and that is apparently just what the Shah set out to do. Through the government-owned national airline, Iran Air—a common type of channel for such efforts—arrangements were made to hire the American public relations firm of Carl Byoir & Associates to undertake the promotional campaign.

Unfortunately for Byoir, at about the time it began its effort, events and images turned against Iran. The Northrup Corporation was implicated in the bribing of an Iranian prince, terrorist attacks resulted in the deaths of several American military and diplomatic officials; and Iran became, for the first time since developing its oil wealth, a net borrower in international financial markets. Iran gained in visibility in the news, but its image became sharply more negative. Six months into the campaign, Iran hired a second consulting firm, Ruder and Finn, and Byoir resigned its contract in a huff.

During Ruder and Finn's first months on the job, the volume of news coverage of Iran dropped significantly—this, you will remember, was a desirable outcome under the changed conditions of high visibility and high negatives—while accounts appeared in the American press on such topics as the development of the country's urban centers, the importance of United States corporations in the Iranian economy, the stability and continuity of the government, steps toward ending corruption, and even the Shah's plans to reconstruct a reception hall first built by the famous Persian ruler Xerxes. Not bad for starters. But then the roof fell in on the effort.

In January of 1976, the *New York Times* published the fact that Marion Javits, whose husband Jacob coincidentally sat on the Foreign Relations Committee of the United States Senate, was employed by Ruder and Finn on the Iranian contract. In fact, she had herself been the one to bring the contract into the firm for an expected fee of $67,500. The *Times* followed with fully fourteen related stories, many on the front page, and Senator Javits, by his own account greatly embarrassed, pressured his wife to resign from the account.[11] While this was not good for Ruder and Finn, it was a disaster for the Shah's government, which saw its news image return to the same dizzying heights of negativity that had occasioned the switch in consultants. Months of successful work wiped out in an instant. Worse than that, the United States government began to talk about cutting off arms shipments to Iran, which was looking more and more like a pariah among nations. At this, the Shah became so frustrated that he told *U.S. News and World Report* that Iran "can hurt [the United States] as badly if not more so than you can hurt us" if the flow of American military support were cut. Ten days later, Ruder and Finn resigned its contract.

The key event here was the revelation of the Marion Javits connection—made all the more titillating by the appearance of a conflict of interest which it created. This revelation—and the extensive history of Iran's communication campaigns that accompanied it in the press—made clear to journalists and the public the extent of the manipulative effort. As a result, people raised their defenses, and the effort backfired. Such instances are rare, but they do occur.

An interesting variation on this theme occurred in Denver during a local debate in May of 1989 over whether or not to build a new airport to serve the city. A local business group hired Roger Ailes, who had designed several of the most strongly negative advertisements of the 1988 Bush campaign, to prepare a media campaign against airport development. Within hours of the time the first Ailes spot aired, however, pro-airport forces called a news conference to denounce Ailes as a "slash-and-burn media manipulator" and a "master of the slick and sleazy"; and, not incidentally, to link his clients and their viewpoint to this characterization.[12] These charges may have had some impact, as the airport proposal was subsequently approved by voters. They clearly became the model for a political tactic, attacks on the records of opposing consultants, that has been widely adopted since then, for example, by Senators Paul Simon (Democrat of Illinois—versus Roger Ailes) and Mitch McConnell (Republican of Kentucky—versus Democratic consultant Frank Greer) in their 1990 races.[13] People do not like to feel that they are being taken advantage of, and when, on rare occasions, they see such efforts at work, they will rebel.

Then, there is the more general influence-limiting inertia of public opinion itself. When it comes to our attitudes about politicians or foreign countries or government policies or the media—or anything else, for that matter—most of us tend to be small-"c" conservatives: we like what we have and we do not intend to change it. We tend to be comfortable with who we are, and our political and other opinions make up a good bit of our individual characters. Those opinions define us for others—they know who we are by the opinions we display—and they define us for ourselves as well. I am a Republican. I don't trust the Communists. I was in sympathy with the prodemocracy demonstrators in China. I feel good about myself, and I will defend my views against all comers.

From the perspective of a would-be strategic communicator—especially one who would like to persuade us to a different point of view—

this can be a serious problem, rather like planning an assault on a mountain fortress using grappling hooks and rope ladders when you know that the fortress is supplied with unlimited quantities of boiling oil. A frontal assault simply will not work. Instead, it is necessary to induce in the defenders a false sense of security, then to lure them out to work the fields below the fortress. Away from their protective shelter, they are quite vulnerable. And that, in fact, is essentially what many strategic communicators do. Rather than *persuade* people of the correctness of a given viewpoint—where persuasion implies a conscious process of decision making—they induce people to lower their guards, or they "attack" at the least expected times, aiming not to persuade, but to *influence* or to *manipulate*—both terms that suggest a more passive audience. This avoidance of the defenses against persuasion, and the careful insertion of strategic messages to just the right people at just the right time in just the right way, is the theme that unifies many of the practices we have examined here.

This approach tends to work, not because people have no defenses against it, but because they seldom man the barricades. When it comes to matters of politics, most people demonstrate a fairly high degree of disinterest. While it is true that we tend to *have* political opinions, most of us tend not to wear them out through overuse. Other things—home, family, job, church, the latest woes of the Cleveland Indians—these things are simply more important. We read the news, as noted, not to *be* informed, but to *feel* informed. To fulfill our civic responsibility. To maintain our sense of attachment to the political life of our society. And that is enough.

What this means is that, for most of us—even many who find politics *interesting*—such matters do not matter, at least not much. So we simply do not bother thinking much about them. We take in the images and messages from the news and other sources, but we do not consciously process them. We do not defend against them, because we do not see ourselves as under attack.

The point here is that a personal defense against manipulative communication—in the form of individual resistance to persuasion—is available if we choose to use it. That we do not choose to do so very often creates opportunities for the strategic communicators. That the option is there, to be called upon in times of evident need—as in the Iran-Javits controversy—acts as a constraint. But many less blatant efforts pass us by unnoticed.

Finally, though it is still quite rare, there is a growing realization—but not yet a resentment—among journalists themselves that the media are vulnerable to the trivializing influences of strategic communication. On the one hand, columnist David Broder has noted that "the forces that shape history are people and ideas. Journalism focuses on the former, believing that 'names make news.' But often it is the ideas whose consequences are more significant."[14] What journalists need to do, Broder seems to suggest, is to treat news makers less as personalities per se, and more as representatives of specific policies or ideas, and, by extension, events less as isolated happenings, and more as components in a larger political context. That sounds pretty good.

Indeed, with respect to elections, Broder has suggested, and even lobbied his fellow journalists for, a five-point program to overcome cynicism and to restore what he terms "sanity" to the process. Broder suggests that journalists should reclaim from candidates and consultants the determination of the campaign agenda, inoculate voters against negative tactics by reminding them of how they were manipulated the last time around, interrogate the candidates mercilessly about all messages issued in their names, investigate every advertising claim made by a candidate, and denounce those judged through the previous steps to be engaged in demagoguery.[15] Broder helped to convince his own paper, the *Washington Post*, to provide readers with comparisons of the performance of particular political consultants during the 1990 election season as they worked for candidates in differing states and regions.[16]

In at least one respect, Judy Woodruff, chief Washington correspondent for the "MacNeil/Lehrer NewsHour," has gone even further. Pointing out the obvious—that journalists have what strategic communicators want: control over credible access to the audience—she suggested that, when manipulative efforts get out of hand, journalists should pull the plug.[17] Just say, "No!" No issues, no air time. No substance, no exposure. Force the politicians and their backroom strategists to conform more closely to the content of the democratic myth rather than merely to its rituals. Indeed, in the summer following the 1988 presidential race, ABC News considered one such policy, that of assigning camera crews to cover such photo opportunities as Bush's visit to the flag factory or Michael Dukakis's rather comical ride in a battle tank, but declining to air the resulting footage unless the candidate also makes himself available for questions.[18] Making such judg-

ments is a risky business, rife with the potential for a fundamental
conflict between politicians and journalists that could, as have other
such conflicts in the past, damage the media as much as their ostensi-
ble adversaries—but it is within the range of possibilities.

Consultant Victor Kamber has called not only for better news, but
for more of it. He would require all television stations to carry at least
two hours of news each day without commercials on the assumption
that the extra time would be devoted to matters of substance.[19] Similarly, another journalist, Paul Taylor, has suggested that each presidential candidate in 1992 be given five minutes of network air time
every night during the campaign, which he or she is *required* to fill by
speaking to the camera, while still others would compel candidates, as
a condition of accepting public financing, to participate in restructured
and more substantive televised debates.[20]

But, as usual, there is a second hand. (Wasn't it Harry Truman—
frustrated with the diversity of economic opinion and advice he received—who said he hoped one day to meet an economist with only
one hand?) In this case, it is captured in a letter to the *Washington Post*
from political consultant Greg Schneiders, who dismissed Broder's
suggestions (and, by extension, the others) as the equivalent of a
"neighborhood watch" approach that addresses symptoms rather than
causes of the problem.[21] A headline that appeared in the same newspaper some four months into the Bush presidency read: "Press Corps to
Bush: Manipulate Us!" Gerald Seib, White House correspondent for
the *Wall Street Journal*, quoted in the *Post* article, described the frus-
trations then being expressed by his colleagues, who had become ac-
customed to the careful staging of presidential appearances in the
Reagan White House: "People who did stories about the cynical, manipulative Reagan presidency," he observed, "are now complaining
about the unfocused, unpackaged Bush presidency. . . . If you try to
manipulate the press, you'll be accused of manipulation. If you don't,
you'll be accused of incompetence."[22] Sometimes, it seems, the pursuit of the sacred trust takes some strange turns.

Where, then, are we to find the white knight come to rescue our
political process from the onslaught of strategic communication? Of all
of the potential lines of defense—the force of events or direct experience with them, the countervailing machinations of opposing forces,
the uneven distribution of strategic communication skills, the effron-
tery felt by the public when manipulative efforts are exposed, and

journalistic recognition of the dangers inherent in the myopia of the profession—none, by itself, seems to hold much promise. That is not, to be sure, an optimistic view, but it is, I think, a realistic one. Consider the options.

Historical forces on a scale that can move whole societies are, at least within the confines of the present argument, virtually beyond control, and are uncommon in any event. Even where they can be channeled or directed—as through the adoption of development policies that encourage migration to or from urban areas—the factors that define newsworthiness are not readily subject to manipulation if they are present at all, and cannot be counted on in the near term to offset the conduct or portrayal of specific people or events. Historical forces move nations—or prevent them from moving—but in themselves make no "news." Urban migration—though it changes the lives of millions—does not make a sound, let alone a sound *bite*.

Personal experience with events, obviating the need of people to depend on media accounts for their knowledge and understanding of events, and thereby depriving strategic communicators of the principal tools of their trade, has unlimited potential as a defensive mechanism, except for one small detail: no one individual can possibly have enough personal experiences to significantly limit his or her dependency on mediated information. I do believe that Neil Armstrong walked on the moon—did take a "giant leap for mankind"—but I do not, *cannot,* know that for a fact except as it is conveyed to me by the media. And as much as I may travel or as many interesting people as I may meet, I cannot be everywhere at all times. In fact, most of the time I am at home or at work performing the very mundane tasks that make up the greater part of each of our lives. The potential of individual experience as a defense against strategic communication can *never* be fully, or even significantly, realized. It is, for all practical purposes, mere illusion.

The notion that opposing forces presenting competing images can defend the polity against the manipulations of strategic communicators—a media-era mutation, perhaps, of the so-called marketplace of ideas, and one possibly captured best in the so-called fairness doctrine, which calls upon broadcasters to provide equal treatment of opposing views—derives its appeal from the idea that we live in a so-called pluralist society, one in which the diversity of the people is reflected in a plethora of groups organized to represent specific interests or viewpoints. Those who see our political system in these terms argue that because all, or at least most, views are represented by one or more groups, and because all groups are given a voice in decision making, the policies we pursue will be broadly representative of the public interest. In the present context, this would translate into a veritable symphony of political talk, with many voices blending—albeit with some solo performances here and there—harmoniously into consensus. Leaving aside the obvious and most asked questions about this notion of pluralism—Are there enough voices to represent all interests? Are the voices equally loud? Is everyone working from the same piece of music?—relying on a mixture of competition and cooperation between opposing forces to protect ourselves from the adverse effects of strategic communication overlooks one thing: *all* of these opposing forces— or surely all of those that are likely to be effective—use the *same* devices. *All are strategic communicators.* In effect, then, while relying on opposing forces to offset one another may broaden our repertoire of stereotypes, it does not counteract stereotypic thinking. While it may increase the number of images available, it does not devalue image *making.* To the contrary, it positively encourages it. No, the road to salvation does not lead through Pluralist Gap.

Nor—for all the oft-heard complaints about the poor quality of workmanship in American-made products, can we rely on the failings of our strategic communicators to protect us. Contemporary strategic communication is a home-grown industry whose basic technology is still developed and controlled principally in the United States. We have a high-quality work force and an industry structure that, for all its recent mergers and acquisitions, continues to reward innovation and entrepreneurial skill. Training programs run by political parties and others are proliferating, and the export market is booming. As in any industry, some firms provide better products than others. But we cannot hope or expect that low-quality providers will flourish, predominate, or even long survive in the current environment. This is not an activity that will, if left to its own devices, self-destruct.

For its own part, public recognition of manipulative efforts is very limited, and comes to the fore principally during the biennial periods of political campaigning. Stop the negative ads. Say more about the issues. Watch out for those Republican handlers, says Dukakis (through his handlers). It is time for this bird to fly on its own, says would-be Vice President Quayle. But—leaving aside the not insubstantial disingenuousness of such comments—these flurries of concern miss the mark. When taken as part of the overall phenomenon of strategic political communication, political campaigns are anomalies. They are highly public, event-specific, behavior-directed efforts. They are designed to be seen, to be recognized as competitive with one another, and to be related to an expected citizen action—voting—on a certain date, election day. Then they disappear. And what happens the rest of the time (and even while these campaigns are in progress)? Laws are passed, policies are set, nations interact—*all with the aid of strategic communication*. And in those instances, the science—and it is that in part—of strategic communication is devoted to *avoiding* public notice, to finding ways *around* the prospective barriers. The record is one of remarkable achievement. No hope here.

Nor are journalists—Broder and a few others to the contrary notwithstanding—likely to provide the ultimate answer. For in the end, even the most insightful and altruistic of journalists will draw the line at actual participation in political events. Journalists are, by definition, witnesses to events, not protagonists in them, and in a real and legitimate way, a more active involvement would, at least within the context of their structure of professional values, constitute a conflict of interest. Journalists can identify problems—at which they tend to be quite good—and point the way to solutions—at which they are less good—but their training and inclination limit them to reporting on the responses of others and, except as it pertains directly to journalistic practice, avoiding taking action themselves.

No, given the present set of incentives and institutionalized patterns of behavior, none of these factors alone will be the determinant of fundamental change in our way of doing politics, and none is even likely to provide the impetus for such change. But that is not to say that each of them, in its own way, cannot contribute to a solution. The key is to find some device to encourage change in all of them together.

While that may sound like a big job, Americans do have some recent experience in building, or in some cases *re*building, democracy. That experience has come in Latin America, Eastern Europe, and elsewhere—places where neither institutions nor, in most cases, the political culture offered much foundation for democratic practice, but where expressions of popular will mandated political change. Through a combination of private and governmental action—through corporations, citizens groups, party organizations, and such government-supported agencies as the National Endowment for Democracy—the United States has nurtured new democracies around the world. And while the final results of these manifold experiments are not yet in, many of the early returns look promising. Larry Hansen, a long-time student of such issues who prepared a report on the state of American democracy for the Joyce Foundation and the Aspen Institute, came to the conclusion that something of the same response might work at home.[23] That, it seems to me, is an idea worthy of exploration.

Perhaps the place to start is with a domestic counterpart of the National Endowment for Democracy, one whose purpose is to identify and foster ways of improving the quantity and quality of citizen participation in political life, enhancing the quality of our political dialogue, raising the standards of practice in political campaigns and politics generally and in the journalistic coverage of these events, and in general restoring the rewards of public service through politics so that more thoughtful, courageous, and productive people are encouraged to compete for public office. Perhaps what we need to do is to establish an Institute for American Democracy.

To be sure, there are many individuals and groups in all parts of the political system—even among the strategic communicators themselves—who are already addressing the issues raised in this book. David Broder, whose journalistic effort we have described; the Public Agenda Foundation, which for some years has stimulated local discussion of national issues; Les Francis and Larry Hansen, who have begun an effort to improve practices within the professional community; local groups of political activists around the country. These folks and others have pointed the way. In one six-week period during the spring of 1990 alone, at least nine major conferences—bringing together journalists, academics, political consultants, and others—were held to address some of the questions we have raised here—especially those relating to political campaigning.[24] In effect, there is abroad in the country something of a mass movement—a movement to restore meaning to American democracy, to reassert the importance of substance over appearance—but it is a movement that has not yet taken shape, found central leadership, or, importantly, settled on a specific objective.

Without each of these efforts and others like them, a return to the politics of substance cannot occur. They are critical. But the weakness of relatively unorganized and more or less amorphous movements like the one we see at the moment—whether aimed at political reform or some other objective—is that they come and go; historically they tend to have had little staying power. And the shortcoming of specific efforts at reform—whether of political campaigns, news practices, or citizen participation—is that, in isolation, they too will wither as the principal movers and shakers—and the mass public—lose interest.

Yet the need for political reform is both deep and enduring. It encompasses not merely the activities of political consultants, candidates, or politicians in general, but the basic political orientations of the American people. And addressing it will require more than talk, or even legislation; it will require fundamental political education on a grand scale. For that reason, the best near-term objective toward which people concerned about the deleterious effects of a politics based in strategic communication might strive is to find some way of institutionalizing their movement—of converting the present high levels of awareness and frustration extant among some of the people into an organization with staying power for all of the time. That is where an Institute for American Democracy—in effect, a public trust charged with safeguarding and enhancing our 200-year investment in people power—begins to make sense.

The structure and functioning of such an institute would necessarily reflect the conditions that have given rise to it. First and foremost, it would need to be independent of both government and all partisan politics. This is the case for the simple reason that the objective of the institute is to encourage—in an even-handed manner—democratic reforms throughout our political system; the parties and government, with their associated networks of consultants and lobbyists, will be among the primary targets of the reform effort. When the fox is in the henhouse, egg production tends to decline. At the same time, though, it is a fact that politicians do, and will continue to, run the political system. They are the ones who might be asked to implement some number of the proposed reforms—and their exclusion from its deliberations would not merely deprive the institute of their expertise, but would assure that few would take its recommendations seriously. In practical terms, this probably means that each major party should be equally represented in whatever form of governing board might be developed, but at the same time, that together they should not hold a majority of votes. Other votes might go to journalists, academics, foundation leaders, citizen representatives, and the like. It also means that the chief executive of the institute must be insulated from day-to-day political pressures. Perhaps the best model here would be that of the comptroller general of the United States—the official who heads the General Accounting Office, the congressional watchdog agency—who is appointed by the president (subject to congressional approval) to a nonrenewable term of fifteen years. And it means that the budget of the institute must be insulated from politics as well. This might be accomplished by supporting the activities of the institute through a tax checkoff system similar to that presently used for the public financing of presidential campaigns, through foundation grants, or by some similar device.

As far as its functions are concerned, the institute might undertake a variety of programs. Outreach, for example, might be accomplished through programs modeled after those of the Public Agenda Foundation, which include raising the quality of citizens' participation in policy making by giving them substantive information about policy choices and a forum for developing and expressing meaningful opinions. Research might be accomplished through grants to scholars whose work addresses ways to improve the quality of leadership and political participation. Education in the political process might be accomplished through the development of television series and classroom materials similar to those developed on a variety of other subjects by the Annenberg/CPB Project. Broadening the base of institutional support for democratic reform might be accomplished by coordinating conferences or other activities of foundations or citizens' groups. And political pressure for change, without which the institute would be ineffective, might be generated through the judicious release of position statements designed to call attention to shortcomings in political practice and violations of the democratic spirit. Perhaps the institute might even issue an annual grade—what Hansen has termed a National Assessment of Democracy—summarizing the performance of the American political system. But most important of all, what an Institute for American Democracy might accomplish would be to serve as a constant and a steady voice for meaningfulness in political life. It might make the demand for substance a real and potent political issue over a long enough time to make a difference.

In the final analysis, what such an institute or any alternative effort would *have* to accomplish would be to find ways of restructuring the current incentives that promote strategic political communication, of giving each player—political consultants, politicians, journalists, the public—his or her own reasons for doing things differently. For only then will new thinking replace old—really thinking replace not thinking—in our daily political life. Only then—when all of the key players have their *own* reasons for changing—will their needs to fulfill their respective responsibilities truly equate with the needs of the American people for political survival in the face of coming political challenges. Without that, the Institute itself—or any other initiative we might take—would be no more than an empty symbol of the urge toward a renewal of meaningful politics.

In this latter regard, a 1987 exchange in the White House rose garden between White House reporters and a group of school teachers and principals whose achievements were being recognized by the president in a brief ceremony, may be instructive. The reporters remained silent as they covered the ceremony, but as it ended and the president moved to leave, they began shouting questions about the then-pending nomination of Robert Bork to the Supreme Court. At this, the educators expressed outrage. "You're taking away from the joy of the whole occasion for us," said one. "This is *our* day," said another. "Why don't you ask him about the positive side?" asked a third. " . . . I think all of us here are very disappointed in you." It will not be easy.[25]

Notes

1. Personal conversation with Wilbur Garrett, March 1986, and subsequent correspondence and personal conversation with Steve McCurry, August 1989.
2. *New York Times,* 27 July 1969.
3. Jonathan Kolatch, "Could There Have Been a Revolution Without Television?" *TV Guide,* 31 May 1986, p. 6.
4. Patrick E. Tyler, "Kurds Disappoint Iraqi PR Effort," *Washington Post,* 18 September 1988, p. A30.
5. Eleanor Randolph, "Venture in Managing News Backfires," *Washington Post,* 3 March 1989, p. A17.
6. The memorandum is reproduced in "How a PR Firm Executed the Alar Scare," *Wall Street Journal,* 3 October 1989.
7. Ann Devroy, "For This President, the Medium Is Not the Message," *Washington Post,* 30 April 1989, p. A18.
8. Ann Devroy, "Las Vegas Ad Man Joins Bush's Staff," *Washington Post,* 1 August 1989, p. A4.
9. "President Left Some Drug Aides on the Tarmac," *Washington Post,* 16 February 1990, A21.
10. Portions of the discussion that follows are based on Jarol B. Manheim and

Robert B. Albritton, "Public Relations in the Public Eye: Two Case Studies of the Failure of Public Information Campaigns," *Political Communication and Persuasion* 3 (1986), pp. 265–91.

11. Marilyn Bender, "Marion Javits Issue Focuses Unwelcome Spotlight on Publicizing of Foreign Clients," *New York Times,* 27 February 1976, p. 6; and Jacob K. Javits, *Javits: The Autobiography of a Public Man* (Boston: Houghton Mifflin, 1981).

12. "Negative Ad Wizard Becomes Part of the Issue," *Washington Post,* 9 May 1989, p. A6.

13. Paul Taylor, "Campaigns Take Aim against Consultants," *Washington Post,* 15 February 1990, p. 1.

14. "The Self-Interest Decade Is Over," *Washington Post,* 29 January 1989, p. D7.

15. David Broder, "Five Ways to Put Some Sanity Back in Elections," *Washington Post,* 14 January 1990, pp. B1, B4.

16. Personal conversation, April 1990.

17. "Campaign '88: A Retrospective," forum conducted at The George Washington University, 10 January 1989.

18. R. W. Apple, "Will the Networks Succeed in Getting the Candidates to Talk Substance in 1992?" *New York Times,* 10 May 1989.

19. Victor Kamber, "Negative Campaigning: What to Do About It," *The O'Leary/Kamber Report* 5 (Washington, D.C.: June 1990), pp. 1, 3.

20. Paul Taylor, "The Five-Minute Fix," *Washington Post,* 15 April 1990, pp. D1, D2; and Walter Goodman, "Toward a Campaign of Substance in '92," *New York Times,* 20 March 1990, p. C16.

21. "Why Negative Ads? Cynical People Demand Them," *Washington Post,* 20 January 1990, p. A17.

22. David Ignatius, "Press Corps to Bush: Manipulate Us!" *Washington Post,* 7 May 1989, p. B1.

23. Personal conversations, January and May 1990.

24. Michael Oreskes, "If Politics Is Broke, Can Talk Fix It?" *New York Times,* 6 April 1990, p. A12.

25. Christopher Connell, "Conflict of Interests: Educators, Reporters Square Off," *Roanoke Times & World News,* 6 October 1987, pp. A1, A8.

11 ALL OF THE PEOPLE, ALL THE TIME

Tell us of his fight with Douglas—
How his spirit never quails;
Tell us of his manly bearing,
Of his skill in splitting rails.

Tell us he's a second Webster,
Or, if better, Henry Clay;
That he's full of genial humor—
Placid as a summer's day.

Call him Abe, or call him Abram—
Abraham—'tis all the same,
Abe will smell as sweet as either,
We don't care about the name.

Say he's capable and honest,
Loves his country's good alone;
Never drank a drop of whiskey—
Wouldn't know it from a stone.

Tell again about the cord wood,
Seven cords or more per day;
How each night he seeks his closet,
There, alone, to kneel and pray[.]

Tell us he resembles Jackson,
Save he wears a larger boot,
And is broader 'cross the shoulders,
And is taller by a foot.

Any lie you tell we'll swallow —
Swallow any kind of mixture;
But oh! don't, we beg and pray you —
Don't, for God's sake, show his picture.

"Lincoln's Picture," Democratic campaign song, 1860[1]

◆ ◆ ◆ ◆

Historians tell us that he was prone to dark moments of gloom and self-doubt, but when it came to the willingness and ability of his fellow citizens to preserve democracy, Abraham Lincoln was an optimist. He believed in their innate capability to cut through the demagoguery and utter claptrap of much political rhetoric—in the ultimate wisdom of their political judgment. You *cannot*, he asserted, fool all of the people all the time.

Abraham Lincoln did not live in the era of strategic political communication.

That is not to say that Lincoln was wrong when he observed that one cannot fool all of the people all the time, but it does suggest that—given the hindsight provided by our *contemporary* political life—he may have misread the implications of his assertion. For the fact—or at least the principal operating assumption of the strategic communicators—is that it is not necessary to fool all of the people all the time if one is to achieve power and to exercise it freely. The only requirement is that one fool—*manipulate* is a better word—*some*, perhaps even most, of the people so that they will, at the very least, acquiesce in one's decisions, and will, when needed, mobilize to show their support. And as we have seen, those who engage in such practices have developed diverse and effective devices for bringing this about.

Two of the central themes in democratic thinking are leadership and responsiveness. To Lincoln, leadership was a form of responsiveness. It was the responsibility of the political leader to ascertain the needs of the nation, to design policies—even the most difficult of policies—to address and serve those needs, and to educate the people to their own best interests. And that he did. But to the politician schooled in the era of strategic communication, *responsiveness is a form of leadership*. If it is anything, strategic political communication is responsive to a fault. Indeed, as an instrument of political leadership, its central emphasis on responsiveness may be its *critical* fault. Does one lead from the front of the pack, from the middle, or from the rear? To the extent that polls, focus groups, feel-good machines, pulse-takers, and the like *permit* a political leader to measure public sentiment, do they not also *compel* him or her to follow it? To do otherwise is to risk much. If the dangers of demogracy are great in an election campaign, they are far greater still as a philosophy of government. They give a whole new meaning to yet another of Lincoln's well-turned phrases: "government of the people, by the people, for the people."

Quite irrespective of their intended short-term objectives, which are typically much more mundane, the techniques and instruments of strategic political communication—when viewed in the aggregate—are well on their way to producing a citizenry that is deprived of the basic skills of civic involvement and is, as a direct consequence, not merely vulnerable to demagogic appeals of a scale, intensity, and sophistication that Abraham Lincoln never imagined, but actually *conditioned to accept them, even to demand them.*

This does not mean that strategic political communicators are inherently evil persons who set out to undermine the infrastructure of democracy. Quite to the contrary, their objective is to use that very infrastructure of public opinion and citizen participation to advantage. The problem is that they fail to perceive the longer-term damage caused to the political system by the strategies and tactics that serve their immediate needs so well.

The interests of the political system are served when democracy is viewed as an ideal, and when the myth of the free press and the free people is more or less an accurate representation of the way things really work. But communication strategists tend toward a much more mechanistic view—democracy is defined for them as a landscape of values and attitudes, patterns of individual and group behavior that they must traverse to obtain power, either for themselves or for their clients. They are a political version of the military's Special Forces, trained to live off the land—to use the attitudes, behaviors, interests, and opportunities that they encounter—as they cross it. If, in their wake, they disrupt an ecosystem or two, that is of little concern—not because they are, necessarily, uncaring, but rather because they are unseeing.

Ours is not a uniformly Orwellian world, however, and not everyone is likely to suffer equally the deprivation of political literacy that strategic communication so strongly encourages. Those who are better educated and more affluent, who have greater opportunity and ability to participate directly in political activity, and who rely less on television than on print for their information about the political world, will be spared somewhat—not immune, surely, but affected less—if for no other reason than their lesser dependence on mediated and manipulated information. As we have seen in chapter 8 and elsewhere, there already exist some significant inequalities among the information gathering and processing abilities of "the people." These tend to be reinforced and even augmented by strategic communication practices, which place no inherent value on the citizen except as a member of the audience for some particular message.

In effect, our society is being divided into three classes.

The first of these comprises an elite consisting of persons who are in direct contact with political reality, whether as political operatives or journalists or in some other capacity. What sets this group apart—and gives it real power—is, first, the ability of its members independently to test that reality against their own experience, and second, the opportunity to shape perceptions of reality for the larger public. Members of the elite operate upstream—they are the ones who have access to raw, unprocessed political information, and who, as a group, package that information for subsequent distribution to the larger public. Even they do not have perfect information—President Bush responded to one news conference question about events in China in 1989 by noting that "I'm trying to say that I don't know. And I'm trying to say you don't know. And he doesn't know. She doesn't know. And nobody knows. . . . And that's the way the . . . system works."[2]—but they have more and better of it than does anyone else. It was Francis Bacon who observed in 1597 that knowledge is power. Our knowledge-based elite of some four centuries hence puts the truth to the maxim.

Our second class (of) citizen comprises a politically literate minority consisting of persons at the receiving end of the information pipeline. These are individuals who possess to some significant degree the skills needed to isolate and evaluate the products of strategic political communication and to respond accordingly. Demographically, they probably resemble members of the elite more than they do other members of the public. They are comparatively well educated, and probably more affluent than the average citizen. They may read widely, and surely watch the news on television regularly. What sets them apart from the elite is their social location—their place in social and political life—which places them downstream in the flow of political communication.

These individuals could—by skill and understanding—join the elite, if time, motivation, occupation, or other factors led them in that direction. Instead, however, they fall victim to the misperception that, by widely seeking political information, they are well informed.

But it is the third class (of) citizens, comprising the majority of Americans, persons who lack political skills or motivation, who are best equipped to fulfill the role of victims of strategic communication. These individuals do not know much about politics, and do not care that they do not know. In their preferences, they sway with the political breezes. Some—perhaps half—vote, though few of these more often than in the quadrennial presidential elections. They are easily influenced, easily disillusioned. But most important of all, they are—for all practical political purposes—functionally illiterate. They have lost—or have never developed—the skills requisite for gaining influence over the many ways that political decisions can directly affect their lives. They are helpless to recognize, let alone to resist effectively, the manipulations and other machinations of those to whom they have, by default, ceded power. How can a people among whom Joseph Wapner, the judge on the television program "The People's Court," has name recognition of 54 percent while William H. Rehnquist, chief justice of the United States Supreme Court, has only 9 percent—leading, incidentally, all but one other justice, Sandra Day O'Connor, in that regard—begin to *understand* its government, let alone to govern itself?[3]

Under some circumstances, this tripartite division of the polity might not make any difference. If, for example, the most knowledgeable, active, and influential persons were able to get everything they wanted from the political system, *and* if they wanted the very same things—had the same policy agenda—as those at the bottom of the pile, then the interests of the mass public would be served even as the political system responded only to the self-interests of a small minority. In a study of this question some years ago, however, political scientists Sidney Verba and Norman Nie concluded that something of the opposite was the case. Comparing the policy preferences and political opinions of the most active and the least active citizens, they found significant areas of disagreement as to what government and the political system should do, and how it should be accomplished. As might be expected, the system was most responsive to those who were most affluent, most knowledgeable, and most involved.[4] This was the case, however, not because of their status, but because they were the only ones effectively registering demands. Even a political process that is truly open and responsive will benefit a minority if no one else raises his or her voice.

Lest those at the top begin to feel too cocky, however, they might do well to bear in mind the fact that they do constitute a very small minority of the citizenry, and that in politics, numbers do count. Indeed, one of the greatest dangers such persons may confront in a situation like the one we have described, is that, precisely because they have no value to the majority of persons in the society, or, indeed, may have a *negative* value, skills and issues that pertain directly to the free and meaningful flow of information—things like education and press freedoms, the very wellsprings of power and influence—become objects of class conflict. In some circumstances, such issues can be used by the elite and the minority to improve their position at the expense of the majority—as, for example, by restricting access to higher education by eliminating affirmative action or student financial support programs. But they can as easily be withheld from the minority by a majority which does not understand or value their significance. Indeed, this is precisely the sort of issue on which demagogic leadership can be built—ironically, perhaps, using the very tools of strategic political communication that helped so much to bring about the necessary preconditions in the first place.

Walt Whitman once observed that "to have great poets you must have great audiences also." The communication strategies we have explored in these pages require audiences as well—audiences of docile, uninformed, disinterested, and distracted persons who are susceptible to systematic manipulation. There is an argument that democracy requires the same—that if all of its citizens followed every issue intently and regularly spoke their minds, such a system would inevitably collapse of its own weight. Some must speak, but most must not. Indeed, some scholars go so far as to argue that "the people" are not democrats at all—that if they spoke, they would say the wrong thing. Democracy would fail because it is the elite, not the *demos*, that is the true repository of democratic values.[5] From that perspective, strategic political communication, with its elitist and manipulative tendencies, may be seen as delivering democracy *from* evil rather than *to* it.

For my part, I am not that trusting—either of the mass American public *or* of an elite. Neither has given much cause for confidence in recent years.

There is no likelihood whatsoever that all of the citizens of the United States—or even a majority of them—will ever become fully involved in the political process as thinking, reasoning citizens. But there is a distinct possibility that many will enter the political arena—finding community in their distrust of government and angered by the accumulating levels of frustration they feel—to make their will felt. And there is a serious danger that a political elite drawn by the logic of mass manipulation will distort the processes of democracy and turn these upon themselves—that the potential of strategic political communication to foster and pander to the basest urges of the polity will be realized.

It seems, then, that the only viable constituency for a renewal of meaningfully democratic politics is to be found in the middle. Reform will come, not from all of the people, but from some of them—those who are able to appreciate the scope of the problem and the need to fashion a solution. And the lesson of this book is that we must find a way to mobilize that some of the people while their numbers, skills, and influence are still up to the task.

Notes

1. Reprinted in Harold Holzer, Gabor S. Borritt, and Mark E. Neely, Jr., *The Lincoln Image: Abraham Lincoln and the Popular Print* (New York: Charles Scribner's Sons, 1984), p. 2.

2. "Transcript of President Bush's News Conference," *Washington Post,* 9 June 1989, p. A18.

3. These results of a nationwide survey are reported in Richard Morin, "Wapner v. Rehnquist: No Contest," *Washington Post,* 23 June 1989, p. A21. O'Connor scored 23 percent. The other justices, in order of their name recognition, scored as follows: Anthony Kennedy, 7 percent; Antonin Scalia, 6 percent; Thurgood Marshall, 5 percent; Harry Blackmun, 4 percent; William Brennan, Jr., and Byron White, 3 percent each; and John Paul Stevens, 1 percent.

4. Sidney Verba and Norman Nie, *Participation in America: Political Democracy and Social Equality* (New York: Harper & Row, 1972).

5. Thomas R. Dye and Harmon Zeigler, *The Irony of Democracy,* 7th ed. (Monterey, Calif.: Brooks/Cole, 1987).

REFERENCES

Arlen, Michael J. *Thirty Seconds*. New York: Farrar, Straus & Giroux, 1980.

Bennett, W. Lance. *News: The Politics of Illusion*, second edition. New York: Longman, 1988.

Blair, Gwenda. *Almost Golden: Jessica Savitch and the Selling of Television News*. New York: Simon & Schuster, 1988.

Boorstin, Daniel J. *The Image: A Guide to Pseudo-Events in America*. New York: Harper & Row, 1964.

Cohen, Raymond. *Theatre of Power: The Art of Diplomatic Signalling*. London: Longman, 1987.

Cornwell, Elmer E., Jr. *Presidential Leadership of Public Opinion*. Bloomington: Indiana University Press, 1965.

Crouse, Timothy. *The Boys on the Bus: Riding With the Campaign Press Corps*. New York: Random House, 1972.

Dahl, Robert A. *Democracy and Its Critics*. New Haven, Conn.: Yale University Press, 1989.

Diamond, Edwin and Stephen Bates. *The Spot: The Rise of Political Advertising on Television*. Cambridge, Mass.: MIT Press, 1984.

Edelman, Murray. *The Symbolic Uses of Politics*. Urbana: University of Illinois Press, 1964.

————. *Politics as Symbolic Action: Mass Arousal & Quiescence*. Chicago: Markham, 1971.

————. *Constructing the Political Spectacle*. Chicago: University of Chicago Press, 1988.

Elder, Charles D. and Roger W. Cobb. *The Political Uses of Symbols*. New York: Longman, 1983.

Entman, Robert M. *Democracy without Citizens: Media and the Decay of American Politics*. New York: Oxford University Press, 1989.

Epstein, Edward Jay. *News from Nowhere: Television and the News*. New York: Random House, 1973.

Gans, Herbert J. *Deciding What's News*. New York: Random House, 1979.

Graber, Doris A. *Processing the News: How People Tame the Information Tide*, second edition. New York: Longman, 1988.

Green, Fitzhugh. *American Propaganda Abroad: From Benjamin Franklin to Ronald Reagan*. New York: Hippocrene Books, 1988.

Halberstam, David. *The Powers That Be*. New York: Alfred A. Knopf, 1979.

Kelley, Stanley, Jr. *Professional Public Relations and Political Power*. Baltimore, Md.: Johns Hopkins Press, 1956.

Kern, Montague. *30-Second Politics*. New York: Praeger, 1989.

Kosinski, Jerzy. *Being There*. New York: Harcourt Brace Jovanovich, 1971.

Kubey, Robert, and Mihaly Csikszentmihalyi. *Television and the Quality of Life*. Hillsdale, N.J.: Lawrence Erlbaum Associates, 1990.

Lang, Gladys E., and Kurt Lang. *Politics and Television Re-Viewed*. Beverly Hills, Calif.: Sage, 1984.

Laudon, Kenneth C. *Communications Technology and Democratic Participation*. New York: Praeger, 1977.

Linsky, Martin. *Impact: How the Press Affects Federal Policymaking*. New York: W. W. Norton, 1986.

Lippmann, Walter. *Public Opinion*. New York: Free Press, 1965.

Manheim, Jarol B. *The Politics Within: A Primer in Political Attitudes and Behavior*, second edition. New York: Longman, 1982.

Margolis, Michael, and Gary A. Mauser, eds. *Manipulating Public Opinion: Essays on Public Opinion as a Dependent Variable*. Pacific Grove, Calif.: Brooks/Cole, 1989.

Martel, Myles. *Political Campaign Debates: Images, Strategies and Tactics*. New York: Longman, 1983.

Mauser, Gary A. *Political Marketing: An Approach to Campaign Strategy*. New York: Praeger, 1983.

Nimmo, Dan. *The Political Persuaders: The Techniques of Modern Election Campaigns*. Englewood Cliffs, N.J.: Prentice-Hall, 1970.

Nimmo, Dan, and James E. Combs. *Subliminal Politics: Myths & Mythmakers in America*. Englewood Cliffs, N.J.: Prentice-Hall, 1980.

Nimmo, Dan, and James E. Combs. *Mediated Political Realities*. New York: Longman, 1983.

Oudes, Bruce. *From: The President: Richard Nixon's Secret Files*. New York: Harper & Row, 1989.

Paletz, David L., and Robert M. Entman. *Media Power Politics*. New York: Free Press, 1981.

Rosenbloom, David Lee. *The Election Men: Professional Campaign Managers and American Democracy*. New York: Quadrangle Books, 1973.

Sabato, Larry J. *The Rise of Political Consultants: New Ways of Winning Elections*. New York: Basic Books, 1981.

Savage, Robert L., James Combs, and Dan Nimmo. *The Orwellian Moment: Hindsight and Foresight in the Post-1984 World*. Fayetteville: University of Arkansas Press, 1989.

Schmid, Alex P., and Janny de Graaf. *Violence as Communication: Insurgent Terrorism and the Western News Media*. Beverly Hills, Calif.: Sage, 1982.

Sigal, Leon V. *Reporters and Officials: The Organization and Politics of Newsmaking*. Lexington, Mass.: D.C. Heath, 1973.

Smith, Hedrick. *The Power Game: How Washington Works*. New York: Random House, 1988.

Turow, Joseph. *Media Industries: The Production of News and Entertainment*. New York: Longman, 1984.

INDEX

ABOUT THE AUTHOR

Jarol B. Manheim is professor of political communication and political science and director of the political communication program at The George Washington University. He is the author of numerous books in political science, and his research on strategic political communication has been published in the leading journals of communication, journalism, and political science. His commentaries on American politics and policy have appeared in the *New York Times* and the *Washington Post*.